DISENCHANTING

LES

BONS TEMPS

Post-Contemporary Interventions

Series Editors:

Stanley Fish and Fredric Jameson

For Don Spinelli,
with gratitude
and friendship;
Charles, November 2002

DISENCHANTING LES BONS TEMPS

Identity and Authenticity in Cajun Music and Dance

Charles J. Stivale

Duke University Press   Durham and London 2003

© 2003 Duke University Press
All rights reserved
Printed in the United States of America on acid-free paper ∞
Typeset in Scala by Keystone Typesetting, Inc.
Library of Congress Cataloging-in-Publication Data
appear on the last printed page of this book.

"C'était la valse après jouer . . ."

To Marian,
and
to all those who did not make it along the way,
in death and in life

CONTENTS

ACKNOWLEDGMENTS

Even when you think you're writing on your own, you're always doing it
with someone else you can't always name.—Gilles Deleuze, *Negotiations*

This book is made up of many steps—dance steps, music steps, and steps
of research, composition, and editing. Although Gilles Deleuze is no
doubt correct that one cannot always name those with whom one writes,
I can at least attempt to thank the many individuals who have helped me
through these steps.

For the dance steps, I owe a debt of gratitude and love to Lezlie Hart
Stivale, who said yes to stepping out and to a lot more besides; to Rand
Speyrer for his efforts on behalf of Cajun dance, music, and culture; to
Thérèse Puyau for showing me how to follow so that I could lead; and to
our friends in Erath, Louisiana, for their friendship, then and now. I also
want to acknowledge my great affection for the regular dancers in the
many different venues that I have frequented in New Orleans, Lafayette,
and Ann Arbor, especially the Sunday afternoon crowd at Tipitina's.

For the music steps, there is simply not enough space to thank the
many musicians who have graced us with their creativity. For making a
special difference, I thank Bruce Daigrepont, Wayne Toups, Ann Savoy,
Marc Savoy, Michael Doucet, Zachary Richard, Steve Riley, David Greely,
Christine Balfa, and Dirk Powell, and the scores of musicians, sung and
unsung, who inspired these musicians on their creative paths.

For the steps in research and writing, I thank the Wayne State University Humanities Center, especially Walter Edwards, and the Wayne State Office of Research and Sponsored Programs for financial support; Janet Langlois, Mireille Rosello, and Paul Patton for the opportunities to present the initial work that helped me to undertake this project; and the Conjunctures Working Group for keeping me going and on track. For editorial encouragement and patience, I thank Peter Wissoker and Douglas Kellner, and especially Candice Ward and J. Reynolds Smith at Duke University Press. I owe special thanks to Carl Brasseaux and Rhonda Case Severn for their scholarly generosity; to Theresa Antes, Raffaele De Benedictis, Andrea di Tommaso, Michael Giordano, Donald Haase, Louise Jefferson, Louis Kibler, Lawrence Lombard, Lawrence Scaff, Donald Spinelli, and Sandra Van Burkleo for collegial support at Wayne State University; to the Wayne State Foreign Language Technology Center, and especially Bruce Roffi, for years of superb technical assistance; to Jennifer Slack, Christa Albrecht-Crane, Gordon Coonfield, and Patricia Sotirin for their encouragement in the final steps; and to Kristin Dziczeck, Carol Lessure, and Gary Kaluzny for their energy and initiative in developing the Cajun and zydeco dance and music scene in southeastern Michigan.

Any text as it develops requires nurturing and assistance from readers and writers who make suggestions for revisions and further development. Hence I owe special thanks to Martin Allor, John Barberet, Ron Day, Petrus de Kock, Les Essif, Rae Beth Gordon, Ron Greene, John Isbell, Doris Y. Kadish, Tom Klingler, Marie-Pierre Le Hir, Mary Makris, Jean-Philippe Mathy, E. Nicole Meyer, William Olmsted, Paul Patton, Denis Provencher, John Rouse, Greg Seigworth, Jennifer Daryl Slack, Louise Speed, Lezlie Hart Stivale, and Gayle Zachmann for critical and moral support without which I could not have moved forward. Finally, this project and my other research endeavors in cultural studies would not be possible without the continuing encouragement and friendship of Lawrence Grossberg.

Needless to say, even with this considerable support, responsibility for the views expressed and analyses undertaken in this study, and any lapses therein, are entirely my own.

Finally, I acknowledge with gratitude the different authors, musicians, editors, and publishers who have granted specific permissions, as cited herewith:

Lynda Barry has granted permission to reprint epigraphs from *The Good Times Are Killing Me* (Seattle: Sasquatch Books, copyright 1988, 1998).

Baxter Black has granted permission to reprint an epigraph from his essay "Cajun Dance," in *On the Edge of Common Sense*, 17 July 2000.

Michel Brulé and Les Éditions des Intouchables have granted permission to reprint notes and poetry from Zachary Richard's *Voyage de nuit* (Montréal: Les Éditions des Intouchables, 2001) and *Feu* (Montréal: Les Éditions des Intouchables, 2001).

Yves Chiasson has granted permission to reprint his song "Petit Codiac" (Les Éditions Zéro Degré Celsius), as printed in Zachary Richard's *Cap Enragé* (Audiogram Records ADCD 10093; 1996).

Bruce Daigrepont and Bayou Pon Pon Music, Metairie, Louisiana, have granted permission to reprint lyrics from "Laissez Faire," "Disco et Fais Do-Do," and "Marksville Two-Step" on *Stir Up the Roux* (1987).

Michael Doucet has granted permission to reprint the lyrics and translation of "La Chanson de Mardi Gras" (BeauSoleil, *Live from the Left Coast* 1991), "Les Flammes d'Enfer" (BeauSoleil, *Bayou Cadillac* 1989), and "Recherche d'Acadie" (BeauSoleil, *Cajunization* 1999).

Flat Town Music, Ville Platte, Louisiana, has granted permission to reprint the transcription and translation of Nathan Abshire's "Pinegrove Blues," copyright 1967, and Dewey Balfa's "My True Love," copyright 1965.

"Laissez Faire," "Marksville Two-Step," and "Disco et Fais Do Do," by Bruce Daigrepont, copyright Happy Valley Music, all rights reserved, are used by permission of Happy Valley Music.

Gérald Leblanc and Les Éditions Perce-Neige have granted permission to reprint poetry from Zachary Richard's *Faire récolte* (Moncton, Canada: Les Éditions Perce-Neige, 1997).

Lyrics to Shirley Bergeron and Lee Lavergne's "Old Home Waltz" are reprinted by permission, courtesy of Mardi Gras Records/Jon Music, Metairie, Louisiana.

Zachary Richard has granted permission to reprint lyrics, notes, and poetry from *Voyage de nuit* (Montréal: Les Éditions des Intouchables, 2001), *Cap Enragé* (Audiogram Records ADCD 10093; 1996), *Faire récolte* (Moncton, Canada: Les Éditions Perce-Neige, 1997), and *Feu* (Montréal: Les Éditions des Intouchables, 2001).

Melissa Samluk has granted permission to reprint material from her master's examination, Department of Romance Languages and Literature, Wayne State University.

Chris Myers, managing director of Peter Lang Publishing, has granted permission to reprint chapter 4, a version of which is to be published in *Animations (of Deleuze and Guattari)*, edited by Jennifer Daryl Slack.

Richard J. Golsan, editor of *South Central Review*, has granted permission to reprint " 'Spaces of Affect': Versions and Visions of Cajun Cultural History," *South Central Review* 11.4 (1994): 15–25.

Lawrence Grossberg and Della Pollock, editors of *Cultural Studies*, have granted permission to reprint "Becoming-Cajun," *Cultural Studies* 14.2 (2000): 147–76.

DISENCHANTING LES BONS TEMPS

Introduction

"The Good Times Are Killing Me"

.
.
.

Do you ever wonder what is music? Who invented it and what for and all that? And why hearing a certain song can make a whole entire time of your life suddenly rise up and stick in your brain?—Lynda Barry, *The Good Times Are Killing Me*

This study began on the dance floor, with experiences of joy and pain. The sources of joy shall become evident in the following pages—the music, the movement, the musicians, the many friends and dance partners with whom I have shared time and space on and off the dance floor. The pain is from the loss of many of these same experiences and friends, mostly due to different sorts of distance and, early on, through death. Whereas the joyful experiences exist as fond memories and still as activities as near as the closest dance hall, I have come to understand that the painful experiences—of loss of place, loss of friends and loved ones, even loss of self—also must remain thriving at the very heart of Cajun and Creole music. Indeed, the names of legendary musicians who have passed on—tragically, like Amédé Ardoin, Iry LeJeune, Will Balfa, and Rodney Balfa, and prematurely, like Dewey Balfa, Tommy Comeaux, and Beau Jocque—hover above this musical expression as a reminder of just how fleeting the joy of its experience can be. Zachary Richard sums up the paradox of *les bons temps*, the good times that just keep on rolling, in this way: "The basic contradiction of Cajun music . . . is that you have songs which are about nothing but heartache, loneliness, loss—loss of love, loss of property, loss of stature in the society, all of these things—on this music that is absolutely joyful. So it's this incredible contradiction that is part of the Cajun soul, I think. You know, that even in pain you celebrate" (qtd. in Mouton 1999, 40).

This paradox lies at the heart of understanding what I call the Cajun dance arena (which is necessarily a music arena as well), and this volume examines the different means by which identity and authenticity are constructed within and in relation to this arena.[1] These constructions encompass recent Cajun cultural history, but through the music and dance forms they also stretch back to the origins of Cajun and Creole culture in southern Louisiana. Moreover, these constructions not only raise fundamental issues about Cajun and Creole identities and what constitutes authenticity in relation to them but also about questions of popular memory, of cultural representation, and of social exclusion. In this study, I conjoin my understanding of Cajun dance and music culture to these different questions and issues.

Furthermore, I situate my study of constructions of identity and authenticity in the Cajun dance and music arena in relation to the ongoing disciplinary dialogue between, on one hand, French and francophone cultural studies and, on the other, various Anglo-American modes of pursuing cultural studies and research. As Fredric Jameson has noted, one difficulty in defining "the desire called Cultural Studies" as a program of research and study lies precisely in its "relationship to the established disciplines" (1993, 18). Although I return to the question of definition in chapter 1, I conceptualize the goals of this study as located at a juncture in between disciplines, with a hybrid approach derived from a number of critical sources, most notably from the works of Gilles Deleuze and Félix Guattari. I hope in this way to enliven and enrich the understanding of a genuine, if not entirely indigenous, American form of cultural expression with the scholarly tools available in the interdisciplinary fields of contemporary cultural studies.

To meet this cross-disciplinary challenge, I undertake my reflection on Louisiana Cajun music and dance and their cultural representations as a means of "disenchanting *les bons temps*." This French phrase derives from the familiar Louisiana declaration *laissez les bons temps rouler*, let the good times roll, employed by Louisiana residents and nonresidents alike to characterize the spirit of the stereotypically carefree approach to life in the Pelican State.[2] Yet, although it is seemingly an unambiguous evocation of joie de vivre, this expression also places an exuberant face on the hard times and pain at the heart of Cajun and Creole cultural life.

As for the term "disenchanting," it is located in a number of discourses.[3] For my purposes, I borrow it from Sylvia Wynter (1987) in order to demystify different facets of the cultural representations that sustain the spirit and myth of *les bons temps* while also celebrating this very spirit and myth. One might well wonder why such demystification need be undertaken at all. I explain more fully in chapter 1 the steps that helped me to conceptualize this project, but here I will only point out that the constructions of identity and authenticity in the Cajun dance and music arena manifest ways in which contemporary societies and social groups deploy cultural representations for a broad range of strategic and ideological ends.

The dual facets of joy and pain in *les bons temps* have an almost logical counterpart in the contradictory thrust: on one hand, these facets help cultural agents to promote Cajun culture to as wide a market as possible (through tourism, music, dance, and food, and often conflating Cajun and Creole in the process). On the other hand, some of the same cultural agents (and many others) often demand respect for the "authenticity" of this (singular) "tradition." In making such a demand, these agents sometimes fail to recognize that the natural development of forms of cultural expression results in their escaping such tightly controlled traditional boundaries. This line of cultural flight is all the more likely to be uncontrollable when it also results from national and international strategies of promotion.[4] In this sense, my study seeks to join a number of remarkable recent works as an exploration of the conjuncture of practices by local cultural agents and the effects of these practices on wider, global representations.[5]

Alongside this project of demystification of *les bons temps*, however, I insist on the crucial impetus within this study of stating the complementary enchantment of *les bons temps*. Indeed, I had considered repeatedly setting off the prefix "dis" with parentheses—that is, as "(dis)enchanting"—in order to communicate scripturally this dual emphasis. In any case, rather than "declining" *les bons temps*—that is, "an ambiguous gesture of refusal and participation at the same time" (Rosello 1998, 13)—I conceptualize this project as at once celebrating the paradox of joy and pain inherent to practices of the Cajun dance and music arena and pursuing the critique of frequent distortions in representations of these very practices. For, even when the cultural agents active in this arena contribute to such representations, one can understand their activity as a form of "minority discourse," a form of fabulation that Deleuze describes as "catch[ing] someone in the act of legending"—that is, "to catch the movement of constitution of a people" (1995, 125–26).

This dual strategy of disenchanting informs the overall organization of the chapters that follow. I begin by explaining how this project evolved, starting from the passion I developed as a fan of Cajun music and a dance practitioner, the scholarly interest that grew slowly from this personal affinity, and the challenges that arose during the project's realization. Thus, in chapter 1, "Becoming-Cajun," I trace my own becomings—personal and professional—by focusing on a poorly understood and relatively little discussed form of American music and dance expressions with a unique heritage in French and francophone cultures. I then examine how these expressions may be linked and how they contribute to various modes of Cajun self-representation, constitution of identity (although the plural, "identities," is a more precise term), and concerns for authenticity. The opening development provides the bases for actively disenchanting *les bons temps* through the twofold thrust of celebration and critique. By celebrating the thematics of the Cajun music repertoire (chapter 2) and the dance arena in terms of its spaces of affects (chapter 4), I am better able to examine and critique various modes of visual representations (chapter 3) as well as different borders of inclusion and exclusion in related sociocultural practices (chapter 5).

However, this project has also developed in terms of the aforementioned disciplinary intersections between French studies and overlapping strains of cultural studies—as understood and as ever evolving in North American, British, and Australian language, literature, and communication programs. Thus, in the opening chapter I also contrast different perspectives developed by critics and commentators of the current critical conjuncture. My purpose in doing this is twofold: First, I seek to clarify how disciplinary tensions arising from questions of definition relate to the framework outlined here. I also wish to emphasize the debt I owe to diverse practices of Anglo-American cultural studies and to the rich conceptual field articulated by French and francophone theorists. This dual impetus helps me to develop my critical analyses as ways of opening particular cultural forms and practices to scrutiny and understanding in the context of their sociocultural elaboration. Second, I consider these forms and practices as different manifestations of the notion of the "minor" in artistic expression. That is, by their very existence and continued development, these modes of expression consistently challenge and disturb the "major" or dominant cultural modes on a number of levels while, nonetheless, succumbing to the sociocultural "capture" of these same dominant modes.[6]

Finally, to highlight the complex views of Cajun cultural heritage, identities, and their manifestation through musical and dance expressions, I conclude chapter 1 with a brief glimpse at how these issues intersect with conflicts of globality and locality. By introducing and comparing the practices of three Cajun musicians—Zachary Richard, Marc Savoy, and Michael Doucet—who will reappear in subsequent chapters, I provide details about how the very efforts to accommodate demands for authenticity participate in the shifting construction of "identity" by extending and influencing the processes of cultural (self-)representation.[7]

I approach this broad topic in four chapters that focus on distinct facets of musical and dance expressions. In chapter 2, "(Geo)graphies of *(Dé)paysement*: Dislocation and Unsettling in the Cajun Music Repertoire," I examine the affirmation of Cajun identity prevalent in many lyrics that glorify rather stereotypically an ebullient Cajun way of life, the myth of *les bons temps*. In so doing, I locate within the musical repertoire the shifting yet recurrent thematics of place and displacements, both geographical and affective, in order to reflect on the plaintive sadness that constitutes the necessary underside of the enthusiasm in the myth of *les bons temps*. In the chapter's final section, I locate these toponymic, thematic, and performative relations within the poetic and musical expression of one exemplary Cajun musician, Zachary Richard, especially in his two collections of verse—*Voyage de nuit: Cahier de poésie, 1975–1979* (2001) and *Faire récolte* (1997)—and his 1996 album *Cap Enragé*. Based on lyrical evidence from recent Cajun recordings, the predominantly textual orientation of this chapter derives from my firm belief that we can only proceed to discuss the subsequent forms of cultural representation by first having accounted for some key thematic elements at the heart of the myth of *les bons temps*.[8]

In chapter 3, " 'J'ai Été au Bal': Cajun Sights and Sounds," I develop a critique of various filmic representations of Cajun identities in different examples of cinema, documentaries, and Cajun dance instructional videos. I consider these examples (in the production of which many Cajuns

have willingly participated) as ways in which the filmmakers and producers implicitly develop varying definitions of Cajun identity in relation
to the dominant American culture surrounding and engulfing Cajun
culture. As a visual counterpart to the lyrical complexity explored in the
previous chapter, chapter 3 addresses at once the shifting border between
the authentic and the stereotypical, and the linguistic, discursive, and
sociopolitical facets that constitute the "minor(ity)" status of Cajun culture and identity. I focus, first, on precise scenes from two films that
purportedly portray Cajun culture: the final *fais do-do* sequence in the
little-known film *Southern Comfort* (1981) and the central *bal de maison*
(house dance) sequence in the well-known film *The Big Easy* (1987). I
then turn to several versions and visions of Cajun culture and music
representations in documentary films by Les Blank featuring Marc and
Ann Savoy in prominent roles, including *French Dance Tonight* (1989),
J'ai Été au Bal (1989), and *Marc and Ann* (1991). Finally, I address the
confluence of cultural affirmation and commercial initiatives in Cajun
dance instructional videos that entrepreneurs have produced since 1987
—for example *I Love to Cajun Dance* (Cecil 1988), *Cajun Dance Instruction*
(Michaul's ca. 1992), *Allons Danser* (Speyrer 1987), and *Introduction to
Cajun Dancing* and *Advanced Cajun Dancing* (Speyrer and Speyrer 1993a
and 1993b). The analyses in these three sections demonstrate how the
representation of presumably authentic Cajun identities and cultural
practices contributes to the construction of these identities and thereby
inherently extends the disenchantment of *les bons temps* in the very act of
their celebration.

I shift my focus into the field of the music and dance venues themselves in chapter 4, "Feeling the Event: Spaces of Affects and the Cajun
Dance Arena." I explore the "thisness" of these events, the very special
intensities of speed and movement that combine in order both to transform each event and yet also to retain its specificity in relation to the
Cajun dance and music arena. Although creating the most theoretically
demanding chapter, this approach helps to animate the active relationship of dance and music within the event of movement, sensation, and
affects. By examining a range of experiences in Cajun dance and music
venues in terms of the spaces of affects in which they unfold, I propose to
conceptualize more fully how bodies constituted within the sensory and
territorial field of the dance arena can engage with and expand the field
through the simultaneous experiences of sound, sight, touch, and scent.
These conjoined elements of the dance and music event constitute the

vital assemblage of dancers, spectators, and musicians within dynamic spatiotemporal becomings. Thus, drawing on my dance experience at different Cajun dance and music venues, I emphasize the variations in and effects of performances by, notably, Michael Doucet and BeauSoleil and Wayne Toups and ZydeCajun.

In chapter 5, "Disenchanting *Les Bons Temps*," I consider the sociopolitical tensions that underlie *les bons temps*. That is, having established the links between self-representation of Cajun identities, the performance as "event," and the territorial aspects of the Cajun dance and music arena, I consider how the different appeals to Cajun identity and authenticity are troubled both by linguistic isolation and by racial and social practices that inherently attempt to protect the dance and music forms from intrusion by variously defined "others," both inside and outside Louisiana. This disenchantment of prevalent mythologies of identity and authenticity corresponds to the order of analyses in the preceding chapters: first, of the musical repertoire (studied in chapter 2) in terms of modes of instrumentation and selected lyrics in Cajun music and zydeco; second, of documentaries (considered in chapter 3) in terms of statements and images about race relations in the origins of Cajun music; and, third, of the dance arena (described in chapter 4) in terms of particular exclusionary practices that have occurred in different clubs and festivals.

Having thus reflected on the disenchantment of *les bons temps*, I return in chapter 6 to their inherent force of enchantment and hope by considering a number of current initiatives in Cajun music that speak to the joyful prospects for *les bons temps* in this century.[9] These initiatives include, but are not limited to, the emergence of women's voices in the male-dominated Cajun music scene, the plethora of teenage and even preteen musicians performing Cajun music, and collaborations between Cajun and zydeco musicians on a growing number of projects. It is true that however much one might wish the contrary, the tensions and exclusions identified in chapter 5 are likely never to disappear entirely. Yet, with grassroots initiatives like Action Cadienne, led by Zachary Richard to introduce Cajun French language to children and, more generally, into daily life, or Christine Balfa's efforts to stimulate greater knowledge of Cajun cultural practices through the Louisiana Folk Roots organization, different forms of alliances can emerge and serve as examples of affirmative practices that are at once cultural and pedagogical.[10]

In the end, this study is inspired by the paradoxical message—of joy

and pain, of love and loss, of rootedness and displacement—that one dis-
covers in the music and that Cajun dancers practice in seeking out the
next music and dance venue, knowing that it will be over in all too short a
time. This study is also inspired by the same spirit that animates Lynda
Barry's *The Good Times Are Killing Me* (1988), from which I have borrowed the title of this introduction and have used for the introduction and
chapter 6 epigraphs.[11] In Barry's novel, the character Edna Arkins tries to
recall the good times, yet she can only do so by confronting the many
painful experiences of her past. Her experiences raise difficult questions
about identity and authenticity around the vexed issues of race and gender, and yet are also mediated by the joyful sounds and feelings of music
and dance in her childhood. That Barry's own creativity is inspired by a
broad range of musical practices, including Cajun and zydeco, is evident
in the portraits and commentaries that constitute the novel's wonderful
"Music Notebook" in its appendix. Besides these lovely portraits, Barry
also provides an original cover portrait appearing on the videocassette
carton of Blank and Strachwitz's *J'ai Été au Bal* (1989b) as well as for the
1990 audiocassette and CD of the documentary's musical selections. This
individual devotion translates the complex mix of emotions and practices
and of movement and feeling in the Cajun dance and music arena. We
can thus better understand the intensity of investment that lies in the
constructions of identities and claims to authenticity subsumed by the
myth of *les bons temps.*

1

Becoming-Cajun

.

.

.

In the same way [as a body], a musical form will depend on a complex relation between speeds and slownesses of sound particles. It is not just a matter of music but of how to live: it is by speed and slowness that one slips in among things, that one connects with something else. One never commences; one never has a *tabula rasa*; one slips in, enters in the middle; one takes up or lays down rhythm.—Gilles Deleuze, *Spinoza: Practical Philosophy*

During an all too brief four-year period in the mid-to-late 1980s, I began to devote myself actively to the truly pleasurable pursuits of "becoming-Cajun," a "Cajun-by-choice" as many native and nonnative Louisianans are often inclined to say. This pursuit was an avocation born of a happy coincidence of geography (living in New Orleans), personal interests (a desire to become familiar with the region's folk practices and culture), and personal encounters with a diverse group of Cajun dance and music aficionados. Subsequently, despite a job-related move to Detroit, I refused to let go of the rewarding activities and enriching friendships that becoming-Cajun had afforded. Thus, from 1990 onward, I developed a scholarly project that has allowed me to pursue and enjoy Cajun dance and music as well as the many friendships that have grown from this pursuit. In this chapter, I reflect on the circumstances that led me to this project on Cajun dance and music spaces and practices. The chapter also provides an opportunity to consider the difficulties—personal, scholarly, and theoretical—that have arisen in pursuing this project and thereby allow me to clarify certain problems pertaining to the current institutional and disciplinary conjuncture.

Through this reflection on the relation between the personal and the scholarly, I want to emphasize something important that tends to disappear all too often in such discussions and publications—namely, the experiences of personal pleasure that originally inspire research, the experiences of reflection that propel the research forward, and, yes, the doubts that often require one to redirect a project partially or entirely in order to continue.[1] Hence, my use of the personal is a strategic trajectory for considering the motivations and professional choices that have contributed to developing an ongoing critical project, as well as for exploring my in-between status as scholar and participant/observer in relation to the dance and music arena that I discuss.[2] This exploration also examines how the personal, the pleasurable, and the reflective often encounter tensions and even certain forms of conflict when linked to a "disciplinary" domain. Given that cultural studies has become victim of its own success, I begin by tracing a particular example of how "cultural studies travels" (Grossberg 1997b, 343–44; see also Grossberg 1996a) both geographically within a life and disciplinarily in relation to something that has come to be known as French cultural studies. In tracing this trajectory, I also consider ways in which a particular theoretical engagement—in my case, an engagement with works by Gilles Deleuze and Félix Guattari—might offer complementary, practical lines of "becoming" in relation to contemporary events, problems, debates, and cultural practices.

Personal Steps

After moving to Louisiana in 1986 to teach French at Tulane University, I slowly adapted to the many manifestations of New Orleans music culture, and I revised a series of misconceptions about the varieties of New Orleans music as distinct from Cajun musical expression (see Hannusch 1985). I learned, for example, that whereas the French origins of New Orleans were based on aristocratic and imperial fiats for gradual urban development, the introduction of the *exilés acadiens* (Acadians exiled by the British from New Brunswick and Nova Scotia in 1755) into Louisiana occurred fairly quickly in the mid-to-late eighteenth century through a deliberate process of rural resettlement toward the bayous west of New Orleans and even further west beyond the Atchafalaya Basin in the swamps and on the prairies of southwestern Louisiana (see Brasseaux 1987, 1991, and 1992). I also learned of the many difficulties that rural Cajuns suffered in terms of the increasing Americanization of Louisiana society throughout the nineteenth and early twentieth centuries, particularly with the 1921 constitutional interdiction on offering instruction in French in the public schools (see Dormon 1983, 68–71).

Early on, I began to perceive the implicit political impact of Cajun sounds within the New Orleans context. For example, the weekly Cajun music hours in Cajun French, transmitted on one or two local New Orleans radio stations, challenged the hegemony both of English and of the blues, rhythm and blues, and jazz-based idioms that dominate New Orleans musical sounds. In fact, these shows occasionally included specific references to the repression of Cajun identity that occurred throughout much of the twentieth century. These deliberate interventions constituted a musical and linguistic challenge to the more "refined" sensibilities both of the New Orleans French language tradition and of the community's fairly insular cultural practices. Initially, however, I hesitated to venture into the *pays inconnus* (unknown countries) of the bar and music scene without having some familiarity with the social protocols, indeed the social "languages," spoken there. Although I now see this hesitation as a fairly normal function of a certain culture shock, I correctly intuited something special about the Cajun music and dance scene that I would soon better understand.

Having studied the works of Deleuze and Guattari for a number of years, I found the New Orleans social context all the more important both for my experiences therein and for subsequent critical reflections. Most evidently, questions both of "minor language" and of "territorialization" gradually became apparent through the extreme complexity of sociocultural relations in south Louisiana (see Deleuze and Guattari 1986, 1987). As an outsider learning to negotiate various cultural milieus, I began to distinguish how French language, already "minor" in relation to the dominant English surrounding it, could itself be de- and reterritorialized. That is, Cajun French in Louisiana has always been something of a poor cousin in relation to the New Orleans French language with its origins in the French aristocracy (see Ancelet 1988; Phillips 1983). *La langue cadjine*, as it is sometimes known, suffered the same fate as the Acadian settlers themselves, first deterritorialized through exile and physical displacement and then linguistically through the language's evolution over two centuries and its growing distinction from a "major" French as well as the territorializing dominance of American English.

Yet in recent years the Cajun cultural renaissance and Cajun music's commercialization (in advertising and films as well as through recordings) have served to reterritorialize *la langue cadjine*: on the one hand, the mix of Cajun and Louisiana representations is often quite distorted and the language itself still remains incomprehensible within American mass culture (see Ancelet 1990). On the other hand, the Cajun dialect has at least been resituated within increasingly familiar sociocultural and economic coordinates as a form of homegrown cultural and linguistic exoticism, so near and yet so far. In this sense, the potentially subversive impact that this "minor language" may have once possessed in relation to the dominant colonial English has been dissipated by dint of the dialect's "capture" within recognizable parameters, if not linguistically comprehensible ones for all who are attracted to things Cajun. And yet, quite bluntly, time takes its toll inexorably, and like the Louisiana Gulf coastline the Cajun linguistic territory itself recedes. That is, as an older generation of Cajun French speakers disappears and as few Louisianans grow up speaking the language, efforts to jump-start Cajun French in southern Louisiana through educational programs face a daunting challenge (one to which I return in chapter 6).

Of these diverse facets, however, I was only dimly aware as I sought to familiarize myself with a select Cajun sound and movement. This effort constituted the first phase in what I call becoming-Cajun. While I develop this term more fully below, I can define it here provisionally as a gradual cultural familiarization with the indigenous francophone culture close by. My understanding of this becoming was twofold, at once opening myself to local cultural practices by engaging in them and thereby situating these practices as possible sociopolitical enunciations of the "minor." In January 1987, Lezlie Hart Stivale and I participated in a three-week introductory course in Cajun dance—the rudiments of the Cajun waltz, two-step, and jitterbug—offered by Rand Speyrer (see Plater, Speyrer, and Speyrer 1993). Although teaching and research demands that winter prevented me from putting these lessons into practice, Rand's course syllabus (presented orally) included a basic introduction to Cajun musicians and musical traditions. Thus, I began to purchase records and tapes of a few musicians, for example, Bruce

Daigrepont (*Stir Up the Roux*, 1987), Filé (*Cajun Dance Band*, 1987), Wayne Toups with ZydeCajun, (*ZydeCajun*, 1986, and *Johnnie Can't Dance*, 1988), and one compilation (*La Musique Chez Mulate's*, 1986). At that point, not knowing how or if I would continue dancing, I collected and listened to the music as much from linguistic and aesthetic curiosity as from a desire for diversion and recreation.

The second phase of this becoming consisted of passing through successive turning points during spring and summer 1987. In late April, Lezlie and I renewed our contacts with Cajun sound and movement as well as with Rand Speyrer and other friends when we decided to repeat Rand's introductory course, then take advantage of his generous offer to serve as unofficial host for a trip to the Mamou Cajun Music Festival in early June. We New Orleans tourists spent some remarkably recreative time in Mamou with Cajuns and non-Cajuns from various parts of southwestern Louisiana and out of state, as well as with our friends from New Orleans. Above all, we danced and danced, all day at the festival and most of the evening at a local dance restaurant, Randol's. Attending the 1987 Mamou festival was the beginning of a different way of life for us, in Louisiana and beyond, by providing new openings for friendships and deep cultural enrichment.

The third phase of becoming covered the following three years of intense dance activity in New Orleans and southwestern Louisiana, including participation in regular Cajun music and dance venues in New Orleans area bars and dance halls; travel to festivals inside and outside New Orleans (e.g., the annual Mamou Festival and the Lafayette Festivals Acadiens); and connection to a network of dancers who would contact us for local performances of particular musicians or groups. Besides individual activities, we participated in the folk dance group that Rand Speyrer organized, performing an eight-couple contredanse routine at different convention-related events in New Orleans and Lafayette. These brief performances also yielded some paid activities—for example, performances with a live Cajun band at different tour group dinners and occasionally assisting Rand with large introductory dance classes. Above all, these varied pursuits helped us become close friends with a very wide group of Louisianans, both in the New Orleans area and in Acadiana (around Lafayette), and my enthusiasm for this activity spread slowly to my often incredulous and skeptical colleagues in academe. Frankly, had the personal and social aspect of these activities been less enjoyable, I doubt that I would have had an interest in pursuing them as a research project.

Scholarly Steps

To address this second aspect of becoming-Cajun, I must reflect on two conjoined facets of my post–New Orleans experience: first, the factors that impelled me to undertake research in an area that I had initially pursued solely as an avocation; and, second, the specific steps of this project. Both of these facets came together early in the project when I began to understand more fully the tragic circumstances that brought the Cajuns to Louisiana in the first place.

An introductory overview of these Cajun origins must mention that l'Acadie (Acadia; Nova Scotia and New Brunswick) was colonized by French settlers in 1602, but after the English colonization of French Canada in the early eighteenth century the descendants of the settlers in Acadia refused to forswear their Catholic faith and pledge allegiance to the British king. Following decades of tension between Protestant British military authorities and the French-speaking Catholic population, the governor of Nova Scotia, Charles Lawrence, took steps in 1754 and 1755 to isolate and then expel the Acadians from the Bay of Fundy region—a mass deportation known as *le grand dérangement* (the great upheaval). After several more decades of forced separation and wandering along various circuitous routes, most of the expelled Acadians arrived and resettled in southern Louisiana between 1765 and 1785 (see Brasseaux 1987; Dormon 1983; and Griffiths 1973).

The Acadian refugees were welcomed in Louisiana for the products of their farming and cattle raising ventures, which would eventually provide the New Orleans area with the food products as well as the general economic development that were sorely needed. On arrival the refugees were given Spanish land grants (Louisiana remained under Spanish control until 1803) with the condition that they had to accept assignment to specific regions, including the southwestern prairies of the Opelousas and Attakapas areas west of the Atchafalaya River, and the forests and bayous of the Mississippi River of the Cabannocé area to the west and southwest of New Orleans. Nonetheless, the mostly rural Acadians, whose name evolved by deformation to "Cajuns," adapted well and quickly in their new environment, and their prosperity continued unabated throughout the nineteenth century. However, after the Civil War most of their socioeconomic structures collapsed and were not rebuilt until well into the twentieth century. The subsequent assimilation of the Cajuns to American culture occurred quite slowly until after World War II, then accelerated with their exposure to cultural and technological influences from outside the region (see Severn 1991; Ancelet 1989a).

Cajun music and dance practices developed in social gatherings held in the rural communities. The *bals de maison* (house dances) were held in the homes of individuals, where they were also called *fais do-do*, literally "go to sleep," in reference to mothers encouraging their children to fall asleep in a nearby room so the adults could dance. Eventually this tradition extended beyond the private homes to dances held in public halls.[3] The music is a blend of German, Spanish, Scottish, Irish, Anglo-American, Afro-Caribbean, and Native American influences with a base of French and French Acadian folk traditions. Similarly, the instruments are from other traditions: the guitar from Spain, the violin from France, and the diatonic accordion from Germany. Although the Acadian refugees arrived without instruments and their musicians had to mime the fiddle sounds, "by the late 1770s most of the fiddlers had achieved a comfortable existence and enjoyed the leisure time to make, or the financial resources to purchase, new instruments" (Brasseaux 1987, 147). The subsequent introduction of other, imported instruments, such as the accordion in the later nineteenth century, had an impact both on the compositions and the sound of the evolving Cajun music, because "limited in notes and keys, [the accordion] simplified Cajun music as songs that it could not play tended to fade from the scene" (Ancelet 1989a, 21; see also Comeaux 1978). The accordion also came to dominate the fiddle because its power responded increasingly to the need for musicians to be heard over the large crowds that assembled in the public dance halls in the early twentieth century (see Plater, Speyrer, and Speyrer 1993, 22).

In the late 1920s, the availability of recordings began to extend the music of southern Louisiana, and over the next thirty years the fortunes of Cajun music were linked to the successive waves of musical influences that usually overwhelmed the rural form (e.g., Nashville and Texas country swing and the big band influences of the 1930s). Indeed, Cajun music was relegated to a distinctly secondary position as rural clubs provided the styles drawn from other regions (Texas) and national trends (swing bands) that would attract more customers. However, with the return of

GIS to Louisiana following World War II came a slow but growing interest in local musical expression that lasted into the 1950s. The popularity of Cajun music waned yet again with the rise of rock and roll (and its Louisiana version, swamp pop) in the late 1950s (see Broven 1983, 179–245) and especially in the 1960s with the British musical invasion. Still, from the late 1950s onward, various national folk festivals began to nurture a growing interest in ethnic musical expression in America (see Filene 2000, 183–232). The late, great Dewey Balfa returned to Louisiana from a standing ovation at the 1964 Newport Folk Festival and became the ambassador of Louisiana Cajun music charged with bringing it into greater view and encouraging younger musicians to adopt and adapt French Cajun musical forms.[4] The Cajun cultural renaissance has since proceeded on a number of fronts, notably linguistic, pedagogical, and culinary, but also, as mentioned above, through the diffusion of an array of folk initiatives such as the Cajun Heritage Museum and the Liberty Theater, both in Eunice, Louisiana, as part of the Jean Lafitte National Park system.[5]

This rich and complex history of the Cajuns in Louisiana inspired me to study Cajun cultural practices, but I also had other motivations for developing this project. While living in New Orleans, I wanted to maintain a separation between my professional life and my social activities; once in Detroit, however, I sought ways to return regularly to Louisiana to see friends, dance, and hear Cajun music, and also to pursue the ideas I had developed while living there. Specifically, at different Cajun dance and music events, I had noticed the affective transformation of the same physical space from one evening or week to the next (in clubs and restaurants) or one year to the next (at festivals). I was struck by the ways in which the different bands, crowds, available dance space, and even the atmosphere induced by weather all would combine in each venue to create familiar and yet always renewed sensations and possibilities for movement and creative expression. From these observations, I raised some working questions: How do various forms of Cajun music—that is, diverse forms of musical interpretation by different Cajun bands—cause the dance spaces to differ affectively depending on locations, between city and country sites, and even between different sites in the city and sites in the country? A second question immediately followed: How do the different configurations of audiences—less in terms of sheer numbers than in terms of relative dance passivity or activity, and even purpose and intensity in attending the venue (from curiosity to full interaction)—

contribute to that transformation of physical space and to the band's response and interchange with the audience? In other words, what is the nature of an event, and to what extent do such transformations yield different modes of spaces of affects?

I take up these questions more fully later in this chapter; here I want to consider how I pursued the fourth phase of this project of becoming— that is, how I negotiated the practical terms of moving the personal into the scholarly domain. A paper I presented at the 1991 Midwest MLA meeting gave me the opportunity to contrast the musical interpretations of three Cajun musicians, Bruce Daigrepont, Marc Savoy, and Wayne Toups, and notably, the particular ways in which they each express a sense of Cajun identity (see chapter 2). That early paper led me to develop a forty-five minute audio, video, and live dance performance/workshop that I (with Lezlie Stivale or another partner) have presented on a number of occasions. This work allowed me, in turn, to prepare a grant proposal that provided financial support for field study, in summer 1992, which then led to two successful proposals that helped me to extend my research through different conference presentations and publications (see Stivale 1994 and 1997a). Also, in 1994 and 1995, the prospectus of the project's earlier version, with the working title "Spaces of Affect: Forms and Feeling in Cajun Dance Culture," initially elicited some encouraging editorial responses for book publication. However, although I found no sustained interest from presses, I became aware of several theoretical perspectives (outlined in the following sections), specifically concerning the construction of identity and authenticity, that contributed to this project.

Moreover, as the project's scholarly and theoretical aspects developed concurrently with disciplinary concerns, I began to address directly the relation between French studies and cultural studies, particularly the orientation of the former toward the latter.[6] The emergence of cultural studies in relation to North American French studies coincided with a conservative backlash in the United States against questions about the canon and multiculturalism. Indeed, in the early 1990s, French studies experienced its own "culture wars" in the guise of a polemic about which French texts should (or should not) be included in a proper French curriculum in North America.[7] Despite provoking a certain level of rancor, this debate produced as a salutary outcome a number of thoughtful articles on the impact of "cultural studies" in the French curriculum.[8]

Noteworthy among these essays is Marie-Pierre Le Hir's affirmative emphasis on the need for dialogue between French and Anglo-American cultural studies. Le Hir's call for "bridging disciplinary boundaries" emphasizes that the role of cultural studies is not "to passively contribute to the reproduction of the literature field but to produce knowledge in spite of and against disciplinary constraints" (1997, 182).[9] Furthermore, Le Hir argues in conclusion for a mode of French studies that would take the best from both French and Anglo-American approaches; that is, French studies should be conceived not as "an antiliterature discipline, but an intellectual one devoted to the comparative exploration of knowledge production in France and the United States" (188).[10]

Two commentaries on how French teachers might conduct programs in French studies exemplify this project quite precisely. In complementary essays (1996 and 1998), Tom Conley first reflects on the purpose of the volume he edited with Steven Ungar (1996) and then outlines the fading attraction of an earlier conception of French studies, one focusing on elucidation and stylistic analysis of the French canon through an alignment of *explication de texte* with the New Criticism.[11] In contrast to the failed "civilizing project" of the early conception, it is understandable, says Conley, that many students and scholars so indoctrinated now "embrace culture studies as a welcome alternative to the *dictée*, the *explication de texte*, or close reading of preordained literary masterpieces" (1996, 274). Rejecting what can now be understood as hegemonic "operations inherited from nineteenth-century colonial practices," today's "spiritual children of the generation trained in the postwar years," Conley argues, are turning away from the lessons of French teachers who "produced the highest standards of linguistic refinement, but otherwise lived pitifully isolated lives in a mixed and bustling world" (275). This exodus from things patently French, says Conley, has an explanation beyond the impulsion of Freudian mechanics: "Not having grown into the patrician culture of France, but living at a moment when the demarcations established by nineteenth-century geography no longer exists, they see how the spatial, linguistic, and paternal borders that produce identity appear archaic in view of current world problems" (275). Conley clearly emphasizes here the perspectives that he elaborates more fully in his subsequent essay about "putting French Studies on the map." Specifically, he urges us to "think of literature [by] considering spatialities of discourses and their representations," and more generally, to "discern welters of issues—economic, historical, psychoanalytical—that prompt us to reconstruct the past in order to alter the ways we inhabit the present" (1998, 25).

A second perspective on French studies is Sandy Petrey's position statement in the *Diacritics* issue "Doing French Studies" (1998), in which he forcefully opposes the "either/or model" (literary studies *or* cultural studies) exemplified, in his view, by Russell Berman's essay in *Profession 1997*, titled "Reform and Continuity: Graduate Education toward a Foreign Cultural Literacy" (1998).[12] The result of any dominant pedagogical focus in French studies other than literary, Petrey maintains, will be "to condemn ourselves to watered-down, dumbed-down versions of history, political science, art, economics, sociology, and the many other areas pertinent to things French" (12). However, it is not simply a matter of choosing between literary studies and cultural studies because Petrey judges such a choice to be "horribly misguided, something like imposing a choice between breathing and eating" (12). Rather, "if the curriculum is organized around the ways literature represents culture and identity, domination and resistance, mental and discursive self-understanding, then the problems of exclusion and those of inclusion are solved at the same time" (15). Petrey agrees with critics that "the airless enclosure of formalist analysis is by no means the only way to approach literature," and so he exhorts us: "Let us be interdisciplinary from within our discipline, literary studies, not from the deluded impression that we are above and outside disciplines because we find all of them engaging" (16). Petrey concludes frankly that rather than shifting the emphasis from literary to cultural studies, "the productive transformations [that French departments seek] will come not through changing what we teach but changing how we teach it" (22). This transformation would mean maintaining French studies's "definition as programs in language *and literature*," while infusing them with "new life" through "the interdisciplinary orientation of cultural studies" (22).

My purpose in reviewing these divergent positions is twofold: In terms of the research narrative developed here, I need to situate my "field position" at the juncture between French and Anglo-American theoretical and critical divides. In doing so, I must also indicate to colleagues in other disciplines (and in other countries) that I recognize the extent to which references to a purported Anglo-American model are certainly at once too monolithic and too vague (given the complex development of cultural studies on both sides of the Atlantic and in other geographical sites and intellectual practices). Nevertheless, these diverse critical approaches and analyses associated broadly with cultural studies are having an indisputable and often unsettling impact in many fields, and not only in the field of national literary studies.[13] Although my views are not necessarily in the majority in my field, I see this impact as altogether salutary in allowing us to trace new parameters both in teaching and in research; for example, we can now help students develop a rich, non-Anglophone cultural and linguistic awareness while encouraging them to question the ideological underpinnings of a homogeneous and canonical "Frenchness." Just as Ungar and Conley ask, among other important questions, "how and by what means identity can be a useful historical artifact in the domain of cultural studies" (1996, 279), my own scholarly initiative has been to deploy concepts developed by Deleuze and Guattari and other theorists as possible tools for understanding particular critical and cultural practices, no matter in what field these practices might reside (see Stivale 1998; also Grossberg 1997b, 344–45). Following Grossberg's reflections on the cultural studies "crossroads blues," this initiative would pursue cultural studies that think of theory as a "strategic resource" and, quite possibly, one that might "enabl[e] agency and action" (1998, 79).[14]

In terms of the research project I describe here, these debates in French studies have helped me to reflect more fully on the theoretical problems that I have faced, and to ask new questions, seek new answers, and recast the initial project entirely. Specifically, these discussions have led me to reflect on how spatial, linguistic, and paternal borders in Acadiana, to paraphrase Conley (1998, 25), contribute to the production and construction of identity through the perspective of claims to authenticity. Moreover, these discussions have helped me understand how I can conceptualize the cultural practices that constitute the Cajun dance and music arena in terms of a "minor" expression that challenges, albeit in a limited way, the dominant cultural forces in American musical and linguistic artistic practice.

Theoretical Steps

Two terms that constituted the original conceptual framework for this research remain here without adequate definition: spaces of affects and becoming-Cajun. Moreover, a third term, that of cultural studies itself, needs further definition, and I will return to it later. My earlier conception of this study focused primarily on a process of reconstitution of feeling that contributes to an ever-renewed creation of spaces of affects. I argue that this affective renewal occurs through the dynamic and creative exchange between musicians and fans in multiple dance sites in and outside southern Louisiana. The formulation spaces of affects serves a dual function: first, it expresses the transformation of Cajun dance arenas by the moving, fleeting, and yet intense circulation of feeling evoked through the evolving music and dance forms in which dancers, spectators, and musicians participate. Second, the formulation also helps me to envisage how these variable collective assemblages of speed and affect circulate intensely between musicians and dancers/spectators and are based on the mutual "relations of movement and rest" and the capacities of participants on both sides of the stage front "to affect and be affected" in interactive exchange (Deleuze and Guattari 1987, 261).[15] Finally, these reconfigurations of spatial practices in Cajun dance venues are affective investments through which the body, understood as more than simply a semantic space and less than a unity defining our identity, "is placed into an apparently immediate relation to the world" (Grossberg 1986, 185).

For the expression becoming-Cajun, I have borrowed syntax from Deleuze and Guattari (1987; [plateau 10]: "1730: Becoming-Intense, Becoming-Animal, Becoming-Imperceptible"), and I understand this term to function in a number of ways. On the one hand, becoming relates directly to the "minor" expressive force of Cajun music and language in the sense of displacing and disturbing (or deterritorializing) dominant English-language musical expression and, in so doing, creating a collective enunciation that has its own powerful political force, if only locally.[16] On the other hand, I also understand becoming-Cajun in a more literal sense, as both a temporal passage through successive experiential phases and an experimental and spatial process of engagement with diverse cultural practices. One crucial and highly complex problematic that has emerged in my study is the importance of a search for "authenticity" within this passage and process. I should note here that this search is no less important for nonnative Louisianans (some of whom designate themselves as Cajuns-by-choice) than for Cajuns themselves as they both contribute to and resist various modes of representing Cajun identities.

We can discern a manifestation of this complex becoming in the often conflicting views of the Cajun cultural heritage. Notably, with the integrity of an inherited music and dance tradition perceived as being threatened by the influences of innovative contemporary music and dance forms, some fans (Cajuns and non-Cajuns alike) often resist such innovation by professing the need to preserve what they understand as originary and authentic forms (see M. Savoy 1988). At the same time, however, many entrepreneurs and cultural revivalists have successfully exploited the increasing demand inside as well as from outside Louisiana for cultural forms that showcase Cajun identity (see Ancelet 1992a). Recalling Lipsitz's reminder about popular culture—that "hegemony is not just imposed on society from the top; it is struggled for from below" (1990, 15)—we can understand that the very efforts to accommodate such demands for authenticity participate in the shifting construction of identity by extending and influencing the processes of cultural (self)-representation.

In order to consider these issues, I need first to address several related concerns, both methodological and ontological. Regarding the forms of methodology I adopt in this study, my training in research and literary criticism gave me a background in textual analysis and in archival study. Thus, my initial task was to take extensive notes and acquire documents from two sites, the Louisiana Archive at Tulane University and the Center for Louisiana Studies at the University of Southwestern Louisiana (now the University of Louisiana at Lafayette). I also met a number of local spokespersons on Cajun folklore and dance (e.g., Ann Allen Savoy and Barry Jean Ancelet), and my correspondence with Rhonda Case Severn, who completed an extensive NEH project on Cajun folklore (1991), provided me with another valuable set of documents. Thus, in terms of scholarly research this project quickly took on some predictable, but no less important, contours.

Another methodological question concerned on-site research. Without training in sociological or ethnographic methodologies of fieldwork and data gathering, I had to determine quickly just what I would do as research in the dance spaces that initially constituted the focus of this project. I gradually understood that in my role as a participant/observer I could undertake activities with other participants in these sites and thus not limit myself to a strictly note-taking role on the sidelines. Indeed, the role solely of observer would have been all the more inappropriate given that active dance participation in these sites is a crucial, not to mention enjoyable, part of the reconstitution of "spaces of affects." While I would soon recognize a number of different forms of such participation (and adapt accordingly), I decided from the start to interact fully in these sites and with their participants by dancing and socializing as much as conditions permitted, recording notes later for subsequent consultation. Yet, in terms of the actual analysis of dance and music practices that I develop in chapter 4, I decided against attempting an ethnographic focus in order to explore these practices in terms of the dance and music event—that is, both the limitations and potentials in terms of spaces of affects in each venue.[17]

These considerations lead to a related concern, one raised by interlocutors in different discussion formats, regarding the need and even appropriateness of theorizing the Cajun dance and music arena in the ways that I do in this study. One interlocutor posed the issue by stating that while it was clear what Cajun dance and music do for me, it was much less obvious what I do for Cajun dance and music. I can only suggest that through my theoretical engagement with issues of representation and the construction of identity and authenticity in the Cajun dance and music arena I can best take both serious and respectful account of this domain of cultural activity. All too often when I have spoken about my research in this domain I have encountered wry smiles, often from curiosity and sympathy but also from an attitude of incredulity, suggesting that perhaps not everything in society needs to be scrutinized from a theoretical perspective, especially not Cajun dance and music. However, as a scholar in French and francophone studies as well as a fan of Cajun and zydeco dance and music, I maintain that leaving well enough alone—that is, treating the Cajun cultural arena as a pastoral reserve somehow beyond theory—hardly constitutes a critically respectful regard toward these cultural practices. In short, my purpose in bringing different theoretical perspectives to bear on diverse facets of this particular sociocultural arena is to open possibilities for a greater understanding and appreciation of these dance and music practices, precisely in contrast to the focal mythologies and sociocultural constructions with which they are imbued.

These reflections oblige me to address two ontological concerns: first, my relation as a nonnative Louisianan and non-Cajun to the culture and folk practices that I propose to study; and, second, my need to pursue interpretive readings that engage the different cultural forms, to the extent possible, on their own terms but without abandoning the possibilities of engaging them critically as well. From a literal perspective, the concept becoming-Cajun is ironic because it is evident that as a francophone Italian American, I can never become Cajun, not even by choice as Cajun dance and music fans would have it. Yet, this limited understanding of becoming-Cajun—that is, one that eschews a broader understanding of becoming in terms of the disturbing force inherent to Cajun musical and linguistic expression—points to the very problem with the concept of authenticity itself. No doubt, my own authenticity in relation to becoming might readily be challenged from the perspective of what Timothy Taylor identifies as an "authenticity of positionality," a "person's positionality as racialized, ethnicized, subaltern, and premodern" (1997, 21).[18] However, discussion of authenticity presumes an acceptable definition of what the term signifies, and recent studies have shown its definition to be extremely complex, variable, and often limited in range.[19]

In this context, one might well raise questions about the status of outsiders' views in relation to indigenous cultural practices, but it would seem altogether evident that research on Cajun cultural practices need not be limited to those experts who themselves would somehow stake claims to one or several forms of Cajun authenticity, through what Bennett (1993) calls a "charismatic closure."[20] Still, one might pose a complementary challenge to my authenticity from the perspective of my status as tourist (MacCannell 1999) and as tourist as theorist (Van den Abbeele 1980). Thus, the passage and process that I combine in the term becoming-Cajun might be construed in successive steps: first, the twofold manifestation of my personal search to make sense of the Louisiana experience relates initially to a quest for the authentic as an actual tourist, as sightseer and visitor both in urban and rural venues and in a variety of dance and music experiences. Then, the second phase began to unfold, my professional quest as an interpretive creature attempting to dissociate myself from the mass of tourists while seeking theories with which I might explain the passage and process—the becomings—of my quest. Conjoined to the first construction is my passage from accepting the mystification of staged authenticity in the "front regions" of diverse tourist encounters toward demystifying, and then disenchanting, those front regions by dint of a deeper understanding of aspects of the back regions and of exclusions from the front regions.[21]

However, the search for authenticity on the part of the cultural tourist is also a part of the native Cajun's experience. That is, difficulties pertain to being Cajun because the very hybridity of Cajun identity—the socio-cultural in-between of diverse ethnic origins, social classes, and racial groups—renders any fixed or stable Cajun identity quite impossible, despite claims to the contrary. Over the two centuries since the *grand dé-rangement* that brought the Acadian exiles to Louisiana, the mix of this group with the indigenous population already inhabiting the territory as well as with successive waves of immigrants resulted in a very ethnically diverse population to which the designation Cajun is usually generically attributed (see Brasseaux 1992, 38–39). Furthermore, by dint of geo-graphical proximity, many residents of the Cajun region with no blood ties to this heritage have nonetheless become Cajun—that is, they have been assimilated to the Cajun population thanks in large part to the Ca-jun renaissance that developed onward from the mid-1960s. Indeed, the word Cajun not only has pejorative origins as used by Anglo-Americans in the nineteenth century to signify "white trash," but also it was used indiscriminately "to refer to all persons of French descent and low eco-nomic standing, regardless of their ethnic affiliation" (Brasseaux 1992, 104).[22]

Moreover, as Ancelet notes regarding the growing phenomenon of the "cultural tourism experiment" in southern Louisiana, community orga-nizers have found it necessary to take steps to orient visitors, and even to exclude "inappropriate outsiders" from certain events (like the annual Mardi Gras rides) (Ancelet 1992a, 259–60). Other efforts, such as the weekly live radio show *Rendez-Vous des Cajuns* (which is almost entirely in Cajun French and is broadcast from the Liberty Theater in Eunice, Louisiana), have provided the much-needed service of bringing the Ca-jun heritage back to local Cajuns themselves, and the Louisiana Folk Roots initiative (see chapter 6) offers an active engagement with overlap-ping cultural practices between Cajun and Creole cultures. However, such efforts do not go without careful planning; to the remark by Marc Savoy: "What's worse [than the Cajuns having been discovered nation-ally] is that the Cajuns have discovered themselves" (qtd. in Ancelet 1992a, 264), Ancelet responds: "It is unreasonable to expect the Cajuns to remain lost somewhere in the nineteenth century. If we are going to open ourselves to the outside, we should at least try to do it well and *in our own terms*" (1992a, 264; emphasis added). Ancelet's words echo a view expressed by Jean E. Jackson on cultural authenticity in comparing culture to a jazz musician's repertoire: "The individual pieces come out of a tradition, but improvisation always occurs. . . . Just as a jazz artist's music depends on engaging an audience and fellow musicians, so does a culture come into existence because a 'we' and a 'they' interact" (1995, 18).

Hence, the self-representation of Cajun identity through its very construction "in our own terms" has been a deliberate part of the local organization efforts that have contributed to the Cajun renaissance (see Ancelet 1999). This initiative relates directly to my second ontological concern, that of addressing these cultural practices on their own terms. One manifestation of this concern is my deliberate decision to limit this study in terms of distinctions between Cajun music and zydeco. Whereas the former is commonly understood to be a musical expression originally developed by descendants of the Acadian settlers relocated in southern Louisiana (see Ancelet 1989a), the latter is a term derived quite recently (since the 1960s) to designate the music of Louisianans of African American and Caribbean origins, the so-called Creoles.[23] My choice to focus primarily on Cajun music, dance forms, and venues, rather than on zydeco forms and sites, arises from heeding Linda Alcoff's advice that we "strive to create wherever possible the conditions for dialogue and the practice of speaking with and to rather than speaking for others" (1991–92, 21, 23). By limiting my focus, I might better "speak with" the proponents of Cajun cultural forms, although, as I will emphasize later, the influence of zydeco on Cajun music is not only unmistakable but crucial, especially in terms of the difficulties regarding claims to authenticity. That is, the proximity of zydeco dance and musical forms to the expressions of Cajun music and dance has contributed immeasurably both to Cajun's richness and to the tensions about maintaining strict boundaries around would-be traditional and authentic cultural forms. That this tension cannot be ignored provides the main fulcrum for disenchanting *les bons temps*, which I explore in chapter 5.[24]

The inherent volatility of the term and concept of authenticity for constructing identity renders it quite important for this study. For if one agrees that in the mid-1980s things Cajun became "hot" in the conjoined senses of spicy and popular, one still has to answer questions that arise with the notion of things Cajun: What is Cajun and, especially, what is authentically Cajun? The issues of authenticity become even more complex when one considers, on the one hand, the stigma that many Cajun-French speakers still feel exists generally on speaking French outside their community and, on the other hand, the unfamiliarity of many younger Cajuns with French in any form. These questions are all the more pertinent, but seldom examined closely, in terms of folk practices such as Cajun dance and music. As James Clifford reminds us, "claims to purity are in any event always subverted by the need to stage authenticity *in opposition to* external, often dominating alternatives"; and he concludes, "If authenticity is relational, there can be no essence except as a political, cultural invention, a local tactic" (1988, 12). As a way to introduce the topics that I address in the following chapters, I wish to consider the manifestations of authenticity in relation to several Cajun musicians, on whose practices I will focus more closely in later chapters.

Staging Authenticity

I propose here to situate briefly the broad concepts of globality and locality in relation to the vexing question of authenticity by discussing the work and positions of three Cajun musicians: Zachary Richard, Marc Savoy, and Michael Doucet. As I will argue, each of these accomplished artists encompasses a practice in relation at once to global/local issues and to constructing identity and authenticity. Despite sharing a fervent love for things Cajun, the first two musicians, Richard and Savoy, have been in many ways polar opposites in their approaches to global/local issues and interventions regarding their artistic and cultural practices, while Doucet's approach could be characterized as hybrid in terms of these same practices (Ancelet 1999, 141). Marc Savoy abandoned touring early in his career as a musician in the 1960s due to his avowed disgust with the marketing of Cajun music, both within and beyond Louisiana. At the same time, however, he opened a music store specializing in building quality diatonic accordions, the kind used in Cajun music (Ancelet 1999, 129–33; Nyhan, Rollins, and Babb 1997, 117). In his decision to quit touring and start a business, he made a fervent statement about the importance of his conception of the local and the authentic as well as about his belief in using quality instruments as part of the Cajun musical heritage.

Zachary Richard, on the other hand, having begun his career as musician with Michael Doucet in the early 1970s, focused his energies on a particular expression of cultural politics that employed French Cajun music and language globally, particularly in Québec and France. Richard did this deliberately in order to affirm his Acadian roots and to deploy the authentic in the broadest set possible of geographical contexts and cultural relations (Ancelet 1999, 93–95; Nyhan, Rollins, and Babb 1997, 108–10). Meanwhile, after traveling to France with Richard in the mid-1970s, Doucet chose to explore his Cajun heritage within Louisiana under the symbol of Joseph Broussard *dit* (called) Beausoleil, the Acadian resistance fighter who organized against the 1755 forced exile and later settled in Louisiana near Lafayette (see Segura 1983). Thus, by pursuing his interest in Cajun music and forming the now renowned band Beau-Soleil (with several members of his earlier group, Coteau [see Mouton 1997]), Doucet has readily embraced all facets of the Cajun musical and cultural experience, especially as a frequent and learned participant in educational initiatives on Cajun folklore and music. In this way, he has skillfully melded the global and the local by means of the outreach of the commercial (quite successful) practice with the local practice of educating the public on Cajun folk culture.[25]

Zachary Richard's approach to these folk cultural practices has been tactical in the sense that de Certeau employs the term tactic—that is, so that it might "vigilantly mak[e] use of the cracks that particular conjunctions open in the surveillance of the proprietary owners" (1984, 37). Throughout his career, Richard has varied his locale, focus, and even artistic genres, as illustrated by his three collections of poetry (1997, 2001a, 2001c). Even if, as de Certeau contends, the tactic "does not have the options of projecting a global plan, nor of totalizing the adversary within a distinct, visible, and objectifiable space" (1984, 37; translation modified), Richard has deployed his music and related activities in order to create an authenticity, a Cajun "essence . . . as a political, cultural invention" (Clifford 1988, 12). Besides producing records on his own RZ label, Richard has more recently produced a video, *Against the Tide: The Story of the Cajun People of Louisiana* (1999), which documents the settlement of the Acadians in Louisiana in the eighteenth century.[26]

During the 1970s, early in his career, Richard joined the French separatist movement in Québec and attempted to preach French separatism in Louisiana as well. Richard admits to "the naïveté of a young militant" in employing shock tactics in the 1970s in order to express the "fever" of his militancy regarding his Acadian heritage, notably at the second Tribute to Cajun Music festival in 1975, during which "no one understood what we were trying to do . . . and [they] wondered why I was so angry" (Ancelet 1999, 95–97). Having in the 1980s settled in his native Scott, Louisiana, he has remained an active spokesperson on behalf of Cajun culture and the preservation of French, leading an effort called Action Cadienne dedicated to teaching French throughout the twenty-two parishes of Acadiana ("Action Cadienne" 1995; Nyhan, Rollins, and Babb 1997, 109–10). However, Richard's music career, especially his most recent original albums, *Cap Enragé* (1996) and *Coeur Fidèle* (2000c), continue to prove his iconoclastic stance: "Musicalogically, I'm probably closer to Bob Dylan than to [the 1950s Cajun accordionist] Aldus Roger, but listen to the songs. I've never repudiated anything about my heritage. I'm very proud of it. I just want to go beyond the *bons temps rouler* thing and achieve a status as a singer-songwriter as opposed to just a butt-shaking yahoo" (Orteza 1998a, 22).[27]

As for Marc Savoy, he has contributed in important ways to the Cajun folk heritage as an active musician, through his craftsmanship as accordion builder, and through his role as local cultural leader in and around Eunice, particularly with his music center where musicians gather for jam sessions on a weekly basis. He has steadfastly defined the authentic as what de Certeau calls a "strategy" for maintaining tradition (see M. Savoy 1988). De Certeau sees the "strategy" as a means of "postulat[ing] a *place* that can be delimited as its *own* and serv[ing] as the base from which relations with an *exteriority* composed of targets or threats . . . can be managed" (1984, 36). Although no doubt supportive of the musical, folk, and heritage community in his environment, Savoy's example concentrates a strategically narrow focus, of both positionality and primality, that safeguards a defense of Cajun authenticity. For example, Savoy has written that when Cajun music in the 1960s and 1970s turned into "typical American music sung in French and played on the Cajun accordion," he and a few others "gave up the dance hall scene strictly because we were not going to contribute to the birth of this mutation" (1988, 11). He explains that "our Cajun music here had become so crossbred with country and western that it had degenerated to the point that it seemed it was to be lost forever" (Ancelet 1999, 135). He maintains that "the failure was not necessarily that of the Cajun musicians alone, but rather the audience they played for . . . the pressure brought to bear upon [musicians] by [the] public" (Ancelet 1999, 135–36). Evoking his roots on the rural Louisiana farm, Savoy concludes that "if you breed an ass to a horse you develop something which cannot perpetuate itself" (1988, 12; cf. Ancelet 1999, 135). In chapter 3, I situate more fully the perspectives of Marc Savoy and Ann Savoy in relation to the visual representation of these cultural practices.

Although the delineation, indeed binary, of Richard/tactics versus Savoy/strategies is no doubt too clear-cut, this focus on the musicians' cultural and political practices serves as a means to emphasize the necessary in-betweenness of cultural hybridity (Bhabha 1994, 38) that may help us better comprehend the musicians' tactical and strategic interventions, however these might be configured and distributed. For this in-betweenness is a means by which the global and the local are negotiated, as "culture reaches out to create a symbolic textuality, to give the alienating everyday an aura of selfhood, a promise of pleasure" (Bhabha 1994, 172). The third artist in this configuration, Michael Doucet, incarnates this practice in ways that are quite complex. With his group BeauSoleil, he has helped to develop a musical sound that magnificently interprets the music from the traditional Cajun repertoire, yet that also reaches out with an eclectic mix of compositions and instrumentation that diverse audiences can enjoy. Doucet has described BeauSoleil's purpose perhaps with the highest praise in its simplicity, that of being a "Cajun dance band" (qtd. in McKeon 1997). However, he also has given a more all-encompassing statement of BeauSoleil's mission: "The ideal of Beau-Soleil from the 'blue album' [*The Spirit of Cajun Music* (1976)] on, (has been) to show the entire gamut of French music in southwest Louisiana, which is not just two-steps and waltzes, but the different artists and individuals who created those songs and different styles" (qtd. in Mouton 1997, 44).

The diversity and the sheer fun and exuberance in the hybridity of BeauSoleil's performances are reflected in the array of songs that they perform live and record regularly on each album. The 1989 *Bayou Cadillac* album provides some perfect examples: describing the album's "Hey Baby, Quoi Ça Dit?" (colloquial for "how are you doing?") on a 1990 *Austin City Limits* performance as the "original Tex-Mex-Cajun-American song," Doucet sings the Augie Meyer lyrics that combine Cajun French with Spanish and English set to a rapid Tex-Mex beat. Another song (and the album's title), "Bayou Cadillac," is a pun on "buy you [a] cadillac" from the blues lyrics included in the medley of songs "Not

Fade Away," "Bo Diddley," and "Iko Iko." And the song with which this album closes, "Island Zydeco," reflects the hybrid mix that BeauSoleil continues throughout the 1990s: not only does much of their music adopt the rhythms and instrumentation of zydeco, they also create many tunes with a Caribbean flavor, for example, "Danse Caribe" (*L'Amour ou la Folie* 1997) and "Cubano Bayou" (*Cajunization* 1999).

However, another quite important manifestation of Michael Doucet's career is the Savoy-Doucet Cajun Band, the trio that he formed with Marc Savoy and Ann Savoy.[28] In this role, Doucet sees himself simply as a fiddle player, and not the leader of a band, therefore able simply to "play and have a great time" (qtd. in McKeon 1997). In viewing Ed McKeon's 1997 documentary *The Savoy-Doucet Band: Pour on the Pepper*, one might be tempted to take Doucet's remarks about his role at face value. I believe, however, that this collaborative effort, especially his musical interchange with the Savoys, transforms the tactical/strategic facets of the struggle for authenticity into something altogether hybrid, in-between, and quite extraordinary. It is evident that besides their Cajun heritage, Doucet and Marc Savoy share an educated knowledge of the Cajun musical repertoire gleaned from years of collaboration in their youth with legendary older musicians such as Dennis McGee, Dewey Balfa, and Canray Fontenot. The result in their collaboration is that even if each of them tends toward diametrically opposite styles—Savoy steadfastly traditional, Doucet improvisational and progressive—their music creates a strong communicative bond that takes the group ever further and beyond convenient qualifiers.

One section toward the end of *The Savoy-Doucet Band* reveals this hybridity quite effectively by means of a well-edited juxtaposition between their performance of the Cajun classic "Les Flammes d'Enfer" and successive interview comments by Ann Savoy, Doucet, and then Marc Savoy. After Ann Savoy's rendition of the opening verse of "Les Flammes d'Enfer" in a live concert setting, the interview clip provides her appraisal of the superb technical skills of both Marc Savoy and Doucet. She maintains that both can take their respective instruments to places that no other musician can reach, although Marc does so "in a more traditional vein than Mike." Then, following only a brief shot of Doucet playing his fiddle while Marc Savoy shouts encouragement in the background, Doucet comments that because he and Marc have played so often together in so many different venues, they have established a necessary and intuitive communication between each other in performance. The video shifts again to their live musical performance, and Doucet states in voice-over that because both he and Savoy adopt the different styles of the fiddlers and accordionists they have known, they do more than traverse the musical history together: "You can create what these people have given us. If you witness that, it can sound like two things: either like Cajun music and chank-a-chank, or if you know something about it, you can just hear all this stuff, and you just go 'Wow! What was that?!' because we can never do that again, we can never do it the same way again, and that is what's so beautiful, you just do it for the moment."

A segue to the performance focuses briefly on Marc Savoy's accordion and his voice shouting, "Do it now!" and then he makes a statement that contrasts sharply with Doucet's ebullient approach. Says Marc Savoy: "It's fun sometimes to take off, but I don't want my reputation to be based on excursions into left field. . . . I want my reputation to be based upon the fact that we do play old-timey traditional music without all the glitz and the glamour and the structured feeling of modern music." The video segues to Ann Savoy singing another verse of "Les Flammes d'Enfer," followed by Doucet's energetic fiddle solo during which Marc Savoy shouts "C'mon, Michael," Ann wails a Cajun plaint, then Marc Savoy shouts, smiling broadly, "Quit messin' around! Quit messin' around! Do it, Michael! C'mon, c'mon!" As Doucet completes his part, Marc Savoy joins him on accordion and shows the communication to which Doucet referred, over which Marc Savoy's interview voice continues: "I personally think that the things that make Cajun music popular are the things that keep it separate, keep it different, keep it apart from mainstream American music, and if you take this music and have the same attitude as these people on Nashville television or these rock concerts, . . . and try to present it in the same way, it's almost like cutting Sampson's hair—you're destroying the one thing that makes this thing appealing to the rest of the world." The segue focuses finally on the instrumental close of "Les Flammes d'Enfer" with all group members providing the heated musical flourish to which the festival dancers have responded enthusiastically throughout the segment.

What I particularly wish to emphasize in examining the juxtaposition of comments and performance in this segment is a crucial point about authenticity: even though certain aspects of their individual statements, particularly those by Marc Savoy, seem to belie any movement toward a progressive musical expression, the performance itself (at the New Orleans Jazz and Heritage Festival) reveals the sheer joy that Savoy expressed early in the documentary when he said that a music creating such a good vibe "just makes me laugh, that's how much it moves me." In describing in the liner notes to *Live! At the Dance* (1994), a performance of Savoy-Doucet in Berkeley, Dirk Richardson has captured this spirit of the group members' collaboration: "They surrendered themselves to the bliss of the music, staring out at the sea of waltzers, exchanging knowing glances when one or the other let loose a particularly astonishing fusillade of musical phrases. Every third or fourth song, Marc Savoy would get especially worked up, whoop and holler, or shout out encouragement to his Cajun pal 'Come on, Doucet!' urging the fiddler to even higher peaks of expression." Such interchange is an exciting part of all of their live performances, most evident on *Live! At the Dance* and on the more recent *Sam's Big Rooster* (2000).

Furthermore, such a performance helps us conjoin the debate about authenticity with the different terms I have discussed, not just the pairs of globality/locality and tactics/strategies, but also the much discussed but rarely exemplified concept of hybridity. I approach this intersection through another concept, "haecceity," or the "thisness" of an event, which corresponds to what Doucet calls "just do[ing] it for the moment"—that is, the event constituted through the combination of speed and affect (Deleuze and Guattari 1987, 260–65). I return to the thisness of the Cajun dance and music event in chapter 4, but here I wish to argue that through the collaboration of apparent opposites emphasized in McKeon's documentary, Savoy-Doucet expresses an active, musical hybridity, an in-betweenness and haecceity that mitigates, and indeed dissipates in performance, the often polar distinctions maintained in the heat of reflective debate. Whereas such debate is something in which we are often expected to engage in order to prepare the ground for and then develop our work, it is the play that creates the magic, that creates the communication between artists and musicians, and that transcends finally the tactical/strategic differences in order to express, if not clearly to define, a hybrid position beyond the opposition of dualities.

Disenchanting *Les Bons Temps*

In light of these perspectives and multifaceted issues, it is crucial to consider not only the role of cultural representations in constructing identity but also the constructed natures of tradition and authenticity themselves—the intersection of the two forms of authenticity that Timothy Taylor identifies (1997, 21)—in relation to different forms of self-representation in the Cajun dance and music repertoire and arena. I am particularly interested in understanding how many contemporary Cajun groups expand this cultural archive with new compositions, yet still employ the standard repertoire to emphasize sameness, even with new interpretations. That is, many groups tend to situate their music along a constantly shifting border between, on the one hand, the risks of national/global appropriation of these musical forms and, on the other hand, an adherence to a sense of ethnic authenticity, a primality, and sometimes even purity. For some musicians and fans, this process—musicians modernizing traditional and new songs alike—constitutes the natural movement of musical innovation, while for others it represents a dilution or even destruction of the spirit of Cajun music understood as traditional. This conflict recalls a similar one that arose earlier in the past century in the folk music of the 1930s. Recounting the pressure of maintaining the "folkloristic purity" faced by Lead Belly and other folk singers, Benjamin Filene argues that the notion "of a pristine and unchanging traditional music fundamentally misrepresented the reality of folk culture" (2000, 71).

Without attempting to adjudicate such tensions within Cajun culture, I have concluded that the allegiance of dancers and spectators to one music and dance sensibility or another serves as a specific means of representing, and even reconstructing, their cultural identity in relation to, or even as resistance to, the dominant cultural formation. Moreover, this struggle against presumed cultural intrusion by perceived "outside" influences has profound and disturbing sociopolitical effects, and my continuing research and reflection on this struggle is one reason why the project's completion was considerably delayed. However, my reevaluation of this project has caused me to consider further the implications of tradition versus innovation and of authenticity in the context of spaces of affects and becomings. An extraordinary essay by Sylvia Wynter, "On Disenchanting Discourse" (1987), helped me realize that I must explore not only the representations of Cajun identity in various artistic forms but must also disenchant *les bons temps*—that is, problematize further the representation of Cajun cultural practices under scrutiny. One form that this disenchantment could take is to go beyond discussion of traditional versus innovative tensions in order to address the impact of social bias in

1990s Louisiana regarding Cajun folk practices—an issue that I raise in chapter 5.

Still, in reconceptualizing this project in terms of disenchantment, I took considerable time in gaining a clearer understanding of how best to respect both scholarly obligation and personal loyalty as well as how to pursue disenchanting *les bons temps* while also adhering to Alcoff's counsel of not only creating "conditions of dialogue" but also "speaking with and to rather than speaking for" (1991–92, 21, 23). However, I note in Alcoff's advice the key words "to create *wherever possible* the conditions of dialogue" (23; my emphasis), and from this I conclude that one can strive to "speak with and to" without abandoning all critical perspective. Indeed, as Romy Heylen observes, the contemporary Cajun play by David Marcantel, *Mille misères* (A thousand miseries) (subtitled *Laissant le bons temps rouler en Louisiane* [Letting the good times roll in Louisiana]), "exhorts the Cajun community to cease to 'laisser le bons temps rouler' [*sic*], to stop living in the past, singing about the good old days as stereotypical Cajuns do," thereby constituting "a call to arms against outside interference, a demand for Cajuns to commit themselves through militant action to establishing a future for themselves in Louisiana" (1994, 455).

Thus, it is from my enjoyment of the Cajun cultural practices that I have undertaken to consider the diverse manifestations of those practices in dance and music discourse and performance and to engage with the problematics of difference as they relate to the construction of identity and authenticity, bearing in mind Christopher Miller's exhortation to avoid "pledg[ing] allegiance simply and uniformly to one brand of difference and to denigrate or ignore the other" while also avoiding "prescriptive deconstruction" (1998, 5–7). Hence, the shift of emphasis in the current project helps me to establish the more "multidisciplinary, multicultural approach" that Ancelet has called "indispensable for understanding the Cajuns" (1992a, 262). As I suggest in my introduction, this approach consists of understanding disenchantment in a twofold manner: briefly stated, if I presume to critique aspects of the enchantment within Cajun music and dance practices, these judgments will only entail the representations and presumptions of tradition and authenticity that I identify. The enchantment itself is never far from my readings, however critical they may be. Thus, despite the dilemma in "the construction of just representations" inherent to cultural criticism (see Druon 2000, 117–18), the project's current frame and structure now enable me to situate the problems addressed as a cultural studies that straddle the zone in between the local (personal) and the global (scholarly/ theoretical).

These considerations return me to the matter of defining cultural studies, and on this issue I have been inspired by the students in a course I taught on French cultural studies. As the students discussed and developed their own critiques of essays in one of the course's texts, Le Hir and Strand's edited volume *French Cultural Studies* (2000), they noted that a precise definition of French cultural studies was (and remains) quite elusive. Mireille Rosello, the author of one essay in the volume, makes a remarkable and insightful attempt to pursue such a definition. Borrowing from chaos theory to theorize cultural studies "as a provisional and temporary attractor" distinct from the "territories defined by our current specializations," Rosello argues that such a "non-territory would have its own explicit and hidden agendas, it would be a temporarily magic zone of increased agitation, encounters, friction, from which, at certain junctures (after ten years or perhaps even five) we could always stray at will to reach another cluster of both connected and disconnected points" (2000, 96–97).

However, far from implying a weakness in the Le Hir and Strand volume or even in French cultural studies more generally, the apparent lack of a more precise definition points instead to a strength of this burgeoning domain of study, but one that might not seem readily apparent. One student in the French cultural studies seminar, Melissa Samluk, drew from Stephen Greenblatt's definition of culture as the constraints and mobilities bearing on a society—on one hand, the repertoire of models to which individuals must conform and, on the other hand, the possibilities for exceeding these boundaries in creative and critical thinking (1995, 225). As Samluk suggests, "[as] Cultural Studies advocates, researchers and critics function with an autonomy that has not yet allowed for a concrete and stable establishment of what its constraints and mobilities actually are" (2001). We may usefully juxtapose the constant struggle with and between constraints and mobilities to Rosello's image of the "temporarily magic zone of agitation, encounters, friction" in order to discern a general map of the domain of cultural studies. We do not seek to concretize or fix these relational coordinates, for doing so would jeopardize the very vitality of both our scholarly and pedagogical endeavors. Yet, without fixed coordinates, determined methodologies, and precise definitions, our students and more skeptical colleagues will continue to ask how this domain can hope to extend itself toward a continuing, reliable, and reproducible practice.

I would argue that, in fact, these particular traits constitute disciplinary traps that cultural studies should continue to avoid even as its advocates make all efforts to reform the curriculum. Instead, our pedagogy and research can rely on a range of contingent precepts that could at once help us avoid the restrictions of overly determinate constraints and thereby maximize the possibilities of conceptual mobility. Various authors have attempted to detail many of these precepts, and an essay included in my cultural studies course, Cary Nelson's "Always Already Cultural Studies: Two Conferences and a Manifesto" (1997), offers a broad outline of key points that delimits a range of precepts. I seek guidance, however, from the work of Gil Rodman who has observed quite correctly, in his critical book on the legend of Elvis, that cultural studies "is many different things to different people." Yet, the partial list of constitutive features for cultural studies that he finds useful corresponds to four succinct traits: "its radical contextualism, its explicitly political nature, its commitment to theory, and its self-reflexivity" (1996, 19). That is, the thrust of this pedagogy emphasizes that the contexts in which diverse social practices and texts find expression are not static but inherently mobile. Yet these practices and texts are subject to diverse constraints at once social and political in nature—hence the constant oscillation and tension between these poles.

Moreover, the fundamentally sociocultural and political nature of such an approach to texts and practices intersects with the self-reflexive awareness of the reader and the writer, the student and the teacher, and of our shifting positions in relation to the object of study. To those who would object that such a pedagogical and performative intervention simply is not sufficiently political in the sense of direct action and intervention, I would respond that our every course—particularly those with a sociocultural and critical content—yields political dividends that we may never know. But these pedagogical engagements are no less important and effective because through them we contribute to forming citizens able to think for themselves and express themselves in the face of a relentless onslaught of the mass-marketed propaganda that characterizes late capitalism. Finally, in terms of the theoretical grounding of analyses following this pedagogy, here the potential for mobility, for creating "agitation, encounters, friction" is at its maximum. This potential allows writers and readers, students and teachers, to develop a broad range of connections that can bring texts and practices into active interdisciplinary alignments and assemblages.

Approaching this study via the strategy of disenchanting *les bons temps* helps to align my research with these pedagogical and performative precepts. That is, this approach allows me to consider the extent to which the contexts in which *les bons temps* find expression are not static and constitute a crucial element for understanding the dynamic complexity of this myth. Moreover, as I have noted above, the political nature of this project—linking critique to a respect for creating conditions of dialogue—intersects with the self-reflective awareness of my position in relation to this particular object of study. Finally, regarding the theoretical grounding of the following analyses, this approach provides a means for us better to understand the consequences of agency and practices (notably, of Cajuns and their cultural practices) as "articulations of subject-positions into specific places (sites of investment) and spaces (fields of activities) on socially constructed territorialities" (Grossberg 1997b, 366–67). To accomplish this, I will introduce a number of critical concepts in each chapter that can help explain the ways in which the modes of expression in the Cajun dance and music arena develop and, in some cases, lend themselves to diverse forms of representation. At the base of these analyses, however, is my understanding that these cultural practices contribute to a "minor" expression that encompasses the traits that Deleuze attributes to literature, "to set free, in the delirium [of domination], this creation of a health or this invention of a people, that is, a possibility of life" (1997, 4).

To close this chapter, let me recall the steps I propose to follow. In chapter 2, I consider the concept of dislocation / *(dé)paysement* ("uncountrying") in the Cajun music repertoire in terms of the concept of "rooted wandering" related to a form of nomadism, and I extend this thematic reflection to the recent poetry and music of Zachary Richard as a means of understanding one artist's relation to issues of location and identity. In chapter 3, I turn to three visual forms of representation in order to study different ways in which film is used to construct Cajun identities in hybrid fashion—that is, with Cajun cultural agents participating in different ways in the self-representation that communicates various forms of authenticity. In chapter 4, I draw on my own experiences in Cajun dance and music venues to discuss how the vibrant interchange between musicians and dancers, in the thisness of the event, transforms these locations from mere places into spaces of affects. In chapter 5, I consider a number of difficult issues regarding the sociopolitical tensions that underlie *les bons temps* and the cultural practices that constitute the active expression and construction of these "good times." Finally, in chapter 6, I look to recent and ongoing cultural initiatives to seek hopeful signs of concurrent practices in relation, even in sharp contrast, to disenchanting *les bons temps.*

2

(Geo)graphies of *(Dé)paysement*:
Dislocation and Unsettling in the
Cajun Music Repertoire

.

.

.

If the music is merely a re-creation it is pointless, but if it is looking at those who have gone
before for inspiration, and maybe questioning which values have been lost and which
retained, then it is serving its purpose. . . . The fact is, the music has evolved in an unbroken
chain for a very long time specifically to meet the needs of whatever generation plays it at
any time. It is handed to you as a gift and the only thing you can do wrong with it is to keep
it from becoming your own.—Dirk Powell, quoted in Josh Caffery, "Dirk's Due"

That Cajun music and its makers provide an index of *les bons temps* is
readily apparent in a number of ways. One is, of course, the sheer number of songs with the titles, lyrics, and refrains using the expression
laissez les bons temps rouler, both in Cajun music and in zydeco. These
selections range from the fairly bluesy interpretation by Clifton Chenier
(1990) to the highly stylized and even playful versions by Zachary Richard (1980, 2000a, and 2000b) and BeauSoleil (1989a and *Allons en
Louisiane* 1999).

Other indications of *les bons temps* lie in a number of key moments
over the past half century. The start of the Cajun renaissance itself is
linked to an important musical event, the appearance at the 1964 Newport Folk Festival of Gladius Thibodeaux, Louis "Vinesse" Lejeune, and
Dewey Balfa.[1] As a result of the extraordinary response that they received, according to Barry Jean Ancelet, "Dewey Balfa returned a cultural
militant, determined to bring the echo back home" (1999, 29–30).[2] The

second wave of the renaissance can be linked roughly to the appearance in the 1980s of two landmark volumes devoted to Cajun music that are benchmarks of the beginning of the renaissance twenty years earlier: Barry Jean Ancelet's bilingual *Musiciens cadiens et créoles/The Makers of Cajun Music* (1984) and Ann Allen Savoy's *Cajun Music: The Reflection of a People* (1984).[3] This second wave culminates in the faddish burgeoning of national interest in things Cajun from the late 1980s and early 1990s, recently dubbed the "Crawfish Years" on BeauSoleil's *Best of the Crawfish Years* album (on this album, see Orteza 2001). Not only did Paul Simon's 1986 Grammy-winning album *Graceland* include a zydeco-flavored song featuring Rockin' Dopsie and the Zydeco Twisters, the 1987 film *The Big Easy*, according to Michael Doucet, "detonat[ed] the 'Cajun Craze,' allowing non-Louisianans a safe and free ticket to join in the fun" (qtd. in Nyhan, Rollins, and Babb 1997, 5). As Todd Mouton has observed (1997), around this very same time, Doucet and BeauSoleil recorded three albums (1986a, 1986b, 1986c), a fourth that was the soundtrack for the film *Belizaire the Cajun* (1986d), and had music featured in *The Big Easy*.

The alphabetized guidebook by Pat Nyhan, Brian Rollins, and David Babb, titled (appropriately for my purposes) *Let the Good Times Roll! A Guide to Cajun and Zydeco Music* (1997), may well signal a third wave of the renaissance, beginning in the mid-1990s with the waning of the "Cajun craze" and its replacement by ongoing and fervent cultural pursuits in Cajun folklore.[4] Some of the recent musical trends examined in chapter 6—most notably the enrichment of the Cajun music repertoire in performance and recording venues both by an influx of young new performers and by the continued work of musicians from earlier generations—exemplify the nature of the third wave. Yet another manifestation of the third wave would be the concurrent explosion both of interest in zydeco, in Louisiana as well as nationally, and of the different musical trends within zydeco itself. This enlivening and expansion of the already rich forms of zydeco music and dance have also provided grounds both for rivalries between music groups and their fans and for controversies about musical styles, including the now familiar issue (from the Cajun context) of maintaining tradition (see Mouton 1994b; and Tisserand 1996 and 1998).

Underlying this chronological continuity are the "(geo)graphies" of *(dé)paysement* that I propose to locate in the Cajun music repertoire. I employ these terms to indicate two intersecting phenomena: with the term (geo)graphies I refer to the inscriptions of place names and lyrics in the Cajun music repertoire that translate distinct thematic processes of dislocation and unsettling—that is, the forms of *(dé)payement* (literally, "uncountrying") that have characterized Cajun social history. I consider these (geo)graphies to be constitutive of Louisiana Cajun identities to the extent that, through this form of lyrical inscription, Cajun composers and musicians express what has come to be understood as a collective experience of a common Cajun heritage. Furthermore, the use of parentheses in the terms (geo)graphies and *(dé)payement* underscores the precise segments of each term: the "geo" of the "graphies" suggests the importance of specific locales in the performance of the Cajun music repertoire, both the performers' origins and the locales often evoked in the lyrics. For *(dé)payement*, the prefix *dé* (or "un") designates the instability of fixed settlement in these locales, evoked in song and inscribed through lyrical references. This instability is manifested lyrically as the displacement to, from, and between different parts of the *pays*—that is the local region understood as a distinct land or territory.

The shifting movement between unsettling and resettling that constitutes these (geo)graphies of *(dé)payement* emerges in the Cajun music repertoire and remains a recurrent and variable trait in the Cajun oral and musical tradition. One germinal source of this (geo)graphy is the disruptive, forced uprooting that was the originary experience of the Acadian people. As I noted in chapter 1, the Cajuns were originally immigrant French settlers in Canadian Acadia (Nova Scotia and New Brunswick) who were forcibly exiled by the British in 1755, an event known as *le grand dérangement* (the great upheaval). The Acadians were then resettled in southern Louisiana during the second half of the eighteenth century. This experience of uprooting has continued sporadically in Louisiana Cajun culture, especially during the twentieth century, usually for economic reasons. The result of this *(dé)payement*, expressed both thematically and formally in the haunting (geo)graphies of Cajun music, becomes evident through the nostalgia for origins and stability. That is, these inscriptions occur not only in the lyrics but also in the instrumentation and the plaintive interpretations that musicians bring to the repertoire.[5] Hence, by studying such inscriptions in relation to the thematic movements of *(dé)payement*, we can gain a greater understanding of the important intersections between Cajun musical expression and the cultural practices I study in subsequent chapters.

Three aspects of these (geo)graphies concern me here: First, I address the poetic paradox of "rooted errantry" in the Cajun music repertoire by considering briefly the importance within this repertoire of actual toponyms (predominantly, village locales) in the song titles and lyrics of selected contemporary Cajun composers, musicians, and groups. Different textual examples allow me to develop the paradoxical concept of home, at once within the *pays* and also in the circulation away from it with the hope of the traveler's eventual return. Second, I consider the conflict between various forms of uprooting and the bittersweet nostalgia for home, for origins, and for belonging to a territory. I focus in particular on the thematic connection between different expressions of displacement in the predominant love theme in Cajun lyrics, a particularly sentimental form of *(dé)paysement*.[6] Third, I develop the concept of rooted errantry more fully in the works of one notable artist of French Cajun origins, Zachary Richard. Given the breadth of his expanding creative engagement, I consider this errantry in light of his collections of poetry as well as his recent musical compositions.

A Rooted Errantry

In the framework of reflections on the Acadian poetry of the 1970s and 1980s in French Canada, Martine Jacquot refers to this burgeoning poetic movement as "une poésie de l'errance," a poetics of wandering (1988). I wish to consider this particular nomadism as an inflection of the (geo)graphies of *(dé)paysement*—that is, a particularly Cajun experience corresponding to what Edouard Glissant calls a "thinking of errantry." According to Glissant, this thought emerges "from the destructuring of compact national entities that yesterday were still triumphant and [emerges], at the same time, from difficult, uncertain births of new forms of identity that call to us" (1997, 18). He suggests that, "in this context, uprooting can work toward identity, and exile can be seen as beneficial, when these are experienced as a search for the Other (through circular nomadism) rather than as an expansion of territory (an arrowlike nomadism)" (18). This is a "poetics of the Relation" (the title of Glissant's book), and not just of rootedness, through which the "Relation . . . is spoken multilingually," opposing "the totalitarianism of any monolingual intent" (19). Yet, Glissant's Relation acquires an immobile and rooted aspect as well—"a rooted errantry . . . in a will and an Idea" (41)—despite or because of the uprooting: "The poet's word leads from periphery to periphery, and, yes, it reproduces the track of circular nomadism; that is, it makes every periphery into a center; furthermore, it abolishes the very notion of center and periphery" (29).

Just as for Saint-John Perse (to whom Glissant refers in discussing the concept of a rooted errantry), poetry for the Cajuns "has its source in an idea, in a desire" (Glissant 1997, 37), but this idea and desire are quite distinct in Cajun music. This rooted errantry becomes a desire for stability and for home in the face of difficult economic and sociocultural circumstances, but without the luxury of an ideal provenance or possible elsewhere. In turn, this rooted errantry provokes a nomadic paradox that arises from the diasporic origins of Louisiana Cajuns and results in a music that expresses a circularity, at once movement from or within and yearning for a return to origins in some sort of home. This paradox is a dual impulse that simultaneously places emphasis on modes and circumstances of uprooting and displacement and on the stability of community within fixed sociopolitical parameters. In fact, the nomadic origins of Louisiana Cajuns have given way to a distinct form of identity politics through the Cajun renaissance that began in the 1960s as a form of sociocultural affirmation and survival.

For example, at any music and dance venue, whether inside or outside Louisiana, responses to *(dé)paysement* recur not only in the conventions adopted for introducing musicians but also especially in the song titles themselves. Introductions of musicians invariably include their local origins (e.g., "from Mamou, Louisiana, Steve Riley," "from Marksville, Louisiana, Bruce Daigrepont") so that audiences and musicians alike can ground (or root) themselves in the specificity, and even authenticity, of the regional affiliation. Toponyms are also often used to demarcate specific songs, but it is important to recall, as Ann Savoy correctly insists, that songs in an oral tradition are constantly in flux and that a different interpretation of the same song may result in the artist attributing to it a different title. For example, the "Eunice Two-Step" (recorded in 1928 by Amédé Ardoin) becomes "Jolie Catin" in Iry LeJeune's 1948 version (A. Savoy 1984, 15); "La Valse de la Pointe Noire" (located in Acadia Parish near Church Point), recorded in the early 1930s by Angelas LeJeune, is later known as "La Valse de Kaplan" (located in Vermilion Parish) (Ancelet 1989a, 26).

A perusal of song titles on first albums by several contemporary groups (see note 7) suggests just how prevalent toponyms can be. I chose these recordings strategically because each group selected—Filé, the Bruce Daigrepont Band, Steve Riley and the Mamou Playboys, and the Savoy-Doucet Cajun Band—has been an active band playing at various venues in southern Louisiana and elsewhere for a decade or more, and has recorded subsequent albums that reveal similar toponymic traits.[7] These albums suggest how each group draws on and adds to the traditional repertoire not only to produce innovative instrumentation and vocals, but also to produce in fresh combinations songs from this repertoire.

Recordings by these and other groups constitute (geo)graphies not simply in linking the compositions formally to recognizable toponyms and in a proprietary manner to specific sites in Acadiana. In live music and dance venues, the musicians usually announce the title of successive songs to dancers and spectators and thereby situate the song with a specific geographical marker for francophones and nonfrancophones alike (the latter usually and increasingly the dominant group). The song is then rendered all the more recognizable (if not necessarily comprehensible, in Cajun French, to nonfrancophones) by the opening strains and refrain of the relatively limited number of compositions in the Cajun music repertoire. In this way, a sense of home and territory is created despite or because of the physical displacement—of musicians from venue to venue and, more generally, of the Cajuns who have been forced to move. Indeed, the Cajun home tradition constitutes a genre of private, family a cappella singing, distinct from dance hall music.[8]

Through their compositions and performances, contemporary musicians call upon the repertoire as an aural and oral means to demarcate particular music and dance spaces. Moreover, in the case of the traditional "La Danse [or La Chanson] de Mardi Gras" (Mardi Gras song), the Cajun riders in the *courir de Mardi Gras* are depicted as celebrating an oscillation between home and territory in a particular form of circular errantry that demarcates a cultural ritual belonging to the local *pays*. The usual interpretations of this song (e.g., by Les Frères Michot 1987; and Steve Riley 1995) depict the riders circulating *l'entour du moyeu* (around the hub), located near Grand Mamou in the heart of Cajun prairie country north and west of Lafayette. In BeauSoleil's live recording of this traditional song (1991), Michael Doucet's vocal rendition provides an interesting variation by referring to the home (or music store) of Marc Savoy as one fixed locale in which the Mardi Gras riders congregate: "On ira tous les soirs / Hé, là-bas chez Marc Savoy, / C'est pour avoir un bon temps, / Tout l'après-midi et toute la nuit" (We'll go every night / Over there to Marc Savoy's, / Just to have a good time / All afternoon and all night long).[9]

In this context let us consider a different song, Bruce Daigrepont's "Disco et Fais Do Do," that dramatically depicts the theme of dislocation and communicates the impact of cultural estrangement. Daigrepont's lyrics give rise to a no doubt idealized and nostalgic vision of local practices within the *pays*. Yet the song also shows how home is constructed precisely through those cultural elements that contribute to defining a particular sense of identity:

Disco et Fais Do Do

A peu près cinq ans passés,
    je pouvais pas espérer
Pour quitter la belle Louisiane;
Quitter ma famille,
    quitter mon village
Sortir de la belle Louisiane,
J'aimais pas l'accordéon,
    j'aimais pas le violon,
Je voulais pas parler français.
A cette heure, je suis
    dans la Californie
J'ai changé mon idée.
Refrain:
Je dis Hey-Yah-Yahy,
Je manque la langue Cadjin.
C'est juste en anglais
    parmi les américains.
J'ai manqué Mardi Gras,
Je mange pas du gumbo.
Je va au discos,
Mais je manque le Fais-Do-Do.

J'avais l'habitude
    de changer la station
Quand j'entendais
    les chansons Cadjins.

Moi, je voulais entendre
    la même musique
Pareil comme les américains.
A cette heure, je m'ennuie
    de les vieux Cadjins,
C'est souvent je joue
    leur[s] disques
Et moi, je donnerais
    à peu près deux cent piastres
Pour une livre des écrivisses.

[About five years ago,
I couldn't wait
To leave beautiful Louisiana;
Leave my family, leave my town,
Get out of beautiful Louisiana.
I didn't like the accordion,
I didn't like the violin,
I didn't want to speak French.
Now, I'm in California,
I've changed my mind.
Refrain:
I say Hey-Yah-Yahy,
I miss the Cajun language.
It's all in English here among the Americans.
I missed the Mardi Gras,
I don't eat gumbo,
I go to the disco,
But I miss the Fais-Do-Do!

I used to change the station,
When I heard a Cajun song.
I wanted to hear the same music
Same as the Americans.
Now I'm lonesome for the old Cajuns
It's often I play their records,
And me, I'd give two hundred dollars
For a pound of crawfish.]
(Daigrepont 1987; excerpt. Transcription by Audrey
Babineaux George, translation by Bruce Daigrepont)

(Geo)graphies of *(Dé)paysement*   47

This song suggests commentary from several perspectives, at once linguistic and sociocultural. In terms of cultural *(dé)paysement*, the song reveals the conflict between feelings of belonging and foreignness, even within one's own culture. This conflict arises not only from geographical dislocation and disorientation, but also from a no-doubt idealized sense of linguistic disturbance, expressed eloquently in the refrain, "c'est juste en anglais, parmi les américains" (only in English among Americans). As Glissant has argued, the "poetics of the Relation" is expressed multilingually, and both the sense of home and the estrangement from it derive, in part, from this linguistic isolation. However, Daigrepont's narrator insists paradoxically on a rejuvenation through opposition to the new and the foreign (disco) by access to the old and authentic music, to the communal Cajun event of the *fais do-do* (weekly private house dances), and to genuine Louisiana culinary delights such as "une livre des écrivisses" (a pound of crawfish).

In some ways, then, this *(dé)paysement* serves to express a necessary affirmation of the Cajun sense of identity, even of cultural pride (Mattern 1998, 90), as distinct from the standard American and English-language cultural manifestations. The poetics of Glissant's Relation thus creates a tension between authenticity and (geo)graphies via different forms of territorial inscription in the lyrics, a practice altogether evident in (geo)graphies that depict a mode of internal disruption.

Displacements and *(Dé)paysements*

A second mode of (geo)graphies, the thematic emphasis on movement from and return to a region, offers the most vivid understanding of *(dé)paysement*/dislocation within the shifting definition of Cajun identity. We can understand the paradox of this rooted errantry in light of the concept of nomadism evoked earlier, a paradoxical rooted errantry that takes on additional nuances in light of the development of the concept by Gilles Deleuze and Félix Guattari.[10] In *A Thousand Plateaus*, they consider and contrast the nomadic in relation to an established, royal apparatus of state that hierarchizes and fixes bodies, collective and individual, in place. The nomadic can be understood in this perspective not necessarily or uniquely to be a people traveling in itinerant fashion, but also a people that stays put in order to nomadize on their land—that is, to open themselves to flows and activity that exist in a different relation to the state. In this regard, the role of the family can be crucial for nomadic relations, according to Deleuze and Guattari, given "the secret power [potential (*puissance*)], or strength of solidarity, and the corresponding genealogical mobility that determine [the family's] eminence" in nomadic spatial relations (1987, 366). This perspective helps us better to conceptualize the Cajun rooted errantry as a mode of becoming in-between, or intermezzo, that "has taken on all the consistency and enjoys both an autonomy and a direction of its own" (380).

Deleuze also links this paradoxical sense of the nomad to the concept of deterritorialization and to music, particularly to the lied, which he calls "the voice as a song elevating its chant as a function of its position in relation to the territory: my territory, the territory I no longer have, the territory that I am trying to reach again" (Deleuze and Parnet 1996, "O as in Opera," "V as in Voyages"). Similarly, Deleuze and Guattari describe the lied as "simultaneously the territory, the lost territory, and the earth vector" (1987, 340) and thereby develop the concept of song as refrain, or *ritournelle* (ritornello), the traits of which correspond to Cajun musical practices. That is, the relatively set grouping of themes and standard compositions in the Cajun music repertoire, predominantly waltzes and two-steps, provides a firm basis from which contemporary Cajun musicians now seek new musical forms as well as thematics to explore recent sociocultural developments influencing Cajun society in the late twentieth century. Moreover, Deleuze and Guattari maintain that, for romanticism, to which much Cajun music certainly corresponds, "the territory does not open onto a people, it half-opens onto the Friend, the Loved One; but the Loved One is already dead, and the Friend uncertain, disturbing" (340). And like the romanticism of Latin and Slavic countries, where "everything is put in terms of the theme of a people and the forces of a people," Cajun music unfolds on an "earth that is mediatized by the people, and exists only through the people, . . . [an earth] that is never solitary [but] is always filled by a nomadic population that divides or regroups, contests or laments, attacks or suffers" (340–41).[11]

To consider this theme of to-and-fro movement and rooted errantry, I start with a foundational legend, the movement of *(dé)paysement* that emerges in another song by Bruce Daigrepont, the "Marksville Two-Step" (1987). In this song, Daigrepont offers a celebration of the settlement of the Avoyelles Parish in central Louisiana from which he hails. While emphasizing the importance of family lineage, Daigrepont offers the very simple tale of Marc Éliché's movement and then settlement in the central prairie of what is now Acadiana:

Marksville Two-Step

La roue de wagon, cher,
  à Marc Éliché,
A cassé longtemps passé
Il a trouvé, cher, il a resté
La belle ville
  de cher Marksville
Refrain: On est tous cousins, cher,
On est tous cousines
On est tous voisins,
On est tous voisines
Les bons Cadjins, cher,
  les bonnes Cadjines
La vie est belle,
  dans les Avoyelles.

[The wagon wheel of Marc Éliché
Broke a long time ago
He stayed, he found
The beautiful city of Marksville
Refrain: We're all cousins (men),
We're all cousins (women)
We're all neighbors (men),
We're all neighbors (women),
The good Cajun men,
the good Cajun women,
Life is beautiful,
in Avoyelles.]
(Daigrepont 1987. Transcription by Audrey
Babineaux George, translation by Bruce Daigrepont)

This song presents almost a freeze-frame of the dual impulses of
rooted errantry: the migration of Marc Éliché across Louisiana is seized
at the moment "a long time ago" when the wagon broke down, forcing a
halt which then resulted in settlement by Éliché and others of "la belle
ville de cher Marksville," and the foundation also of an extended family.
With the final line of the refrain, "La vie est belle, dans les Avoyelles,"
Daigrepont idealizes life, then and now, in rural Louisiana, especially
masking what must have been the harsh reality of daily life among set-

tlers who arrived in an unknown country. However, this affirmation as refrain also underscores the significance of the fixity of home, family, and the *pays* as crucial elements of identity.[12]

The thematics of displacement and *(dé)paysement* in the Cajun music repertoire reveal diverse tendencies, and in this and the following sections I focus on their interpretations and on several representative musicians of the 1980s and 1990s. In music by Steve Riley and the Mamou Playboys, for example, these thematics are centripetal—that is, with the musicians maintaining this musical repertoire and, after several years, extending it with original compositions. For Wayne Toups and his earlier group, ZydeCajun, the thematics reach outward, centrifugally, moving gradually away from the standard musical leitmotifs of the Cajun music repertoire and relying little on the instrumentation and arrangements except the Cajun accordion. Toups has drawn, rather, on American rock and roll and rhythm and blues both for themes and for musical "sound," as a deliberate strategy to bring audiences to Cajun music and to inspire Cajuns themselves toward musical innovation within the tradition (to the extent possible). Finally, Bruce Daigrepont has sought a middle ground, relying on thematics and leitmotifs of the *pays* but employing rhythms and instrumentation that, like Toups, seek to reach a broader and younger audience. As Ancelet notes in the liner notes to Daigrepont's third album, *Petit Cadeau* (1994), "[Daigrepont] has infused his original compositions with the elegance of tradition and the vitality of contemporary pop." This contrast of thematic and musical sensibilities provides a view of the intimate relationship of authenticity and (geo)graphies in a living, if endangered, contemporary folk tradition.

Recordings from the 1930s and 1940s have translated the nomadic leitmotif clearly and succinctly in what Ancelet calls the theme of "tu m'as quitté pour t'en aller au Grand Texas" (You left me to go off to Texas) (1989a, 29). One version of the lyrics that define this thematic motif is in a song titled "Grand Texas," interpreted by Chuck Guillory with Preston Manuel and the Rhythm Boys on the documentary *J'ai Été au Bal*:

Grand Texas

Verse 1 and Refrain:
Tu m'as quitté pour t'en aller
    au Grand Texas
T'en aller, toi toute seule,
    au Grand Texas

[Tu connais pas] comment je vas faire,
   moi tout seul,
Tu m'as quitté pour t'en aller,
   pour t'en aller.

[You left me behind to leave for Texas
To leave all by yourself, for Texas
You don't know what I will do, all by myself,
(Since) you left me behind to leave.]
(Traditional; transcription by Barry Jean Ancelet [1989a,
29]; my translation)

The sense of rooted errantry is quite stark in these simple lyrics: the addressee, *tu* (you), goes away from the singer who must stay fixed within the locus of his *pays*. Here, "le Grand Texas" fills the role of the exotic elsewhere, far enough away in an earlier era of limited transportation to constitute a distinct *(dé)paysement*. Moreover, in Ancelet's transcription of the Cajun French, the phrase "toi toute seule" indicates, through the feminine gender endings, that the addressee is a woman. Although a listener might have difficulty hearing the grammatical gender distinction on a recording or in live performance, this particular transcription introduces the implicit theme of heartbreak and lost love, a source of unsettling and *(dé)paysement* that constitutes an internal form of rooted errantry and movement through the shifting emotions of the heart.

The search for love and its frequent loss relate to the first theme because the interlocutor of songs following the "tu m'as quitté pour t'en aller" tradition is usually a departing or departed lover. The reasons for this separation, however, can be other than economic. One example is found in lyrics from a lively two-step by Dewey Balfa, titled variously "Voyage au Mariage" (My true love) (BeauSoleil 1984) and "Voyage d'Amour" (Steve Riley 1998).[13] This song recounts a simple tale of a traveler's journey across Acadiana to rejoin his beloved in order to ask for her hand in marriage:

Voyage au Mariage

J'ai eu nouvelles de ma belle,
Elle était là-bas au Texas.
J'ai passé par Eunice,

Et moi, j'ai acheté
    un pain de cinq sous.
J'arrivais à Basile
Et moi, j'ai acheté
    une canne de sardines,
C'était pour faire le grand voyage
D'ici là-bas au Texas.

Quand j'ai arrivé au Lac Charles,
Moi, j'ai mangé la moitié.
J'ai quitté l'autre moitié,
C'était pour mon déjeuner.
[1 and 3 repeated, then:]
Quand j'ai arrivé chez ma belle,
C'est là ayoù moi, j'ai vu
Que une vieille amitié,
Ca va jamais s'oublier.

Elle est après m'espérer
Avec des larmes dans les yeux.
Elle m'a dit, "Cher vieux nègre,
T'as venu, c'est pour me marier."

[I got word that my love
Was out in Texas.
I passed through Eunice
And bought bread for a nickel.
I arrived in Basile,
And bought a can of sardines
For the long trip
From here to Texas.

When I arrived in Lake Charles,
I ate half for supper.
And kept the other half
For breakfast.
(1 and 3 repeated, then)
When I found my girl,
That's when I understood
That an old love
Is never forgotten.

She's waiting for me
With tears in her eyes.
She said, "My dear,
You've come to marry me."]
(BeauSoleil 1984; traditional. Transcription and
translation by Barry Jean Ancelet)

Here the displacement is voluntary and joyful, with the marital goal explicit, but the very geographical unfolding, the steps of the trip (and also the provisions consumed), seem as important for the narrative as the goal to be attained. That is, the goal is to reach Texas, gradually crossing through southwestern Louisiana, in order to establish the link with the loved one and, presumably, once married then to return. So the circularity of the errantry is at least implied, and the joyful spirit of this two-step lies both in the voyage as well as its ultimate goal.[14]

Another example of this sentimental *(dé)paysement*, also recorded by BeauSoleil (1989a) and many others, is a standard from the Cajun repertoire, "Les Flammes d'Enfer" (The flames of hell). This song hearkens back to the origins of Cajun and Creole forms (the latter now expressed as zydeco) and links the love theme to another leitmotif of *(dé)paysement*, incarceration in prison:

Les Flammes d'Enfer

Oué, asteur, je suis condamné,
Oué, je suis condamné dans la prison,
Prison d'amour, prison d'amour,
Et ma chère bébé, Elle a gardé
    les clefs pour ma liberté.
Refrain: O chère bébé, priez pour moi,
Sauvez mon âme des flammes d'enfer.

[Yes, now I'm condemned,
I'm condemned in a prison,
A prison of love, prison of love,
And my baby holds the keys to my freedom.
Refrain: Oh dear one, pray for me,
Save my soul from the flames of hell.]
(BeauSoleil 1989a, excerpt; traditional. Transcription and
translation by Michael and Sharon Doucet)

This excerpt, taken from the song of imprisonment, suggests the metaphor of love as a prison, a cliché, perhaps, but one that translates the paradox of pain and pleasure that constitutes the disenchantment of *les bons temps*. The choice of examples to depict the theme of sentimental *(dé)paysement* is vast, but to my mind a selection from Wayne Toups's first album (1986), the haunting waltz "Mon Ami" (My friend), succeeds masterfully in relating the quite familiar theme of familial rupture:

Mon Ami

J'étais assis après jongler une journée
Ce qu'arrivé avec mon ami longtemps passé.
Il était un musicien proche toute sa vie
Jusqu'à sa femme l'a quitté avec sa petite fille.
Il (a) dit, "Pourquoi tu me fais ça?
Tu connais les larmes vont tomber.
Pourquoi tu reviens pas avec moi à la maison
Une autre fois, petit coeur, pour une autre chance?"

[I was sitting while thinking one day
About what happened long ago to my friend.
He was a musician nearly his whole life
Until his wife left with his daughter.
He said, "Why'd you do that to me?
You know the tears will fall.
Why don't you come back home with me,
One more time, for one more chance?"]
(Toups 1986; excerpt. Transcription and translation
by Barry Jean Ancelet [1989a])

This tale of a man's separation from his wife and child does not include physical displacement through travel as in the previous lyrics. Rather, it is in the psychological and emotional drama of spousal and parental separation that the song's intensity lies. Furthermore, the plaintive valence of the tale recounted is doubled by the framing device of the composer/narrator's first-person reflection on the pain of "mon ami," all the more poignant with the compassion expressed for a fellow musician. In this sense, the song corresponds well both to the desire *(vouloir)* and to the concept *(idée)* of rooted errantry so evident in Cajun music.

Centrifugal and Centripetal Directions

We can also consider the concept of rooted errantry in the practices pursued by representative Cajun musicians and composers. Notably, in their respective moves from initial to subsequent albums, Bruce Daigrepont and Wayne Toups stand in sharp contrast: Daigrepont's *Coeur des Cajuns* (1989), his second album, contains only his original compositions, instrumentals, and vocals, nearly all in Cajun French, yet all related to the thematics of the Cajun music repertoire. The third album by Daigrepont, *Petit Cadeau* (1994), contains even more personal original songs—for example, about his new daughter, about his uncle's country store, and about the hectic life of a musician. After a five-year hiatus, Daigrepont produced yet another fine album, *Paradis* (1999), in the same vein as the previous ones—that is, offering new interpretations of traditional songs from the repertoire mixed with original compositions. The latter group includes an homage to the Louisiana farmers in his family, songs about faithless love, and several others ("Je Suis Pas un Prisonnier," "Le Diable Est Laché," "Paradis") that reveal Daigrepont's continued rejection of materialist culture as well as the growing importance of religious faith in his music.

Wayne Toups also continued to rely on Cajun standards in his second album (1988), and although his rendition of the title song "Johnnie Can't Dance" is so powerful that it has almost become the standard interpretation for all groups, Toups did little to extend the repertoire itself in this album. Having signed a contract with Polygram/Mercury Records in 1989, Toups's third album, *Blast from the Bayou*, included several songs previously released on the first and second albums, as well as two non-standards, Van Morrison's "Tupelo Honey" and Aaron Neville's "Tell It Like It Is," that Toups regularly included in live performance. The recording does include some new compositions that combine English and French and Cajun and rock in the fusion mix that was the trademark of the zydecajun sound.

The lyrics on Toups's fourth album (the second for Polygram/Mercury), titled *Fish Out of Water* (1991), reveal the complex centrifugal strategy to which I referred earlier. Toups contributed to compositions on only six of the twelve songs, most of which are dominated by the band's main lyricist, Rick Lagneaux, in English or an English-French mix. Toups's contribution to two songs with Lagneaux, "Chisel without the Stone" and "Waiting for You," was a verse for each in Cajun French, and in his own compositions (written with Barry Ancelet under his pen name Jean Arceneaux) he adapted the standard "Les Flammes d'Enfer" as "Rockin' Flames," and contributed two new songs sung in French, "Late in Life" and "Night at the Wheel." The latter belongs to the tradition of sentimental *(dé)paysement*, a courting song that captures well the mix of instrumentation and broadened thematics of pain and joy due to lost love.

Throughout his progression beyond the Cajun music repertoire, Toups has sought to develop a conjunction of instrumental forms (evident even in his original group's name, ZydeCajun) that fuse Cajun with the other dominant regional music, the French Creole rhythm and blues forms of zydeco. More accurately, however, Toups brings rock instrumentation to his music, replacing the fiddle with electric piano and the rhythm guitar with electric lead and bass, while cranking out passionate interpretations on his accordion. Toups has called this music "new wave Cajun, Cajun music of the future, . . . mixed with a little bit of R&B, rock 'n roll, and soul." He continues: "It's played on the diatonic accordion. I still keep my Cajun language in it, but I also sing in English to let the younger generation know what the stories are about, and that keeps it new and interesting" (1990, 162). To reviewers who have asserted that this music is no longer Cajun, Toups emphasizes his authentic Cajun identity, insisting, "They can't take that away from me. They can say whatever they want . . . as long as they say my name," and continues: "I think [zydecajun music] is a whole new way to listen to the music. And we want to get the younger generation involved. That way they can go back to the roots, if they're interested enough. . . . I'm looking out for preserving [Cajun] music for the next generation. Give them something so they can go back and say, 'You left this for us' " (162–63). The success of Toups's strategy is evident not only in his now-classic interpretation of songs like "Johnnie Can't Dance," but especially in the influence of his style on young musicians such as Hunter Hayes (who was seven years old when he released his first CD in 2000), and Damon Troy (2001).[15]

In his subsequent albums and changes of record companies, Toups has maintained the deliberate mix of traditional and innovative music but has dared to branch out in new directions.[16] His return to Louisiana roots and home is marked especially by the 1995 album *Back to the Bayou*. The album resembles *Fish Out of Water* in the combination of original songs (coauthored with Jean Arceneaux/Barry Ancelet) and interpretations of old standards (most notably D. L. Menard's "La Porte d'en Arrière") that move between French and English. Moreover, Toups also includes a solid group of rhythm and blues tunes ("Mine, Mine, Mine," "Take My Hand," "Come On In") that he will reinterpret two years later on the entirely rhythm and blues oriented *Toups* (1997). Ironically, in light of his fervent comments about preserving Cajun music for the next generation, this blues album almost aggressively eschews his trademark zydecajun sound. However, Toups located this album as an important step in his growth as becoming an "artist, period," not just a Cajun artist. Noting his efforts through his career to "turn on a different generation every time and to keep my fan base," Toups judged that the time was right "to highlight my voice more than my musicianship" with an album spotlighting his abilities as "a blue-eyed soul singer" (qtd. in Orteza 1997, 56).

On the two most recent releases, *More Than Just a Little* (1998) and *Little Wooden Box* (2000), this approach has changed considerably. On the former, few of the songs are composed by writers from Louisiana, except the extended version (more than eight minutes long) of a song by Wade Richard and Bobby Terry, "Please Explain," previously included on *Fish Out of Water* (1991). On the most recent release, Toups mixes several songs from the Cajun and zydeco repertoire with some new compositions, most in French. Furthermore, his renditions of "Little Wooden Box" and "Oh, Louisiana" reveal the strongly self-reflective side of his music first made evident on the song (and album) "Fish Out of Water." Thus, given the centrifugal model that I used above to describe Toups's musical project, the (geo)graphies defining his current production clearly emphasize a rooted errantry in the directions of new styles and new sources of creative inspiration yet also a firm resolve not to abandon his Louisiana roots and themes.

"Le Vieux Home" and Territory

A number of compositions by contemporary Cajun musicians point to the complex linguistic and sociocultural issues connected to the tensions between *(dé)paysement* and home, and to the search for roots that extend back to the original *grand dérangement* of the Acadians in the mid-eighteenth century. In many ways, the music of Steve Riley and the Mamou Playboys fulfills the goals of both Daigrepont and Toups in an unexpectedly traditional way. Although the group did not add many original compositions to the Cajun music repertoire in their first few albums (1990, 1992, 1993, 1994), they surely have contributed to rejuvenating the existing music with very polished and spirited interpretations of familiar and not so familiar tunes. Subsequently, on *La Toussaint* (1995), *Friday at Last* (1997), and *Bayou Ruler* (1998), Riley and group members David Greely and Peter Schwarz provide new compositions and rearrangements of older standards in an extraordinarily refreshing mix. In their most recent recording, *Happytown* (2001), they continue this blend of originals and standards but have changed the instrumentation to a distinctly contemporary sound combining the traditional accordion, fiddle, and triangle with percussion, Greely on saxophone, and electric guitars.[17]

This group represents precisely the return to Cajun music by the younger generation that Wayne Toups and many others hoped for in the 1980s, a group that conforms to Dirk Powell's remarks (cited in the epigraph to this chapter) about making the music one's own. The group members have been playing together since their late teens and have now been active on the national and international music scene for a decade. In fact, Steve Riley's talent on both the accordion and fiddle revealed itself so forcefully in the 1980s that the late Dewey Balfa frequently invited Riley to join him and his group at different festival events. Thus, Riley is one of several successors to the Balfa tradition, bringing the musical ability and fervor to the Cajun music repertoire that the slightly older generation of Daigrepont and Toups have manifested throughout their careers.[18]

The lyrics of one song interpreted by Riley and the Mamou Playboys, "Old Home Waltz," provides within it the phrase "the trace of time," which is the title of their Grammy-nominated recording (1993). Hence, this phrase takes on particular significance within this composition, which contains much material ripe for linguistic analysis, notably the apparently curious use of two English words, "home" and "gone," as well as English for the title.[19] However, of particular interest is this song's development of the theme of the sentimental *(dé)paysement*, employing the waltz lament of lost love and of rooted errantry:

Old Home Waltz

Mon vieux *home* est plus le même depuis t'es *gone*.
Ca ressemble juste comme une place abandonnée.
Je suis juste comme un prisonnier qu'a perdu
Son espoir de jamais, ouais, te revoir.

J'ai perdu tous les traces du temps
A guetter l'almanac jour au jour,
A jongler si jamais je vas te revoir
T'en revenir dans le petit croche, toi tout seule.

Je suis après vivre dans l'enfer aujourd'hui
A jongler si jamais je vas te revoir
On pourrait vivre dans le paradis toute notre vie,
Moi et toi, aussi content dans notre vieux *home*.

[My old home is not the same now that you're gone.
It's nothing more than an abandoned place.
I'm just like a prisoner who has lost
All hope of ever seeing you again.

I've lost all trace of time
Staring at the calendar from day to day,
Wondering if I'll ever see you again
Coming down the crooked lane, all alone.

I'm living in hell today
Wondering if I'll ever see you again.
We could be living in heaven all our lives,
You and I, so happy in our old home.]
(Steve Riley 1993; lyrics by Shirley Bergeron and Lee
Lavergne. Transcription and translation by Steve Riley)

The expression of distance between a home eliminated due to affective rupture and a no man's land resulting from this sentimental uprooting recalls the lyrics of the prison song "Les Flammes d'Enfer." Furthermore, the conditional tense of the second-to-last line suggests the dependence on finding an affirmative sentiment to avoid "living in hell."

This loss of home takes on even more stark and depressing proportions in the Schwarz-Greely composition on *Bayou Ruler* (1998) titled "Chez Personne" (literally "at nobody's home," but translated in the CD as "No Man's Land"). Whereas the "Old Home Waltz" is easily located within the thematics of sentimental *(dé)paysement*, the "no man's land" in the 1998 song relates to social indifference and perhaps reflects the emotions the writers feel after so much traveling to performances around the globe. And whereas the "Old Home Waltz" at least holds out the conditional possibility of contentment, "Chez Personne" ends without hope: "Revenants, / Monde gris, / Fait sourd par le silence. / Ni larmes, / ni sourires, / Sans coeur, Chez personne" (Ghosts, / Grey world, / Deafened by silence. / No tears, / No smiles, / No heart, / In No Man's Land). Finally, the earlier composition is recognizable as a waltz while "Chez Personne" employs a 4/4 beat; but it is less a two-step than an anthem with a haunting fiddle tune reminiscent of the "Mardi Gras Song."

The sentimental *(dé)paysement* that often characterizes the plaintive tone of the Cajun waltz stands in thematic and stylistic contrast to the two-step and jitterbug tunes such as Daigrepont's "Marksville Two-Step" and "Laissez Faire" (Let It Be) from his first album (1987). In the latter, which is the opening song of the album, Daigrepont describes almost stereotypically the joyful pastimes of life in Louisiana:

Laissez Faire

[Refrain]
Laissez faire, laissez faire, ma jolie.
Bon temps roulé, allons danser toute la nuit.
Oh, T-Pierre va jouer p'tit fer
Boire la bière et jouer cuillère,
Laissez faire, laissez faire, ma jolie.

. . . .

Travailler c'est trop dur,
Et voler c'est pas bon.
C'est un "va et vient"
Pour avoir rien.
Chère fais attention.
Si toi tu chasse une place comme paradis,
On a ici un beau pays dans la Louisiane.

[Refrain, finale]
[Let it be, let it be, my pretty one.
Good times roll, let's go dance all night long.
Oh, T-Pierre will play the triangle,
Drink beer and play the spoons,
Let it be, let it be, my pretty one.

. . . .

Working is too hard,
And stealing is not good.

It's a going and a coming
To get nothing.
Dear, be careful.
If you're looking for a place like paradise,
We have here a beautiful country in Louisiana.]
(Daigrepont 1987; excerpt. Transcription by Audrey
Babineaux George, translation by Bruce Daigrepont)

As much as this song provides the lively rhythm for performing a two-step or jitterbug, its sentiment communicates the very essence of the myth of *les bons temps*, that is, at once a way to forget the cares of hard work in the pastime of hard play, and also a means of proliferating a stereotype of Cajun joie de vivre, perhaps as a form of wishful and wistful thinking. In the excerpt above, Daigrepont includes lyrics (and title) from another traditional song, "travailler, c'est trop dur," and in Zachary Richard's versions (1977, 1996, 2000a, and 2000b), these lyrics relate the musician's desire to play for his friends so that they might dance because "life is way too short to stir up problems" (my translation). Still, while Daigrepont's upbeat rendition of "Laissez Faire" contrasts with the slower waltzes, their expression of plaintive regrets about love lost, through the complementary *cris* (wails) of the instruments and voices, speaks to a greater loss and nostalgia that waltzes often share with the two-steps that celebrate a simpler and more truly communal time.

Moreover, the geographical location celebrated in the closing line of the verses above makes clear that the two contrasting sentimental styles—of plaintive lament and lively celebration—refer to the nostalgia for origins evident in all Cajun music. We can locate two recent examples of this nostalgia for family and origins on BeauSoleil's *Cajunization* (1999). The recording's opening song (by Michael Doucet) is a lively two-step, "La Terre de Mon Grand-Père" (My grandfather's land) that depicts the land, specifically his grandparents' oak grove and garden, as defining not just "the spirit of my Cajun family" but the very spirit of family itself.

However, it is on another Doucet composition, "Recherche d'Acadie" (In search of Acadia), that the musician translates the terrible vision of his ancestors' dilemma in 1755. In the liner notes, Doucet speaks of his "constant dream" of this vision "watching homes burn and neighbors drown," with the Acadians led to Louisiana by the band's namesake, Beausoleil Broussard:

Recherche d'Acadie

Quand je rêve de ma vie en Acadie
Moi j'ai vu mes voisins et les familles
Devant leurs maisons
Toutes brûlées
A leurs genoux
Ils ont crié
Pourquoi le bon dieu
nous a abandonné?
Recherche d'Acadie

[When I dream of my life in Acadie
I see my neighbors and their families
Outside their houses
Burning down
On their knees
They cried,
"Why has the good Lord
Abandoned us?"
In search of Acadie]
(BeauSoleil 1999, excerpt; lyrics by
Michael Doucet. Transcription and translation
by Michael and Sharon Doucet)

This song stands in sharp contrast to the other songs not only on *Cajunization* but also on most BeauSoleil albums, few of which invest so much emotion into an explicitly personal message.[20] Composed as a haunting waltz like Toups's "Mon Ami," and sustained by Doucet's plaintive interpretation on vocal and fiddle, "Recherche d'Acadie" situates the painful tale firmly within the historical register of the *grand dérangement* of 1755. The song also recalls the finale of Daigrepont's "Laissez Faire" as well as his "Acadie à la Louisiane" (on *Coeur des Cajuns*) because Doucet's composition ends with the descendants of the exiled Acadians, once abandoned and impoverished but now proudly settled and working "La belle terre / Pour l'avenir / Encore notre paradis / Nouvelle Acadie" (The good land / For the future / Once again our paradise / New Acadia [i.e., Louisiana]).[21] As I point out in the next section, this "constant dream" also evokes the topics and tone of music by a contemporary and long-time associate of Doucet, Zachary Richard, not only in the early song

"Réveille," but also quite explicitly in the documentary that Richard produced about the origins of the Cajun people, *Against the Tide* (1999). In both cases, the (geo)graphies of *(dé)paysement* constitute a vital source of creative inspiration as well as personal and existential pain.

Refrains of *Errances* and *Retours*: Zachary Richard

The musical self-representation and affirmation of Cajun identity traced above, although important and real as linguistic and sociocultural phenomena, continuously reconstitute the hybrid ground of what Homi Bhabha calls "an 'in-between' reality": "The inscription of this borderline existence inhabits a stillness of time and a strangeness of framing that creates the discursive 'image' at the crossroads of history and literature, bridging the home and the world" (1994, 13). This formulation also describes quite eloquently the efforts of Cajun writers during the past two decades to create forms of written literary expression within a language that has predominantly remained oral. In local theater, for example, with the encouragement of CODOFIL (Council for the Development of French in Louisiana), the touring company Le Théâtre 'Cadien has "promoted self-expression in the French languages by Cajun people through the performing arts," adopting and adapting plays such as James Fontenot's Civil War romance *Les Attakapas* and David Marcantel's *Mille Misères* (Heylen 1994, 454).[22]

These efforts to create a bridge between the world and home are quite evident in the career and oeuvre of Zachary Richard.[23] In the interview with David Wetsel that precedes *Voyage de nuit: Cahiers de poésie, 1975–79* (2001c), Richard's first collection of poems, he reflects on a comment he made to Ancelet about turning away from angry militancy (1999, 97), affirming to Wetsel that "although I still have these same emotions, in this collection, I make a special place for themes inspired by nature, by the tribe, and by travel" (2001, 14; my translation). To Wetsel's follow-up question of whether Richard considers himself to be a counterculture poet like those he admires, he responds: "The most revolutionary thing that I have done is to plant oak trees. They will be there in a hundred years. It's my commitment to a continuity and to a better earth" (15; my translation). Although Richard had once espoused an angry and militant stance in relation to the forced impoverishment of the Cajun language and heritage, his efforts from the mid-1980s onward have not been devoid of political import. In a profile by Ancelet, Richard states, "I don't think any less of the cause, but I think much more about the means," and when he returned to Louisiana after his militant years of travel in francophone countries in the 1970s, Richard began to refer to himself again by his given name, Ralph. Ancelet comments that Richard "learned important lessons concerning the role of the performer which allow him to step away from the crowds and return home simply as Ralph, Eddie Richard's boy from Scott, with no less concern for the survival of his culture, but with a sense of tempered restraint" (Ancelet 1999, 99).

Such questions of home and its relation to *(dé)paysement* are manifold in Richard's musical and poetic creation. For the displacement from home/*pays*, the return to it and to loved ones—to their nurturing effects and, above all, the relationship between home to and within nature—all constitute fundamental values that Richard expresses in different poetic forms and thematic contexts. Regarding the important connection between home and creation, Richard states:

> My home is a refuge where I can put on another costume and play out another myth: the savage at home. . . . I work much more at writing and composing music when I am here than I ever did when I lived in Montreal, for example. What I create here, I don't have the burning desire [*le feu*] for it to be recognized or even known [elsewhere]. And the satisfaction that I get comes from creating. The place I feel best and most real [*vrai*] is out here in the country, without living out the myth of being bigger than life for other people. (Ancelet 1999, 99)

Although these sentiments suggest that Richard's roots matter most, his creative work in the 1990s shows the extent to which these sentiments are in tension, if not outright conflict, with an active practice of *errance*, the rooted errantry that Glissant discusses. The most obvious examples are the 1996 album *Cap Enragé* and the second collection of verse, *Faire récolte* (Bring in the harvest) (1997). The album was Richard's first recording in French in a decade, due, he says in the album notes, to his feeling "the need to return to this part of myself that is neither more real, nor more comfortable than the other [English-speaking part], but that simply has been there for a long time . . . both parts [being American and being Acadian] give me chills and make me sing for different, but equally valid reasons on both sides" (1996). In this recording, Richard offers a very confident affirmation in French of his French American heritage, with half the songs skillfully and explicitly drawn from either

Acadian or Louisianan sources, yet without the musical (i.e., instrumental and rhythmic) style that would necessarily identify the compositions as Cajun.[24]

From the perspective of the (geo)graphies traced earlier, Richard's selections of Louisiana and Acadian themes and compositions eloquently express the constant shift of geographical and affective referents, between the different regions, from city to country, and from hope to sadness and despair. The one composition on the album not composed by Richard, a song by Yves Chiasson titled "Petit Codiac," is the most distinctive inscription of affective (geo)graphies. With its title designating a river running through southern New Brunswick, the song's lyrics are composed of Acadian place names in the verses and names of Native American and Acadian resistance fighters in the chorus:

> Petit Codiac
>
> Petit Codiac, Rivière Jaune;
> Petit Codiac, Rivière Jaune;
> Petit Codiac, Rivière Bleue.
>
> Petit Codiac, Mic Mac,
> Kouchibouguac.
> Petit Codiac, Petty Coat Jack, Mic Mac,
> Kouchibouguac.
>
> Mississippi Rivière, Rivière Jaune,
> Beaumont Néguac y hé back.
> Kouchibouguac.
> Katché couché couté, Rivière Scoudoc.
> Big cove mic mac, Kouchibouguac.
> Refrain:
> Crazy Horse, BeauSoleil, Louis Rhéal, Jackie Vautour,
> Asteur c'est mon tour.
>
> La Memramcook Ouest, La Memramcook Nord
> Shediac Mic Mac, Kouchibouguac.
> Cap Maringouin, Cap Enragé,
> O Mic Mac jack 'tit mac, Kouchibouguac.
> Refrain[25]
> (Richard 1996; lyrics by Yves Chiasson.
> Transcription by Zachary Richard)

In terms of a rooted errantry, Richard affirms that *Cap Enragé* is a return to "singing in my grandmother's language," and as such, "I feel the pleasure of a prodigal child proud of my wandering [*errance*] but happy that it is over" since this album constitutes both a culmination and a new start: "I have turned toward the East, left for the North, the end of one trip, the start of another" (album notes, my translation). That is, he seems to have embraced fully the French linguistic heritage from which his career as English-language musician had distanced him in the 1980s and early 1990s. Richard has felt that once Louisiana music gained "its rightful place in the pantheon of American musical styles [in the 1980s], now the challenge for me as a songwriter is to go beyond that perception and to create songs that don't necessarily have allusions to 'Jolie Blonde'" (qtd. in Orteza 1998a, 23).

Still, Richard maintains that his "songwriting is very anchored to south Louisiana, and my style—whatever the purists might say—is very much anchored to the musical traditions of south Louisiana" (qtd. in Orteza 1998a, 22). He locates his earlier albums *Zack's Bon Ton* (1988) and *Mardi Gras Mambo* (1989) in his "Faulknerian mode," the albums being his "Yoknapatawpha County": "I was going to create these universal images and address them to Everyman but in the guise of southwest Louisiana experience" (23). And although Richard claims that he has no political agenda in his writing, he also admits that many of his songs— for example, "No French No More" (1990) and "Sunset on Louisiana" (1992)—"can be perceived as socially conscious songs" (22). Thus, with *Cap Enragé* and its mix of tender ballads and fervent tributes to the Louisiana and Acadian heritage, Richard has reached a maturity and harmony in his music that is reflected more generally in the breadth of his career.[26]

This relative closure on Richard's *errance*, at least linguistic, connects to the more complete sense of home that is manifest in *Faire récolte* (1997). With exactly half of the work dating from 1981, this collection of one hundred poems is in many ways a continuation of the poetic forms and thematics of *Voyage de nuit*. The second half of the poems extend over the next eleven years, with the final two poems, "Migration" and "Brûler la canne" (Burning the cane), dated 26 December and 27 February 1994, respectively. Thus, in this precision of dates and locales and also in the continued oscillation between Louisiana and French-Canadian inspiration, the struggle with *(dé)paysement* and with the rooted errantry of the

1970s continues in these poems in which Richard traces his movement toward the more grounded, harmonious position he achieved in the mid-1990s.

However, there is another sense in which the errantry becomes increasingly immobile (though never static) in this volume: nearly half of the poems are located near rural Scott, Louisiana, at Chênes du Marais, where Richard's home was built and where he formally came to reside on 3 December 1981 (the twelve-syllable poem "Chaleur" [Warmth] is followed by the annotation "Move from the [North Scott] Ghetto," where he formerly resided). Richard marks fully half of the poems in the second, post-1981 section of the collection with the notation "Chênes du Marais," and the poems themselves reveal a forceful sensuality—for example, "Bébé créole" (Creole baby), "Soudainement l'hiver" (Winter suddenly), "Depuis que j'ai aimé" (From the time I have loved)—and also a political intensity, even bitterness, that expresses the intransigence of Richard's social consciousness. Besides the Baudelaire quote in the poem "Têtu" (Stubborn)—"Crieur, pétard, révolutionnaire, / Mon semblable, mon frère, / Je te salue, et je t'embrasse" (Shouter, noisemaker, revolutionary, / My kin, my brother, / I greet and embrace you)—the near rant of "La vérité va peut-être te faire du mal" (The truth may cause you pain) brutally expresses a rejection of self-pity for the Cajuns' linguistic dilemma, summing this up in the near blasphemy of the final verses:

> À l'autel de la Sainte Persecution Complex
> Au nom de la merde, du pisse et du petit pipi,
> Parle français, ou crève maudit.
> [On the altar of the Holy Persecution Complex
> In the name of shit, piss, and the little wee-wee,
> Speak French, or die accursed.]
> (118; my translation)

Besides the newfound maturity, even lusty intensity, in some of these poems, many others correspond fully to Richard's conception of the collection's title in relation to his home, his ten acres of land in rural Louisiana, and to the work of his neighbors there. In the introduction, he explains how he associates this collection with the farmer, both on the superficial level of "planting the seed, tilling the earth, and then harvesting, like receiving an inspiration, working on the verses, and completing the poem," and on the deeper level of the "collaboration with forces that can become adversaries or allies, depending on conditions" (1997, 7; my translation). Here, the farmer and poet "act within a spiritual dimension in which certain elements remain mysterious and uncontrollable." For both of them, success "depends on a power, an energy that can neither be described nor imagined, but that they attempt to reach and to direct in a positive way" (7; my translation).

Richard followed the release of another French-language recording, *Coeur Fidèle* (2000c), with a new volume of verse, the title of which, *Feu* (Fire) (2001a), provides the collection's guiding metaphor: from the outbreak of a fire that engulfed part of his Louisiana property, Richard derives a powerful inspiration for his poetry, the unpredictable character of fire as well as its paradoxical nature: "In a tamed state, fire is man's ally, helping him make life more enjoyable, just like poetry. In its wild state, fire dominates man, forcing him to recreate himself through purification, forcing him, like the poet, to reconstruct his world around him" (2001a, 11). From the perspective examined here, of *errance* and *retours*, this collection resembles the earlier ones in terms of Richard's careful notation of the different geographical locales of composition for many poems, those composed in rural Louisiana (at Chênes du Marais) as well as in Québec, and on to France. However, in the sections that follow the opening selection of poems (titled "Feu" collectively), Richard's attendance at the 1994 Acadian World Congress helped him to create a poetic chronicle (titled "Arrangements pour la catastrophe" [Arrangements for the catastrophe]) of the two-week period from 1 to 15 August 1994.

What is particularly notable in these poems is the difficulty that Richard experiences in finding any certain or clear responses to his many questions about how to define what he calls "my 'Acadianity' ": "I was confused by the enigma of my heritage and its significance, and flabbergasted by the thousands of accidental circumstances which propelled me into this trip and connect me still to the memory of this country that is no longer found on any world map, but continues to be located in the imaginary of the descendants of the 1755 exiles" (2001a, 71; my translation). This dual experience of cultural enrichment and confusion is expressed poignantly and succinctly in the final lines of this section's final poem, "Aller-retour court-circuit" (Round-trip short-circuit): "Ici dans mon pays / Loin de mon pays. Dans deux cent trente-neuf ans / Peut-être je vais mieux comprendre" (Here in my land / Far from my land. In two hundred and thirty-nine years / Maybe I will better understand) (2001a, 105). The next section, "Français d'Amérique" (French people of America), follows up the appeal in "Aller-retour court-circuit" for the protection and preservation of the French language, quite possibly lost now for succeeding generations.

Following the section's opening poem reminiscent of Rimbaud's "Le Bateau ivre," three poems have place names as titles: two from Montréal, "Mon Royal" and "La rue Sherbrooke Street," and one from Louisiana, "Kaplan" (a town south of Lafayette). What the poems share is a crude yet forceful mixture of French and English and poetry and vulgarities, through which Richard starkly translates the simultaneously sexual and linguistic violence wrought on francophone culture globally, both in Québec and Louisiana. The poems in the final section (titled like the last poem, "Un à la traîne" [One lagging behind]) all express an overwhelming sadness, even despair, in light of "two hundred and thirty-nine years of suffering" (133), summed up well by this perhaps unanswerable question in the penultimate poem, "Chignectou": "Comment se défaire de ces images qui me hantent / avec leur tristesse ancrée comme de la saleté / en dessous de mes ongles?" (How to get rid of these images that haunt me / with their sadness imbedded like the filth / underneath my fingernails?) (2001a, 133).

Although Richard has claimed that he has no political agenda in his writing, he also admits that many of his songs "can be perceived as socially conscious" (qtd. in Ortez 1998a, 22), a judgment that seems indisputable in his poetry. Indeed, taking a lesson from his family roots, and no doubt to fight actively against the temptations of despair, he has also committed himself to working to make things grow, and not just on his land: he has been active in southern Louisiana as president of Action Cadienne, the grassroots movement to encourage the development of French language skills through immersion courses in elementary schools.[27] Moreover, joining the recent rapprochement between the Acadians and Cajuns, Richard produced and narrated a fifty-five minute video titled *Against the Tide*, which is a poignant history of the Cajuns of Louisiana. Above all, from the perspective of disenchanting *les bons temps*, Richard has been willing and able to explore from early on, with great clarity and severity, the different aspects of Cajun culture that cause him pain as well as joy. From the early songs of Cajun protest in French (e.g., "Réveille," "La Ballade de Jackie Vautour"), he moved on to create some extraordinarily moving songs in the English phase of his career, most notably on the loss of French language ("No French, No More," 1990) and on the effects of pollution and industrialization on life in Louisiana ("Sunset on Louisiana," 1992).

One can still notice the distinction of linguistic audiences by comparing selections between the American retrospective CD (by Rhino Records) and the French Canadian two-disc anthology. On the latter, there is a strong and deliberate emphasis on Richard's evolution as a songwriter and musician, whereas the American single CD has a greater emphasis on the variety of compositions (see Mouton 1999, 37). There is a difference of tone as well: the American album is more upbeat while the French Canadian production does not shy away from social statements. Not only does the first disc include selections from the early, militant period of Richard's career, among the last five songs on the second disc are three of Richard's most hard-hitting songs: "No French, No More," and "Sunset on Louisiana," as well as the 1999 live version of "La Ballade de Jean Batailleur" (also included on *Cap Enragé*).

Richard's creative work suggests a continuing paradox inherent to the myth of *les bons temps*: on one hand, Cajun musicians and writers, through their exploration of different musical, poetic, and cultural forms, willingly establish the conditions of another form of *(dé)paysement*, beyond Acadiana, through recognition in national and even international markets. Richard's albums *Cap Enragé* and *Coeur Fidèle* were both recorded in France with the French musicians with whom he tours and have garnered prizes unavailable in the English-language markets (double platinum for *Cap Enragé* and gold status for *Coeur Fidèle*). This exploration produces (geo)graphies linked at once to the regional specificity and to new horizons of errantry, no longer rooted in the same way but rather caught in the shifting and conflicting demands of both market and creative forces.

On the other hand, *les bons temps* is a dual-faceted mythology, at once a form of celebration but also a distinct recollection of suffering. Richard closes his most recent album, *Coeur Fidèle*, with a new version of "Réveille" followed by "Contre Vents, Contre Marées," the theme song of the documentary *Against the Tide*. The choice of these selections suggests that both aspects must be maintained—celebration and recollection of suffering—for survival of this cultural expression and affirmation. Richard himself sums up these sentiments in the notes on the French Canadian CD that introduce the final song, "La Ballade de Jean Batailleur": "Il y a dans chacun de nous un Batailleur avec qui on est obligé de s'accomoder. C'est la partie de nous-même qui nous réveille la nuit avec ses cris de souffrance" (In each of us, there is a Batailleur, a fighter, that we have to get used to. It is the part of us that wakes us up at night with its cries of pain; my translation).

3

"J'ai Été au Bal":

Cajun Sights and Sounds

.
.
.

The reason that Cajun music was so attractive to the rest of the world when they first heard it in the '60s was that it was so unlike anything they had heard before, and I think that's what the beauty of Cajun music is: It's not programmed or polished. It has all these elements that are not mainstream. It sounds old. It doesn't have any kind of hype, commercialization or pretentiousness.—Marc Savoy, quoted in Arsenio Orteza, "Taking on the Big Boys"

The celebration of joy and the remembrance of suffering are the two poles that coalesce in the work of many Cajun musicians and composers. Yet, according to the definition of tradition proposed by Marc Savoy, a musician like Zachary Richard could hardly be considered a "traditional musician." Says Savoy: "I realize now that the person who plays the music he loves and identifies with is the one who is less likely to change or mutilate it. The one who is not concerned with whether or not it's marketable is the one I call a traditional musician" (Ancelet 1999, 139). For over twenty-five years, Richard deliberately sought to bring his music to new audiences and to diverse, multilingual markets—indeed, to risk hype and commercialization for the sake of spreading the dual-faceted message of *les bons temps*. To do so, he even eschewed his French linguistic heritage for a time in order to escape facile and limiting market labels. However, he has always attended to the vital importance of the French language, and in his recent recordings he reaffirms his fervent commitment to the history of the Acadian and Cajun peoples and to the diversity of his own musical and poetic expression, both in French and in English.

These observations suggest the limitations of Marc Savoy's definition of the "traditional musician," for no one could accuse Richard of seeking to mutilate the music (or the cultures) with which he so intimately identifies. To understand the hyperbolic thrust in this definition, then, we need to situate the development of the Cajun music and cultural renaissance in relation to the market forces that came to bear on it in the 1980s. Notably, one result of the popularity of things Cajun and things Creole during this time was that various corporations sought to employ Cajun and zydeco rhythms and images as background for marketing a wide array of products. Examples abound, from theme music and primetime television shows to commercials for food and drink. My favorite commercial was one I saw for several months in the early 1990s during televised nightly news programs: a dancing crawfish would cavort happily with a bottle of commercial antacid to a zydeco beat, with blurry images of Cajun-style dancing in the background. As a large African American man with a gold-capped tooth smiled close to the camera, the narrator's very deep, resonant voice concluded, "life is good" (but only if you took the antacid tablets being advertised).

As I suggested in the previous chapter, despite these and other forms of exploitation of Cajun and Creole culture in the mass media, the concurrent cultural affirmation, begun in the 1960s, developed quietly and forcefully in Cajun music and dance through creative and innovative efforts of indigenous Louisiana artists and entrepreneurs. I have identified this affirmation, following comments by Gilles Deleuze (1995), as a paradoxical form of "legending" that seeks to create a people through the power of fabulation. In certain ways, however, the best efforts of these entrepreneurs to promote a vision of Cajun culture have tended to move toward modes of representation and mythmaking that are related to the mass-market advertising evoked above. Although some may find the marketability of the music to be incompatible with the notion of tradition, we can trace the diverse and consistent efforts to market images of Cajun cultural life, efforts in which many of the main spokespersons for Cajun cultural affirmation have participated.

A number of folklife initiatives in the Lafayette area of southern Louisiana deserve scrutiny in this light: for example, the living museums of early Cajun settlements at Acadian Village and Vermilionville around Lafayette; the weekly radio show *Rendez-Vous des Cajuns* at the Eunice Liberty Theater under the auspices of the U.S. Park Service; and the proliferation of festivals in southern Louisiana which, despite different themes emphasized, tend generally to focus on Cajun food, music, and dance.[1] Instead of these local initiatives, I will focus on different genres of film—commercial productions, documentaries, and dance instructional videos—that are meant precisely to reach broad, even global, audiences and to participate, directly or indirectly, in marketing images of Cajun culture. In so doing, I will discuss the confluence of hybridity with issues regarding the cultural affirmation of Cajun identity as revealed in different forms of representation in film. In the opening section of this chapter, I examine the role of Cajun dance and music in key scenes of two films, *Southern Comfort* (1981) and *The Big Easy* (1987). In the second section, I link the preceding discussion of representation of cultural identity to the cultural practices portrayed in two documentaries by the filmmaker Les Blank: his general overview of Cajun music and dance, *J'ai Été au Bal (I Went to the Dance): The Cajun and Zydeco Music of Louisiana* (1989a), and the more specific documentation of Cajun life, culture, and folk practices in his profile of one Cajun couple, Marc and Ann Savoy, in *Marc and Ann* (1991). In the third section, I turn to the commercial initiative of Cajun instructional dance videos that depict and provide instruction in dance practices for the Cajun dance and music arena and also articulate as part of the instructional delivery an image of Cajun identity. The analysis of these instructional tapes serves a dual function: on the one hand, to provide a glimpse at the ways in which local entrepreneurs develop dance as a product in relation to the cultural heritage of which it is an expression; and, on the other hand, to establish a bridge to the discussion of the dance and music venues in chapter 4.

Scenes of Dance and Music: Constructing Minor(ity) Identity

As Louisiana Cajun French has evolved throughout this century, the music and especially the lyrics therein have come to serve as the most lively vehicles for the proliferation of linguistic and artistic expression as well as Cajun style. This expression and style relate to a particular sound or set of sounds that are quite evocative but that have also been exploited for commercial ends. It is the tension between construction of an ethnic identity through music and the exploitation of this cultural form that I wish to explore in this section.

The words "j'ai été au bal" in the chapter title evoke a particularly hybrid and paradoxical type of cultural development. Most recognizably, these words are the title of a standard song in the Cajun music repertoire, the lyrics of which begin: "J'ai été au bal hier soir, / J'vais retourner encore ce soir, / Si l'occasion se présente, / J'vais r'tourner demain soir" (I went to the dance last night, / I'm going back tonight, / And if I get the chance, / I'll go back tomorrow night). The lyrics refer to the locations in which, and, more broadly, the ritual through which, the affirmation of Cajun cultural identity is most frequently manifested—the dance halls, clubs, restaurants, and festivals in southern Louisiana, and beyond Louisiana in the many local events that promote Cajun music and dance year-round in North America, Great Britain, and beyond.[2]

Thus, these lyrics point to the movement between repetition—of musical compositions from the repertoire as well as dance moves—and renewal of the music and dance experience at successive dance and music venues as a key component of such affirmation. However, the opening words, "j'ai été au bal," have also been borrowed by filmmakers Les Blank and Chris Strachwitz as the title of their video documentary (and the accompanying audiocassettes and CD) on the history of Cajun and zydeco music (1989). As such, these words take on a new resonance, utilized to signify a narrative representation of the development of Cajun music and dance forms now commercially available through global marketing.

The matter of minor(ity) identity is at the crux of much debate on taste and styles in music and dance in southern Louisiana. In fact, identity in this region is quite precisely constructed on the basis of many complex attributes, some of which, like the Cajun dialect, are quite distinct although beleaguered, while others are highly problematic (most notably, racial origin). Indeed, many such attributes contribute to defining tradition (in Cajun dance, music, festivities, and rituals) and even of maintaining what some would call purity, and others authenticity, of traditions in the face of perceived threats from outside influences. Hence, these practices contribute to forming a hybrid in-between zone along shifting and variable lines that vary according to different venues and contexts (e.g., club or restaurant; city or country; within Louisiana or outside the state) and agents (e.g., musicians, fans, dancers, spectators). Yet, a fundamental aspect of this in-betweenness strikes me as paradoxical: the fervent desire, expressed by various spokespersons on Cajun culture, to hold on to what they construe as traditional and authentic while simultaneously employing the media and technological means that at once weaken this hold and fail to translate these very values. We may understand the relationship of the horizontal (of inside/outside) to the vertical (above/below) through the distinction of national/global versus regional/local oppositions. As I will demonstrate, different genres in the cinematic domain provide clear examples of this paradoxical situation.

In this light, I place the suffix "ity" of "minor(ity)" in parentheses with two goals in mind: first, because the attribution of minority to this particular social group of predominantly European origins may appear incongruous, the parentheses placed in the term minor(ity) are a way to emphasize nonetheless both the marginal status of this ethnic group of French and French Canadian heritage within American national culture as well as the fact of their predominantly willing integration to this very culture. However, the first use of the parenthetical markers connects to a second use: the specific valence of the term minor as developed by Deleuze and Guattari.[3] In chapter 2, I noted that the characteristics of a "minor" artistic practice—a disturbance of a major language linked to the political impetus and collective expression of this disturbance—are linked to the hybrid in-betweenness of fabulation, of finding the means to invent a people to come. Such expression and its concomitant cultural practices form a nexus with dual locations: on the one hand this nexus is located between increasingly dominant American cultural practices and language and the attempts to maintain and develop Cajun linguistic and cultural specificity; on the other hand this nexus appeals insistently to the Acadian and francophone origins of Cajun music and culture, but also finds vigor in new modes and mixes of artistic creation that open onto the present and future.

Among the many scholars who have deployed the concept of the minor in discussions of artistic production, Fredric Jameson has made particularly cogent use of it, arguing that the minor "has the advantage of cutting across some of our stereotypes or doxa about the political as the subversive, the critical, the negative, by restaging an affiliated conception of art in the new forcefield of what can be called the ideology of marginality and difference" (1992, 173). This codification of the minor, says Jameson, "works within the dominant . . . [to] undermin[e] it by adapting it," such that "selective modes of speaking are 'intensified' in a very special way, transformed into a private language" (173).[4] This conception of aesthetics differs, Jameson concludes, "from that of the breaking of forms," and so "'minor' aesthetics" or "symbolic 'restricted codes' . . . forfeit any grand progress on towards the status of a new hegemonic discourse" (173–74). That is, "unlike Hollywood style, they can never, by definition, become the dominant of a radically new situation or a radically new cultural sphere" (174).

I use the term minor(ity), then, to emphasize the linguistic, discursive, and sociopolitical facets that constitute the "minor" status of Cajun culture and identity, constructed at the nexus of tension and conflict between vertical (above/below) and horizontal (outside/inside) sociocultural relations. Jameson's reference to the hegemonic dominance of "Hollywood style" as distinct from, but connected to, a "'minor' aesthetics," no doubt errs in its own way by essentializing a broad array of dominant practices in film. However, the tension that Jameson underscores provides an entry for considering a number of elements that constitute conflicts inherent to minor(ity) identity. Specifically, I propose to examine two examples of the dominant/dominated dialogue within commercial cinema of the 1980s, *Southern Comfort*, and the more well-known film *The Big Easy*. My purpose here is to extend the study of the construction of *les bons temps* in relation to the Cajun dance and music arena by considering in particular the purported tendency to undermine the dominant by adapting it. I select these films on the notable basis of the filmmakers' use of Cajun dance and music in crucial scenes as part of the narrative construction. Besides their stereotypical value, what makes the scenes in these films of particular interest is the presence in each of prominent musicians whose music and performances are exploited for the purposes of cinematic and sociocultural representation.

Besides notable stylistic differences, these films stand in sharp contrast by one rather remarkable index—their availability. *The Big Easy* is readily accessible on videocassette, DVD, and televised retransmissions to audiences who presumably have limited awareness of the film's complex manipulation and conflation of cultural elements. *Southern Comfort*, on the other hand, has only recently become available on VHS and DVD, and has only occasionally appeared on TV rebroadcasts.[5] Even so, there is little risk of viewers taking the film's plot elements at face value—the Cajuns depicted solely as swamp-dwelling trappers and backwoods misfits. This was not the case for *The Big Easy*; other than questioning the overall cinematic quality of the film, most reviewers seemed to accept it as a faithful representation of cultural life in southern Louisiana, especially of the relatively unproblematic insertion of Cajun culture into New Orleans.[6] Moreover, as I noted in chapter 2, Michael Doucet attributes to this film the spectacular feat of having unleashed the "Cajun craze" in the late 1980s (Nyhan, Rollins, and Babb 1997, 5). Although the causes of this craze certainly relate to more than just one film, the period 1987 to 1994—the peak of what I have called the "second wave" of the Cajun renaissance—encompasses all the visual representations of Cajun dance that I examine in this chapter.[7]

Southern Comfort's lack of availability, as well as its only relative popularity, are somewhat surprising because the film boasts not only an important director, Walter Hill, and a superb ensemble cast, but also a soundtrack by Ry Cooder, most recently of *Buena Vista Social Club* fame.[8] Whereas the tone of *The Big Easy* remains remarkably lighthearted despite its grisly subject of multiple murders and drug-related police corruption, *Southern Comfort*'s dank setting and the increasingly desperate plight of National Guardsmen at the mercy of the rural Louisiana swamp and justifiably vengeful Cajuns seem to weigh down the film with a ponderous and bleak atmosphere. However, this heavy tone is consistent with the inexorable narrative drive toward a seemingly inevitable catharsis in a sequence supposedly set at a rural Cajun encampment. It is in this scene that Cajun music, musicians, and dance play an important role.[9]

Prior to this finale, the rural Cajun culture and the French language are associated with the unseen forces of vengeance when the guardsmen capture a one-armed trapper whose house is abruptly torched by one unit member in a fit of revenge and frustration. The trapper responds to them in a French patois, claiming innocence and bewilderment when he is accused of having killed the unit's leader. His responses are incomprehensible to the captors, and in their collective rage one of them strikes him brutally in the face. Given the allegory with Vietnam that underlies the entire film, the purpose of the French language, the swampy locale, and the gratuitous violence are mainly symbolic, to depict from the protagonists' perspective an incomprehensible setting (the unit is lost from the start) inhabited by incomprehensible people who deserve whatever treatment they get.[10] However, the one-armed Cajun escapes the captors when rescued by one soldier (Hardin, played by Powers Boothe) from torture at the hands of another. When the two guardsmen confront each other with knives, the trapper reveals his hidden knowledge of English as he goads them to fight—shouting "Tue-le," then "Kill him, kill him!"—before heading into the swamp. Later, he reappears toting a rifle when he confronts the last survivors (Hardin and Spencer, played by Keith Carradine), and in return for Hardin's intervention on his behalf earlier, he warily shows them the way out of the swamp, warning that "my [Cajun] buddies, they not nice like me!"

Thus, the final setting at the sparsely populated encampment, where the local people seem entirely unaware of any danger to these evident strangers, underscores the film's desperate and harsh ethos of survival of the fittest. The guardsmen's arrival—on the back of a pickup truck with two pigs soon to be slaughtered—is bluntly symbolic, and when they demand to be taken to a phone immediately the driver insists that they eat and drink first, closing with the ubiquitous "pass a good time with us, *laisse les bons temps rouler*." However, I consider this final sequence (approximately twelve minutes) to be especially important because its crescendo of violence occurs through a direct juxtaposition between the dance and music at the *bal de maison* and the armed confrontation between hunters and the hunted taking place next door. By precise use of editing, the filmmaker structures this sequence so that he locates the wailing musicians and stomping dancers as implied contributors to the confrontation in a nearby house.[11]

Among the four musicians are Dewey Balfa and Marc Savoy, who surely had no inkling about the manner in which the *bal de maison* scene would be employed through careful editing in relation to the finale. For during the initial dance scene, as the guardsmen warily observe the jubilant crowd inside the packed house, a cold and apparently hostile glare from Marc Savoy seems to cast suspicion on Hardin, and with the paranoia thus heightened, Hardin then appears to return the glare through shot/shot-reverse editing. The film then crosscuts between the dance/music scene and hunters and hunted, in two movements: first, the guardsmen, as if stalked, ominously anticipate the appearance of the hunters, while the dance/music scene is juxtaposed to a third scene, the killing and preparations of two pigs for the *boucherie* (slaughter). The confrontation between hunters and hunted erupts just as the innards of one pig spill to the ground, and the final successive scenes of the pig slaughter are juxtaposed to shots of dancing feet and bodies and the musicians' faces while one wails the waltz. The images and screams of two of the Cajun hunters as they are stabbed are interspersed quickly in successive shots with visuals and sounds of the waltz singer's *cris*, the high-pitched, poignant yells that characterize and punctuate Cajun songs (see Reed, Tate, and Bihm 1969). Thus, the musicians along with the dancers serve as a collective vehicle for constructing an apparently authentic folk setting, but unbeknownst to them, their performance serves the filmmaker as a way of depicting their otherness as foreign and, by juxtaposition to the focal events of the plot, as a way of collaborating through images, sound, and movement in the murderous confrontation.

Another *bal de maison* scene, while altogether quite brief (seven minutes), functions in *The Big Easy* as the fulcrum for communicating the film's moral of honesty and justice and the possibility of redemption for its chief protagonist, Remy McSwain (played by Dennis Quaid).[12] All the principal characters have gathered to celebrate the dismissal of charges of police corruption against McSwain who, in fact, used his connections to have an incriminating videotape erased and thus to thwart the open-and-shut case prepared by the prosecuting attorney, Ann Osborne (played by Ellen Barkin). In hopes of reviving his interrupted love affair with Osborne, McSwain has dispatched his Uncle Sos to take her into custody in order to deliver her to the family (and law enforcement) gathering. Osborne's afternoon jog is interrupted by Uncle Sos who wheels his police vehicle onto the bank of a New Orleans bayou, and thus she is caught off-guard, both in terms of her appearance (she is clad in sweaty t-shirt and shorts) and in terms of her apprehension by the friendly but insistent officer (and quite literally avuncular: "Now listen to ya Uncle Sos, chère").

The shot of her angry acceptance of the "incarceration," as a passenger in Uncle Sos's vehicle, is followed via jump cut by a close-up of an accordion. The camera angle then widens immediately as it pulls back to include McSwain on guitar accompanying the established Cajun fiddler, the late Dewey Balfa, as well as other members of his family and band on the well-known Cajun standard "Pinegrove Blues." The camera movement backward then widens to include a number of dancers, some of whom (the least skilled) are actors playing secondary characters in the film, and others (the most skilled, including the first couple and the man with two women) are experienced New Orleans Cajun-style dancers hired as extras for the scene. Several quickly edited shots then juxtapose uniformed police officers with an array of characters dressed and behaving in exaggerated forms of *les bons temps* in what the filmmaker must have deemed typical Cajun fashion, including the brief cigar-in-mouth boogie by actor John Goodman, who plays a corrupt detective in McSwain's unit. Any doubt that the choice of garish clothing in the crowd scene is deliberate is dispelled by the appearance of the police lieutenant Jack Kellom (played by Ned Beatty). Already established as McSwain's peer and his mother's fiancé, Kellom bounds to the porch dressed in someone's impression of a typical Cajun—crawfish hat, suspendered pants, and t-shirt emblazoned with a bottle of hot sauce, declaring, "Do these Cajuns know how to throw a party or what?" He follows this by proposing a toast to McSwain's apparent vindication, prefaced by a peculiar homily of "justice" triumphant.

I wish to emphasize three particular facets of this *bal de maison* sequence that subtly underscore the tensions relating to constructing minor(ity) identity: the depiction of cultural stereotypes and of established Cajun musicians and music; the role of dance, both in narrative and symbolic terms; and the particular, limited use of Cajun French in relation to English. The stereotype of Cajun behavior and social practices is at once the most evident facet of this scene and the most misleading. Leaving the music and dance practices aside for a moment, this entire sequence (as well as the rest of the film) places great emphasis on community and on family relations, with the filmmaker having taken care to represent all generations in the celebration. However, much of the behavior, the clothing, and even the locale seem to affirm the words in the title of an article by Barry Jean Ancelet summing up the stereotypical depiction of Cajuns by Hollywood as "drinking, dancing, brawling gamblers [in this case, police] who spend most of their time in the swamp" (1990). Added peculiarities in the film include New Orleans presented as the capital of Cajun culture (see Ancelet 1990, 14) and the New Orleans Police Department's uniformed officers partying as if belonging to the clan of *les bons temps* Cajuns. Although the appearance of Kellom on the porch seems to place an exclamation point on these incongruities, his Cajun-wannabe garb is actually quite consistent from the perspective of the film's narrative. Given his close relationship with mother McSwain (played by Grace Zabriskie), Kellom in some ways incarnates the outsider to Cajun culture and social practices, the Cajun-by-choice who, like the filmmaker, cannot help but exaggerate the social practices in an attempt to "get it right." The garb also corresponds to the skewed sense of justice that he enunciates in the scene while, in the process, his statement also implicates the celebrating Cajuns in the prevailing distortion of values.

This guilt by association brings me to the particular use here of the Cajun music of Dewey Balfa, family, and friends, whom the filmmakers depict in order to inspire a sense of local authenticity, as was the case in a different manner in the scene from *Southern Comfort*. As I noted above, until Balfa's death in 1992 no other musician better represented the affirmative aspects of the Cajun cultural renaissance from the 1960s onward. However, as the sequence commences, the camera focuses on the accordion, then moves to a wider angle to present McSwain on the porch instrumentally accompanying the principal musicians and vocalists. As in the technique used in *Southern Comfort*, this insertion of the film's protagonist among recognizable Cajun musicians and a local setting establishes a certain authenticity within the narrative. Similarly, the vocals and instrumentation constitute a distinct aural presence of Balfa and company at some level throughout the sequence, and the editing process allows the musicians to return visually as well. Whether in the background of several porch or crowd shots or in different jump cuts, these images seem to signify not only the privileged place of the musicians before the crowd but also to guarantee the site as one of authentic Cajun celebration. This visual signification will continue particularly in the sequence of shots that are set on the front porch shortly after Osborne's arrival.

However, this arrival is not a happy landing, at least not for Osborne who is furious at the deception by Sos and McSwain and also embarrassed by her own sweaty appearance. The hostile environment is signaled by murmurs from the crowd that signal her presence as unwanted—someone mumbles, "What's she doin' here?" Although McSwain's younger brother appears glad to see her, complimenting her on the case that she tried against Remy, Osborne cuts him short with a curt "Hey, I lost," as she heads for the house to call a cab. After completing her call, she has a second encounter, a confrontation with mother McSwain, who had maintained a dignified, yet wounded presence throughout the trial. To her reproach, "You said some pretty hard things about my boy up there," Osborne replies by affirming, simply, but firmly, that indeed she had made such statements. To the mother's retort, "He's a good boy," Osborne shoots back, "He could be a helluva lot better," and the mother laughingly replies, "What you gonna do? You gonna help him with that?" She pauses as Osborne looks down, embarrassed, then says: "You've got your work cut out for you, chère." However, the final exchange is related not to Remy McSwain but rather to Osborne's sweaty appearance, and serves to put the lawyer in her place: when Osborne explains that she's dressed this way because she was running, the mother mutters, "Running?," rolls her eyes, and walks from the porch, leaving Osborne embarrassed, isolated, and now exposed to the gaze of the crowd assembled before the house.

The second tune that the musicians perform follows this exchange, a waltz composed by Clifton Chenier that features McSwain as vocalist singing in English with his gaze directed in serenade manner toward the embarrassed Osborne. The sequence of shots that compose the porch serenade reveals the visual insertion first of the musicians, then of dance, within the narrative and discursive strategies of the cinematic representation. Indeed, because Osborne has refused to speak to McSwain and stands alone waiting for a taxi to remove her from the humiliating situation, Remy needs some emphatic means to attract her attention and thus assumes the central role in the band. However, it is through the use of fairly rapid shot/reverse-shot movements that the filmmaker positions the viewer in a middle ground as celebrant with the musicians and as observer, along with the other celebrants, of the isolated and humiliated woman/outsider.

In distinction to the opening song of the scene, "Pinegrove Blues," which served as an initial, recognizable marker of French Cajun music, the lyrics of the Clifton Chenier song, "You Used to Call Me," have an evident narrative import for McSwain's disrupted relationship with Osborne. More significantly, this serenade performed in English before family and friends employs the full participation of the Cajun band in support of McSwain's transparent tactics to woo Osborne back. The song continues behind the tense dialogue between McSwain and Osborne which he initiates, after putting down his guitar, by singing the lyrics "why don't you call me anymore?" To his invitation to dance with him, Osborne refuses and descends from the porch, but as McSwain stubbornly insists, the crowd of celebrants—men, women, and uniformed offers alike—surrounds the couple and pressures the visibly flustered Osborne to concede, thereby abetting McSwain's tactics.

Osborne yields reluctantly and leads McSwain to the dance floor, and this sequence is crucial not only for emphasizing the importance of both language and dance as part of the filmmaker's narrative and discursive strategies but also for the visual and aural effects created by the film editing that juxtaposes lyrics and dance in tandem. First, as McSwain and Osborne begin to waltz, the jump cut to the vocal performance, followed by Dewey Balfa's solo, introduces the Cajun French version of one verse that McSwain had just sung in his English serenade. Besides again inserting the musicians within the narrative in support of McSwain's tactics, the filmmakers introduce the linguistic difference through Balfa's vocal. The fully framed Balfa and his plaintive lyrics ("Quoi faire, quoi faire, chère, quoi faire, toi tu m'appelles plus au telephone?") enhance the authorizing effect of Cajun linguistic authenticity reproduced throughout this sequence. This effect both connects and contrasts with the much more sporadic use of French throughout the film by the actors as a sort of reality effect (most notably, the repeated familiar endearment cher/chère).

The focus shifts then from the music performance to the tense waltzing couple, and here one notices that the soundtrack makes an aural jump, from the verse that Balfa had been singing to another part of the song. This is a necessary move in order to prepare the subsequent jump cut within the dance sequence to a close-up of the musicians. Whereas dance played the role of contrasting frenzied exuberance with grisly murder in *Southern Comfort*, dance's narrative and symbolic role in *The Big Easy* becomes increasingly evident: just as the sequence's opening song and dance scene establish the space of affects in terms of *les bons temps*, the filmmakers use edited shots and voice-overs in the second dance sequence in order to extend the "authentic" representation of group celebration. It starts with mother McSwain calling, "Allons danser, everybody!" as if to give the maternal guarantee that all difficulties will be resolved. As McSwain and Osborne move onto the dance floor, the mother's call also seems meant to emphasize the salutary, even nurturing effect of the dance event. However, we should also read this dance floor as a marvelous site of confrontation. For while Osborne meets McSwain's gaze in response to his direct challenge to dance, she literally follows his lead in the dance, refusing to meet his gaze, and thus deliberately appears to submit to the group pressure and to the dance conventions only better to respond to McSwain's tactics.

This sequence finally shifts from the dance floor to the sidelines as the couple waltzes off the floor, with the dance arena working in symbolic fashion to turn the moral advantage to Osborne. Despite the image with which the *bal de maison* sequence ends—the dejected Osborne riding off alone in the taxi—she has capably met the dance challenge: having performed dutifully in following McSwain's lead, she then poses her question—"Are you satisfied?"—once they have waltzed away from the group. This challenge seems to startle him, as if the enchantment not only of the dance movement but also of the lyrics, sung yet again in English by the harmonizing singers, would somehow have combined to overcome her steadfast resistance. As Osborne continues to express herself, fervently and succinctly emphasizing the extent to which McSwain has betrayed his community's trust, McSwain seems quite able to shrug off the litany of crimes that he has committed because Osborne speaks a different language than he, one of justice and right. But her final summation, "Face it, Remy, you're not one of the good guys anymore," shifts to terminology that even he can understand, echoing the mother's earlier claim, or hope, that "Remy's a good boy." As if to emphasize the disparity between image and reality, the filmmakers prepare an emphatic, if cloying, final juxtaposition: the head and torso of a little boy emerges conveniently from an open car window next to McSwain, and the boy gazes inquisitively as McSwain stares in bewilderment at Osborne's departure. The dance arena and the lyrics of the Cajun waltz, begun as a serenade and completed with the woman/outsider in McSwain's arms, have failed to produce the intended, seductive magic. Instead, with music and musicians in support, the dance floor has functioned as a site that evokes allegiance to family and community, and in the intense locus of dance and music McSwain's usual jokes and amorous ploys are inadequate in the face of these complex issues.

The *bal de maison* sequence constitutes the moral turning point for the film's narrative because the subsequent scenes, done in rapid succession, show McSwain removing himself from the "Mothers and Orphans" list of payoff recipients; refusing to help the property room officer who abetted his cover-up; and overriding his fellow detectives' objections in order to reorient the murder investigation in a direction that will quickly lead to both legal and moral resolution. It is interesting to note, then, that Cajun music and a form of dance return one final time as if to place an exclamation point on the happy denouement: having exposed the corruption within his own detective unit and killed the perpetrators while saving Ann Osborne (but not his mother's fiancé), McSwain is shown with Osborne lifted in his arms on their wedding day in some well-lit room overlooking the Mississippi River. To the strains of the Cajun "national anthem," "La Jolie Blonde" (adapted and performed by the zydeco artist Buckwheat Zydeco) and with the final credits rolling, McSwain clearly has won the ultimate prize by taking possession of the previously resistant woman, "la jolie blonde" (the pretty blond). Henceforth *les bons temps* will roll, just like the Mississippi River in the scene's background, because Remy has succeeded again in becoming a "good boy."

In this analysis, I have used the film sequences in heuristic fashion as a concise means to foreground the problem of constructing Été minor(ity) identity and its in-betweenness, and thus to consider the related issues of cultural representation and exploitation. Not only does the stereotypical representation of such identity obscure the nuances and complexities of the cultural practices portrayed, the exploitation of actual agents of these practices, particularly the musicians, for both narrative and discursive ends also suggests the power that "the dominant" wields in adapting minor(ity) cultures. Moreover, this process often occurs through the inclusion of these very cultural agents in such exploitation, wittingly or not. Even the limited use of Cajun French (sung and spoken) and the presentation of dance in response to the musical performances effectively allow the filmmakers to employ the most poignant site of cultural expression and of potential family and community harmony.

In the case of *Southern Comfort*, the analogy with the Vietnamese conflict is constructed only from the perspective of the oppressor. That is, the indigenous Cajuns, who are quite in control of their environment and way of life, are situated as an oppressed and impoverished populace who gaily let the good times roll while they resist the foreign invaders by systematic extermination resulting in the surviving invaders' desperate withdrawal. As for *The Big Easy*, the use of the *bal de maison* setting and recognizable Louisiana musicians makes it possible not only to express the film's simplistic moral message but also to bring law and civilization finally to the lawless and the uncivilized. This construction of minor(ity) identity through the Cajun music and dance arena reveals at once the obviously strategic use of specific cultural practices and the filmmakers' awareness of the potential for cinematic representation contained in the skilled deployment of these very practices. And as we have seen with the musicians performing in these scenes, the construction of identity also functions to situate actual cultural agents in between the affirmation of tradition and authenticity and the commercial exploitation of these expressions of affirmation.

Versions and Visions of Cajun Cultural Identity

In the past thirty-five years, documents from an array of critical perspectives have offered different versions of the vision of Cajun identity and history. One perspective employs a heartfelt approach, devoid of scholarly trappings, in seeking to redress misapprehensions of Cajun culture, the most prominent of these being Revon Reed's *Lâche pas la patate* (1976) and Pierre Daigle's *Tears, Love and Laughter* (1972). While Reed's work is the only personal overview of Cajun culture (origins and music) written in Cajun French (and published in Québec), Daigle's volume provides a similar tale as if recounted to Cajun children curious to understand their background. Another personal statement is presented by Trent Angers (1989) who seeks to "spread the truth about Cajuns" and their culture as a refutation of what the author judges to be an array of distorting stereotypes. The more frequent, and more thorough, perspective consists of research based on extant historical documentation that traces Cajun culture from its origins into the nineteenth and twentieth centuries.[13]

In this section, I turn my attention to the documentary genre in order to situate the elements of memory and history and their construction in terms of Cajun cultural identity. Of the three documentaries on Cajun music and culture by the director Les Blank (and colleagues), two were broadcast on PBS. *French Dance Tonight* is, in fact, an hour-long adaptation for television of the 1989 feature-length documentary *J'ai Été au Bal: The Cajun and Zydeco Music of Louisiana*, while a third film, the thirty-minute *Marc and Ann*, presents unused material from the longer documentaries to portray the lives of a married couple from Eunice who appear in *J'ai Été au Bal* and *French Dance Tonight* as musicians and cultural commentators. Whereas the original *J'ai Été au Bal* and its shorter adaptation each chronicle the history both of Cajun music and of the Afro-Caribbean form known as zydeco, the film portrait of Marc and Ann Savoy limits the chronicle to more local and traditional aspects of this same heritage. By comparing the two versions of the music documentary to footage and commentary presented in *Marc and Ann*, I wish to reflect not only on the manner in which cultural history is recalled and represented but also on how such recollection and representation orient and inflect this cultural history as it unfolds as memory in the present.[14]

Narrated by folklore professor Barry Jean Ancelet and Cajun musician Michael Doucet, both music documentaries combine folkloric scholarship, oral history, and musical performance to represent the origins of Cajun music and zydeco. Tracing the music from its beginnings following the 1755 exile of the Acadians, the films show how their Cajun descendants preserved and yet transformed the Celtic and French musical traditions throughout the following centuries. Moreover, the filmmakers and narrators emphasize that one must attribute the distinct flavor of Cajun music to the dynamic interaction between the original roots and the Afro-Caribbean musical tradition developing in the black communities with whom the Cajuns lived, worked, and intermarried.

Thus, the music documentaries trace the importance of the fiddle and the accordion for both traditions from the late nineteenth century to their material reproduction in the 1920s with the first recordings, and how the accordion disappeared under the stigmatizing effect of so-called Americanization during the 1930s and 1940s. The narrators then describe the post–World War II beginnings of the Cajun revival in the 1950s and 1960s with various low points (rock and roll's impact followed by the British musical invasion) as well as peak moments, such as the influence of accordionist Iry LeJeune and, most notably, the success of Gladius Thibodeaux, Louis "Vinesse" Lejeune, and Dewey Balfa at the 1964 Newport Folk Festival. As for zydeco, the name that has dominated all discussion of its development from the 1950s onward is that of Clifton Chenier, who, along with Boozoo Chavis, pioneered early recordings and oriented the musical instrumentation and performances toward the rhythm and blues sound that distinguishes zydeco from Cajun music (see A. Savoy 1984; Ancelet 1989a).

In chapter 5 I consider the construction of Cajun musical history in these documentaries in relation to zydeco and Louisiana Creole culture. Here, however, I direct my attention to the films' representation of more recent relations of Cajun music to the impact of evolving styles and technologies in the American and international music industries. An ongoing and seemingly irreconcilable debate exists in the Cajun cultural sphere (to which I will return) between proponents of two contrasting sociocultural and aesthetic sensibilities. Some musicians and fans favor the fusion of musical forms by innovative trends in Cajun instrumentation and performance, notable examples of which are Filé and Wayne Toups and his former group ZydeCajun. Other fans and musicians prefer to conserve the so-called traditional style of Cajun music that would emulate the *bal de maison* (house dance)—that is, with limited or no amplification and few instruments beyond the accordion, fiddle, triangle, and guitar, as well as little interest in observing audience demands for popular, hybrid forms.[15]

The quote by Marc Savoy in this chapter's epigraph succinctly speaks to this distinction. Moreover, explaining the title of his group's album *With Spirits*, Savoy argues forcefully in this vein: "You don't need to moan, groan, or twist your face around while you play folk music because that isn't natural and natural is what folk music is all about. This tendency constitutes the natural movement of musical innovation while, for others, it means a dilution, even destruction of the spirit of traditional Cajun music" (Savoy-Doucet 1986). From a contrasting perspective, the accordionist and composer Wayne Toups justifies the urgency of creating the fusion expressed in his band's name ZydeCajun. As I observed in chapter 2, Toups has retained his links to Cajun culture and to creating Cajun music, whereas Zachary Richard has gone further afield in his creative work, seeking to compose and perform music first and foremost, without denying his origins in his music, yet without privileging them either.[16]

Many Cajun music fans would dispute Toups's visionary justification of the fusion of musical forms, because the varied demands of aficionados depend necessarily on their diverse musical and sociocultural orientations, calling for a music that conforms to an apparently distinct notion of cultural integrity and authenticity. In *J'ai Été au Bal*, this debate emerges only obliquely at best, while the pbs version, *French Dance Tonight*, is even more streamlined and thus less nuanced. However, both versions of the documentary seem to develop an implicit case in favor of the fusion form within the logic of their sequential movement during the final twenty to thirty minutes. Having brought the historical chronology into the 1970s and 1980s, the filmmakers complete the history of Cajun music in two well-known rural dance arenas (Mulate's in Breaux Bridge and Belizaire's in Crowley) with the spirited and electronically enhanced performances by two groups that straddle the distinct positions of this debate (Michael Doucet and BeauSoleil, and Paul Daigle and Cajun Gold).[17]

J'ai Été au Bal continues then with a succinct examination of developments in zydeco parallel to those in Cajun music through performances and interviews with a half dozen musicians. The crowned king of zydeco, Clifton Chenier, appears in performance later in his career at the 1977 New Orleans Jazz and Heritage Festival. Then, in the 84-minute version of *J'ai Été au Bal*, another performance and interview sequence appears, in a rural setting with the younger musician Rockin' Sidney and the record producer Floyd Soileau discussing the breakthrough success of the song "Don't Mess with My Toot-Toot" (see Morthland 1985; Tisserand 1998). These parallel strains, Cajun music and zydeco, then lead sequentially and, by implication, historically to the film's finale with Wayne Toups and ZydeCajun.

The transition to ZydeCajun's performance does not proceed, however, from the final notes of the previous zydeco tune into the performance of ZydeCajun's "fusion" sound. Rather, in a brief statement, Wayne Toups describes in poignant terms the precarious equilibrium between innovation and tradition: "You add a little herbs and spices of rhythm and blues and a little bit of rock 'n roll—not out of line, there's a border that you can just go by, and you can't cross the border, 'cos then if you cross the border, you get away from your roots. So if you can just add little bits and pieces to it to keep the fresh feeling and the energy to give to the younger generation, but still keep that roots, tortured strong Cajun feeling in your heart, you can go a long ways." Only then do the filmmakers introduce the final number that leads directly into the films' credits, in both versions. This performance by Toups and his band stands in sharp contrast to previous ones by Cajun artists in terms of its setting, instrumentation, and especially Toups's distinctive musical and fashion statements, and the viewer may well wonder about the "border" to which Toups had just referred. Besides the performance's location, in a racetrack carport (a modern version of the traditional *fais do-do*), and the predominantly youthful crowd of dancers there, the instrumental break presents not the traditional fiddle but the electric piano and then lead guitar, followed by Toups's own impassioned performance on electrified accordion. The instrumental finale is Toups's own showcase with the accordionist, clad in a muscle shirt, headband, and garish shorts, emphasizing the transformative power of his interpretation of the first recorded Cajun song, "Allons à Lafayette," with electrified instrumentation and the mixture of Cajun, zydeco, and rock rhythms (see *J'ai Été au Bal* 1990, vol. 2).

The filmmakers of *J'ai Été au Bal* clearly sought to provide an orderly portrait of the movement and intersections of two musical traditions, Cajun and zydeco, without scrambling the lines of the audiovisual chronicle with the vital but complex dialogue that continues between them and to which I return in chapter 5. As I have suggested, the film's sequential logic leads to the implicit conclusion of progress being associated with the fusion of forms (specifically zydeco and rock and roll with Cajun music). However, neither the narration nor the juxtaposition of images emphasizes in a precise manner the ongoing confrontation between traditional and fusion stances. A comparison with the film *Marc and Ann* reveals some of the footage available but unused in the music documentary and confirms the filmmaker's deliberate representational strategies.[18]

One remarkable scene in *J'ai Été au Bal* is the waltz duet of Marc and Ann Savoy (on accordion and guitar, respectively), performed on the back porch of their Eunice farmhouse; this scene is retained in the shorter *French Dance Tonight* only with the song's instrumental bridge and second verse. This brief performance serves in both versions as the focal example of the simple, traditional, and unadorned tradition of home in rural Cajun music. As I noted in chapter 2, this style reflects Marc Savoy's deliberate choice to "[give] up the dance hall scene strictly because [he and a few other musicians] were not going to contribute to the birth of this mutation"—that is, the fusion of Cajun music with country and western and with rock and roll (1988, 11–12).[19] By comparing the footage from which this segment was edited in the music documentary with the central scene in *Marc and Ann*, we not only understand the representation of synchrony between this musical style and the rural, back-porch context, but we can also more fully comprehend the demonstrative function of both setting and performance especially in terms of the careful construction of the film.

In *Marc and Ann* the sequences progress as follows: at approximately midway through the documentary, the filmmaker presents several views of the Saturday morning jam session held at the Savoy music store, shifting from one group of musicians to a second in which the elder statesman of the Cajun fiddle, Dennis McGee, is highlighted. Over this image of McGee's performance, followed directly by a close shot of Marc Savoy seated outdoors, one hears his emphatic expression of utter dismay at the directions taken in contemporary music and performances:

Marc Savoy: [voice-over, as Dennis McGee performs] But in the days when I started playing music, it seemed that the people who were out there were more interested in playing music for the sake of playing music [close shot on Marc Savoy]. You didn't need to stand on your head or cut flips to be popular. You didn't have to break your instrument up to be popular. All you had to do was play good dance music. That's what made you a success and nothing else. But, as it began to get gimmicked up, I became more and more disillusioned with the whole thing until finally I said, I want no part of this, I want no part of where this is going.

Following this statement, the next sequence in *Marc and Ann* continues outdoors, situating the viewer before the Savoys' back porch and, through a subtitle, within the context of a visit to the Savoy farm by a tour group. Whereas both versions of the music documentaries present the couple performing the waltz "J'ai Fait une Grosse Erreur" simply with a close shot intercut with pastoral shots of their farm, the sequence in *Marc and Ann* is edited in an entirely different manner. The opening images of the group's arrival, its members spreading blankets on the grass, precede and then continue during Ann Savoy's voice-over about the secondary importance of actual musical performance in the Cajun dance and music arena:

> Ann: [voice-over] It would be sad to me to see the music get only popular in a commercial way like that, [shot of Ann Savoy taking guitar, joining Marc on porch] to see people coming to stare at the people on a stage in a concert format or eating-while-listening-to-music format 'cos that wasn't the way it ever was. The people who play the music are not stars, they never were, they're just everybody [slow pan left to right of tour group, then returning to porch]. They all played, they hung out, they'll play in the kitchen, they'll play on the porch, they'll play in the dance hall. I don't think in general the people made that big a deal of themselves in the past playing music [pan ends with Savoy child on swing]. Everybody played music.

Despite the incongruous overlay of this statement with a scene in which people come, in fact, to stare and listen, the filmmaker continues with a tight shot on Marc Savoy as he speaks to the tour group about the fundamental, even natural simplicity and order in Cajun music. As in the quotations above, I intersperse Savoy's statement with scene descriptions in order to emphasize how the filmmaker constructs the scene with precise editing:

Marc: [close shot, seated on porch, speaking to tour group] Cajun music is a lot of things, as Ann says in her book, a lot of things to different people. And traditional music is not very much accepted nowadays, it's not very much sought out, there are not too many people who want to hear it [focus pulls back slowly, includes audience on porch, children in foreground]. But just because somebody played rock 'n roll and wants to play Cajun music, there's nothing wrong with that either, there's nothing wrong with rock 'n rolled Cajun music, or there's nothing wrong with country-and-western Cajun music.

[Voice-over] Myself, I don't believe if you took the sheep out there [reverse shot: attentive audience member 1] and tried to breed it with a chicken, I don't believe [laughter, audience member 2] that works out too well, you know. The results of that would be [audience member 3] maybe pretty chaotic. I'd prefer [audience member 4] if I want to eat a sheep, I'll eat the sheep or [close porch shot] if I want to chase a chicken, I'll chase a chicken, but I don't want to chase that kind of thing that'd be a cross between sheep and a chicken [shot pulls back to include child on swing]. I don't know what that would look like. But some of this stuff that's out there nowadays is pretty much the same as a cross between a sheep and a chicken [voice-over: Marc and Ann playing two-step instrumental].

I play music like I heard it when I was a kid, and I work very hard to keep it that way [shot of the Savoys playing their instruments together, very close shot of dogs playing on the ground].

The filmmaker maintains the focus on the Savoys playing their instruments as Ann Savoy sings a verse in French from the two-step "Hé, Mom," and then, as the instrumental part continues, the filmmaker presents an edited panorama of photo stills that show the couple's performances in various concerts and festival venues, together and with different musicians, culminating with a still of their appearance on Garrison Keillor's *A Prairie Home Companion*.

While this and many other films demonstrate clearly Les Blank's skill as a director,[20] it is not clear to what extent he deliberately intended to emphasize the possible contradictions in the couple's stance as Cajun musicians and social commentators. Notably, Ann Savoy's statements about traditional Cajun music not lending itself to concert or restaurant venues contrast with the subsequent sequence of back-porch performance and concert stills, and Marc Savoy's apparent support of Cajun music's evolution (for example, its merging with different musical forms) is undercut by his forthright assertions against any such evolution.[21] In any case, the complex visual and aural construction of this central segment serves to complicate this emphasis: on the one hand, while the sequence's opening slow pan of the tour group provides the viewer with a visual situation of the addressees of Marc Savoy's statement, the pan also places us, as viewing subjects, precisely in that audience. We viewers are implicitly deprived of a critical distance as "we," with Savoy's audience, laugh appreciatively in response to his commentary. Then, the subsequent reaction shots reinsert the viewer, by association, into different sites of that audience through the editing strategy of rapid shot/shot-reverse—that is, 180 degree shifts between the speaker and the backyard group. This structure thus prescribes a homogenizing coherence by defining, according to Kaja Silverman, "a discursive position for the viewing subject which necessitates not only its loss of being, but the repudiation of alternative discourses" (1983, 205–6).

On the other hand, as noted by Mary Ann Doane, the shift between the disembodied voice-over commentary to the direct, visual attribution of this aural component "endows this voice with a certain authority. As a form of direct address, it speaks without mediation to the audience, bypassing the 'characters' and establishing a complicity between itself and the spectator" (1986, 341). Although Doane concludes that the very unlocalizable, disembodied form of this voice "produc[es] its truth" (341), I would argue further that the shift in this sequence between voice-over and voice-direct, combined with the careful editing, determines the "truth" of the Savoys' statements as well as the viewers' necessarily passive acceptance of these "truths." Thus, whatever contradictions the filmmaker may (or may not) have sought to indicate regarding the couple's stance, the filmic construction serves fully to reinforce the authority of their statements.

However, equally significant is the strategic use of footage in *Marc and Ann* that clearly was inappropriate for the uncomplicated tone and purpose of *J'ai Été au Bal* and *French Dance Tonight*. We can situate Marc Savoy's statement within the framework of the debate previously discussed on Cajun musical forms as corresponding to the refusal by many fans and some musicians to accept the recent and ongoing trend toward fusion, calling instead, explicitly or implicitly, for a music that conforms to an unspecified notion of cultural integrity and authenticity.[22] Savoy's stance corresponds to what Richard Terdiman describes as "the conservative character built into social existence and practice" revealed by "materials memory" (1993, 35)—that is, by the very artifacts and practices to which one can point as proof of that cultural specificity. As David Lowenthal argues, "whatever feels distinctive to any group becomes a jealously unshared possession," and in fact, "to serve as a collective symbol heritage must be widely accepted by insiders, yet inaccessible to outsiders" (1994, 48–49).

Yet, even insiders risk falling outside if they are perceived by certain members inside their group as failing to adhere to forms and practices recognized as remaining inside the heritage. Indeed, the instability of this border between the specificity of heritage and the invasive force of the broader sociocultural formation is inherent to the very hybrid articulation of dynamic in-betweenness. As Lawrence Grossberg notes, "This formation [of intersecting cultural practices and configurations of popular sensibilities] is never simple or noncontradictory. . . . And different cultural practices, as well as different popular sensibilities, are constantly opposing, undercutting and reinflecting each other within the unstable formation of everyday life" (1988, 179).

Thus, just as Les Blank's representation of the traditionalist stance reveals the contradictions therein through precise juxtapositions of scenes and statements in *Marc and Ann*, we can also reread ZydeCajun's performance at the end of both versions of the music documentary as a similar critique-by-contrast of the fusion stance. Wayne Toups's moving statement about the shifting border between roots and innovation cited above stands in sharp contrast to the final number he performs with Zyde-Cajun that demonstrates, for many viewers, the extent to which the band has left that border far behind. Yet, as I suggest in chapter 2, the subsequent trajectory of Toups's career reveals that his search for self-expression as a musician, in contrast to Zachary Richard's, has led him back geographically to Louisiana and stylistically within the parameters of the Cajun musical tradition that, in fact, may well simply have caught up with him.

We can further situate these films and this ongoing debate within the framework of discussions of memory and history by drawing on Pierre Nora's development of the concept of *lieux de mémoire* (realms of memory). The music films both draw on and develop further what Nora calls "archival memory," which relies entirely on the materiality of the re-corded and visual trace and thus replaces traditional memory, says Nora, by creating an "expanding dossier" as "evidence before who knows what tribunal of history. The trace negates the sacred but retains its aura" (1996, 9).[23] Whatever the distinctions are that might (and in this case, do) arise within the particular heritage regarding specific collective forms and practices, the archival memory that constitutes these music docu-mentaries succeeds in emphasizing and even sacralizing certain traces (e.g., the family orientation and group celebration as well as certain musical forms) as if to ward off their extinction.

Although also drawing to a great extent from this archival memory, the film *Marc and Ann* actualizes what Nora calls "memory as individual duty," the "atomization of memory (as collective memory is transformed into private memory)" that constitutes a " 'law of remembrance' [with] a great coercive force": "The less collective the experience of memory is, the greater the need for individuals to bear the burden," with salvation "ultimately depend[ing] on discharging a debt that can never be repaid" (1996, 11). John Gillis explains this as the modern dilemma of our being "dependent on several collective memories, but masters of none," mak-ing us "only too aware of the gap between the enormous obligation to remember and the individual's incapacity to do so without the assistance of mechanical reminders, souvenirs, and memory sites" (1994a, 15). In turn, the proliferation of collective memories belonging simultaneously to different groups produces the concomitant proliferation of identities with the result that, "for those who regard the national 'heritage' as a sacred text, the democratization of memory is equivalent to profanation, or, what is worse, cultural suicide" (19).

These distinctions allow us to resituate the traditionalist/fusion de-bate: on one hand, the constraints of "memory as individual duty" would seem to fortify the traditionalist viewpoint, such as Marc Savoy's, for the sake of defending a privileged memory of cultural heritage and practice (Nora 1996, 7). This viewpoint relies on the selective forgetting char-acteristic of modern processes that commemorate heritage (Lowenthal 1994, 49; see also Gillis 1994a, 7). In this case, the elision is partial and even intermittent, bearing on aspects of the historical process that con-stitute the transformations in this very musical heritage. That is, many proponents of Cajun cultural practices frequently, although sometimes warily, emphasize the importance of mutations that Cajun music has undergone periodically in relation to more popular and dominant forms from outside. The continuing fusion of neighboring traditions (e.g., with Creole and Afro-Caribbean forms) occurs nonetheless as an ongoing dialogue of "the word in language" that, Bakhtin argues, "is half someone else's" (1981, 293).

On the other hand, the fusion perspective as enunciated by Toups readily admits the dialogic interaction as part and parcel of the development of that very heritage, welcoming forms and instrumentation from zydeco, rhythm and blues, and rock and roll within a dynamic Cajun idiom. Thus, although Toups is cautious regarding the inherent limits to innovation, he seems, in fact, to emphasize more the archival memory in readily acknowledging the dialogic processes as the transformative nourishment of future musical forms, and the work of Michael Doucet shares this emphasis as well. However, Toups's very caution suggests what both perspectives share in their particular relations to the past—what Nora calls "alienated memory" (1996, 11). For unlike the "sense of discontinuity" that characterizes modern memory, both the traditionalist and fusion stances express a "cult of continuity, this certainty of knowing to whom and to what we are indebted for being what we are. From this came the important notion of 'origins' " (1996, 11–12).

Although one can make the case that these films still remain carefully selective in reviewing uncomfortable facets of these origins (for example, the elided topics of racial and gender discrimination), the "cult of continuity" remains constant and is the foundation on which the renaissance of Cajun heritage is based. Thus, despite their wholly oblique consideration of the debate regarding forms of Cajun musical expression, all three films constitute *lieux de mémoire* to the extent that they fulfill their fundamental purposes, according to Nora, "to stop time, to inhibit forgetting . . . all in order to capture the maximum possible meaning with the fewest possible signs" as well as of assuring their "capacity [of *lieux de mémoire*] for change" (1996, 15). In this way, the films are representations of memory that, says Terdiman, "are the form which the real transformed by our work upon it takes in consciousness. And in that form these representations inform all present practice" (1985, 29).

The description in the promotional material for *Marc and Ann*—"a more personal look at one Cajun family, their appreciation for their culture and their efforts to save it in the face of the encroaching American 'mall culture' "—underscores the tensions inherent in articulating the shifting frontier between the presumed specificity of heritage and the invasive, culturally dominant forces. However, I maintain that the conflict evident in the debate is itself an important part of the same exchange. As such, this process is not only dialogic (that is, responding to the present, always actively negotiating between past and present) but also dialectic, a process that Terdiman describes so succinctly as one "that must always both remember (conserve) and overcome (transform) its referent" (1993, 65). This perspective helps us better to understand the paradox, to which I pointed above, of active forgetting in order to create legends, to fabulate and thereby invent a people to come.

The complexity of this fabulation emerges most poignantly when both reactive and progressive stances are espoused successively, in different forms, by the same proponents of Cajun music. In a letter to the *Times of Acadiana*, Michael Doucet expressed the importance, and the yet inherent difficulties, in these conflicting processes. What matters for the development of contemporary Cajun musical styles, wrote Doucet, is that "musicians are authentic Cajun-French speaking individuals who play the music they strongly feel, enjoy and share [and] that they all express, in spite of the overwhelming adversity of total Americanization, their own story" (1988, 4). Although Doucet has energetically promoted an understanding of the traditional roots of this Cajun musical heritage (e.g., his contribution to the release of the Library of Congress's Lomax recordings [Doucet and Ancelet 1987]), he has also accommodated rather than resisted the "overwhelming adversity of total Americanization" with his group BeauSoleil. As I indicated in chapter 2, the group's performances and recordings throughout the 1990s have consistently included songs that are hybrids of Cajun style and language with other ethnic and regional forms—for example, Tex-Mex, Caribbean, blues, and rock and roll.[24]

Furthermore, let us compare Doucet's position to Pierre Daigle's reflection on additions to the Cajun music repertoire, with reference to his son Paul's work with the group Cajun Gold: "My objective is NOT to preserve Cajun music. Not, if by preserving it, we mean pickle it, put it in a jar where it cannot grow, or change, or reflect the new feeling of our times. My hope is to come up with new tunes, new ideas—some funny, some sad, but always reflecting the honesty and sincerity of our Cajun past, our Cajun heritage. . . . Sometimes I want it to reflect our bilingualism. I want it to sometimes reflect our Americanism; I don't want it to forget that its roots are in the Cajun Experience" (1987, 15–16). While Doucet's words in his letter to the *Times* seem to speak for a "preservation," his and BeauSoleil's practice animates the heritage as Daigle suggests, linking the "roots" of the "Cajun Experience" to the broader cultural exchange in which it is found. It is precisely this apparent contradiction, or rather continuing paradox, that points to the insistent emergence of a hybrid in-betweenness as a fundamental characteristic of Cajun musical expression.

Teaching and Marketing Cajun Dance Culture

The third visual locus for understanding the representation of Cajun identity is found in several dance instructional tapes produced in the late 1980s and early 1990s, including Betty Cecil's *I Love to Cajun Dance* (1988), the New Orleans restaurant Michaul's *Cajun Dance Instruction* (circa 1992), and J. Randolph (Rand) Speyrer's *Allons Danser* (1987) and his two-cassette follow-up, with Cynthia Speyrer (1993), *Introduction to Cajun Dancing* and *Advanced Cajun Dancing*. The production of these dance tapes clearly corresponded to the lively interest in things Cajun that arose as part of the renaissance of the 1980s.

In this section, I will argue that the production and gradual dissemination of these tapes function in dual fashion. On one hand, the tapes serve as a means to affirm Cajun identity by facilitating access to dance and music as distinctly Cajun folk practices. On the other hand, they constitute a distinct mode of representation, indeed of narrating this identity, and as such they contribute to the fabulating function of active creation of a people. The narrative constructions in these instructional dance videos communicate this complex in-betweenness through at least two conjoined facets. First, each tape offers actual instruction of particular dance forms, following a distinct format, order, and selection of steps. Second, each tape situates this instruction within a particular cultural frame as representative of Cajun identity and difference. I will study each facet successively in order to understand how these tapes, like the films previously examined, contribute in hybrid fashion at once to the articulation and manipulation of cultural identity.

I should, however, first clarify the cultural context as well as the production conditions of these tapes. During the 1980s, first in the Lafayette area, then in New Orleans and Baton Rouge, different local dancers began to teach Cajun-style dancing, or at least what had come to be known by that term. For what one learns quickly when reading about the origins of Cajun dance, particularly in home dances known as *fais do-dos*, is how many different steps there were in the nineteenth and early twentieth century, and how limited is the number of steps currently practiced in Cajun dance and music venues (see Duke 1988, 27–44; and Plater, Speyrer, and Speyrer 1993, 30–35). Indeed, in a personal interview (1992b), Barry Jean Ancelet explained that from his perspective it was the Cajun music restaurant phenomenon of the 1980s—that is, the inclusion of dance bands and Cajun dances at Randol's in Lafayette and Mulate's in Breaux Bridge—that was largely responsible for the development of the dance forms (waltz, two-step, and jitterbug) now associated almost uniquely with Cajun dance. Hence, in developing these dance styles, the regular dancers in these venues performed self-consciously in an exhibition mode, and "Cajun culture" soon developed into a product to be consumed by tourists—not just food, music, and dance, but audio and videocassettes, artifacts (e.g., aprons, T-shirts, bandanas, mugs), culinary aids (e.g., hot sauce), and even local brews of beer (e.g., Mulate's brand). This self-consciousness became increasingly prevalent in different venues—for example, at the annual Festivals Acadiens in Lafayette, dancers coped with the dust they stirred up or, in wet weather, the mud they were slogging through while valiantly continuing to dance, rain or shine, hot or (rarely) cold.[25] Thus, the Cajun dance instructional tapes emerged within this context of simultaneous cultural and commercial expansion.

As for the production conditions of these tapes, it was Rand Speyrer who, although certainly not the first dance instructor in southern Louisiana or even in New Orleans, nonetheless led the competitors by producing and releasing his tape *Allons Danser* in summer 1987. Betty Cecil's tape was released in 1988, yet Speyrer's tape remained unequaled until 1993, when he and his partner Cynthia produced and released a two-cassette version (basic and advanced instructional tapes) accompanied by a high-quality instructional book. As a private entrepreneur, Speyrer produced these tapes to support his business of Cajun dance instruction in the New Orleans area to which he devoted himself primarily until the mid-1990s. Betty Cecil's dance instruction activities in Lafayette were much less extensive than Speyrer's, but she was able to combine private funds with some public support to produce the second commercial tape on the market.[26] In contrast, the Michaul's tape was funded and produced by the proprietors of the New Orleans restaurant of the same name. Because the restaurant has regularly featured Cajun dance instruction as well as a variety of musicians and dancing as the thematic backdrop for its business, the tape places strong emphasis on the commercial aspect as a form of cultural manifestion.

Let us consider, then, the first of two conjoined aspects of the hybrid in-betweenness communicated by these tapes, the actual mode of presentation of the dance instruction, and the format, order, and selection of steps. Each tape provides the rudiments for the Cajun waltz (3/4 meter), two-step, and jitterbug (both in 4/4 meter). This instruction is indicative of shared cultural conventions in the Cajun dance idiom, specifically the male lead and female follow, the counterclockwise movement on the floor, and codes regarding personal dance style and etiquette. The latter conventions combine to place certain constraints on one's freedom of expression on the dance floor, necessarily so given the fluid, counterclockwise movement to which all dancers must adhere in performing the waltz and the two-step. These practices may be complicated further in different dance locales (e.g., New Orleans clubs versus rural Louisiana bars and restaurants) in which different dance codes subtly (or even blatantly) are communicated by regular local dancers. Thus, the different sequences of dance instruction overlap implicitly with the second aspect discussed below, the mode of cultural representation transmitted through the dance instruction, because all three productions relate a set of cultural norms that define what it is to "dance Cajun" in a conventional, if not entirely "traditional," manner.

Moreover, the choices made by the producers in terms of tape length, steps demonstrated and repeated, and different presentation formats yield insights about the pedagogical frame developed for basic instruction. The different dance partners and groups depicted in the Cecil tape and the Michaul's tape reveal just how varied the actual instruction can be, both in terms of explanations provided and in the passage from instruction to practice. Also significant in regard to questions of instruction and production in these tapes are the different approaches to presenting the Cajun "jitterbug" (or "jig"), as well as how it is situated in relation to the other two steps; for the choice between the jitterbug and the two-step on dance floors has tended to mark dancers as observing so-called tradition (two-step) or opting for innovation (jitterbug).

Let us consider how the three producers approach the demonstration of the jitterbug.

By way of introduction, Betty Cecil states simply that the jitterbug (the "Cajun jig," as she calls it) is not yet (in 1988) considered traditional, but she hopes that it will be some day. She then proceeds to present the rudimentary dance steps, in the waltz/two-step/jitterbug order. Because her tape is only twenty-nine minutes long, she necessarily must limit the presentation of examples and practice, and for the jitterbug she only presents the basic footwork and three upper-body moves, saving for a final lagniappe section (Louisiana dialect for "a little something extra") a demonstration of several advanced moves "to show some pretty turns so that [viewers] perhaps might learn for themselves." Cecil also situates the instruction on the actual dance floor of a local club, demonstrating the steps first alone and then with a partner. Through careful editing, the practice segments with the partner segue almost seamlessly to the dance floor with a live band and a group of dancers. All in all, the Cecil video is a very spare but quite efficient presentation of the fundamentals; as an experienced dance instructor, Cecil certainly knows that the best way to gain expertise is on the dance floor, for which she provides the necessary first steps.

Having benefited from the experience of preparing the earlier, shorter tape, Speyrer produced the two-cassette follow-up (1993) that redefined the field in several ways. First, the new cassettes combine introductory and advanced presentations with the complete overview in the accompanying illustrated instruction book. Ormonde Plater and Rand and Cynthia Speyrer provide, in this text (1993, 45–50) and in the opening six minutes of the basic dance tape, the seven steps "for passing a good time," and then illustrate and describe each step in both the text and the video. Second, in both versions Rand Speyrer chose to follow (as did Cecil) the order to which his six-session introductory dance lessons also correspond—that is, instruction first in the waltz, then the Cajun two-step, and finally the rudiments of the Cajun jitterbug. Third, and perhaps most important, the presentation of each of the three steps is structured quite precisely: beginning the instructional segments with an opening demonstration of the focal dance step, the Speyrers then systematically break down each step, for men and for women, with carefully staged demonstrations of each step or upper-body move. Finally, they close the first two segments (for the waltz and two-step) with general practice segments set in the New Orleans venue, the dance restaurant Mulate's, reserving the demonstration of the combined jitterbug steps for the studio.

In the basic video, Speyrer quickly explains the jitterbug's development as a mark of the Cajuns' adaptable ingenuity, but he (and his coauthors) situate the Cajun dance tradition in its historical context in the volume *Cajun Dancing*, which is available in addition to the tapes. They note that in some, supposedly traditional, dance circles, this step is viewed as "alien to traditional Cajun dancing [and is] imposed upon the local culture by outsiders trying to play Cajun and by citified Cajuns attempting to discover their heritage" (1993, 38). Yet they maintain, as all these tapes confirm, that this step "has become firmly established in Acadiana" despite the continuing (though weakening) "conservative reaction" (1993, 39). In terms of the instruction, Speyrer devotes nearly half of the basic tape's demonstration time to the two jitterbug steps (shuffle and push-pull/rock steps) and to six upper-body movements. This segment more than doubles the time allotted to the ever-popular jitterbug on the 1987 tape, and in the advanced tape Speyrer adds an additional thirty-five minutes to introducing and practicing fourteen advanced jitterbug moves, as well as providing seventeen minutes devoted to the three-person step, the troika.[27]

In contrast to the primarily studio locations of the Speyrer tapes' dance demonstrations, the Michaul's tape follows Cecil's instruction setting by locating the instruction segments within the producers' Cajun dance restaurant. However, the Michaul's tape differs in a number of ways from Speyrer's and Cecil's tapes, and the demands of the production—to promote the restaurant along with the dance steps—impede the effectiveness of the instruction.

First, after a number of helpful introductory tips, the instructors in the Michaul's tape, Jean-Paul and Thérèse Blanchard, begin with the Cajun jitterbug—that is, the step that tends to have the greatest appeal to new dancers. Rather than make any commentary about the step, as do Speyrer and Cecil, the instructors simply present the jitterbug unproblematically as an object of enjoyment and consumption. This approach is quite appropriate for the tape's overall focus on dancing as a natural part of the Cajun restaurant experience.

Second, like Cecil's tape, Michaul's employs two live bands to accompany the dancers during the practice segments following the demonstration of steps. In contrast to the other productions, however, the instruction of the waltz and two-step is presented in a rather abbreviated fashion in a group setting within the restaurant, and the practice segments, also in the group setting in the dance hall, provide the viewer little opportunity to view closely how to perform the steps just presented. Moreover, the producers' obvious need to present close-up footage of the bands (the Michaul's house band at the time, La Touché, and the Sheryl Cormier Band) detracts somewhat from the ostensible instruction purpose.

Finally, having introduced the three main steps, the producers add two additional demonstration and practice segments. These segments correspond to the fleeting popularity in the early 1990s at many Cajun dance venues of the country music "line dance," a variant dance step known as the Cajun "freeze." Furthermore, the producers commissioned two dancers to create a new version of this step expressly for the tape and accompanied by a song titled "The Michaul's Stomp."

The different approaches in these three productions provide an indication of some of the sociocultural issues that are prevalent in the broader context of Cajun dance and music practices. Yet, with the general orientation in these tapes toward cultural openness to different styles and the primary emphasis on dance instruction, they cannot reasonably address some very real tensions that may arise in any dance venue between insider and outsider, regarding both the dance codes and different styles. As a neophyte at first, then as a more experienced dancer, finding myself within swirling crowds of Cajun dancers in different dance and music venues, I can attest that nothing replaces the experience of live music and the community of dancers, and certainly no instruction tape can prepare one adequately for the actual practice of leading and following a partner on a crowded dance floor. However, tensions may arise when dancers lack the proper contextual awareness, or consideration, by practicing a step that impedes the smooth movement around the dance floor of dancers doing the more fluid two-step. In an earlier version of this section, I planned only to refer to the jitterbug as the step that impeded other couples who wanted to two-step. However, during the 1990s, enhanced forms of waltz moves have appeared in many dance venues (notably, elaborate twirls done with arms extended) that effectively block the smooth flow of this step. Hence, while the question of etiquette and implicit codes can relate simply to the entirely practical concern of allowing dancers to move easily while practicing a particular dance step, these concerns also intersect with questions of cultural exploitation (e.g., of the dance forms for exhibition) and local accessibility and territoriality (e.g., to the dance floor within a limited circle of acquaintances) depending on the dancer's own perspective and social orientation.

Another aspect of hybrid in-betweenness that I wish to consider is the difference of the cultural frames in which the producers situate each set of instructions. The aforementioned production details connect to various tape segments, particularly in the Speyrer and Michaul's tapes, that deliberately frame the instruction as representations of Cajun identity. These framing devices allow us to understand how the tapes constitute visual constructions that function at once to represent while constructing—and likewise, to construct while representing—the sociocultural context for dance performance and for the dissemination of these audiovisual products. Whereas the Speyrer tapes are produced by a private entrepreneur, the Cecil and Michaul's tapes were partially or fully funded by two businesses (respectively, the Lafayette restaurant Randol's and the New Orleans restaurant Michaul's) that regularly feature Cajun dance instruction as well as musicians that function to frame the entertainment in their commercial operations. In this sense, Ancelet's insights (1992b) about the development of Cajun dance as a relatively unself-conscious social practice in relation to its deliberate production as a style in dance and music restaurants find ample support in the New Orleans setting at Michaul's. As a result of these different funding sources, each tape emphasizes different facets of Cajun culture as a way to situate the particular dance instruction presented. These mixed purposes—dancing instruction and marketing commercial services—constitute the hybrid and paradoxical in-betweenness of these cultural practices.

On viewing these different tapes one notices the extent to which Cajun culture and heritage serve as the frame for the dance instruction, but unequally so from one production to the other. The Cecil tape opens with a shot of Betty Cecil on the steps of a cabin at one of the Lafayette heritage sites, Acadian Village. However, because this single exterior shot and her brief opening welcome are the only explicit attempts she makes to juxtapose the dance lessons with the cultural frame (other than on the dance floor), the demonstration of the dance steps and the practice instruction constitute the main priority of this production.

Rand Speyrer's two productions reveal an interesting progression: in the original tape, *Allons Danser* (1987), Speyrer used three well-edited segments of different locations and activities in Acadiana, two as an introduction preceding the instruction ("Allons Danser" and "The Cajuns," five minutes total duration), and the third as a transition between the waltz and the two-step instruction ("The Cajun Tradition," two minutes duration). Thus, with seven of the twenty-seven minutes of instruction devoted to Cajun cultural scenes and narration, it is a credit to Speyrer's organization and presentation style that the remaining segments are so clear and useful as dance instruction. For the 1993 revised and expanded tapes, Speyrer chose to foreground the dance instruction as the primary focus, leaving the cultural segments to the end. For the basic tape, he drew on the original opening segments again (with the voice-over slightly modified) as a fitting conclusion to the more than seventy minutes of instruction. In the advanced tape, Speyrer followed the same strategy, placing at the end of the tape a commercial promotional video that he had produced in 1988 for the Lafayette Chamber of Commerce, in which the images flit quickly between Acadiana locales and different cultural practices.

The Michaul's tape is also intercut with cultural segments, as Speyrer's original tape had been, and the subtitle of the Michaul's video, "A Heritage Preserved," suggests that the instruction of Cajun dance is the very means by which one can participate in the mission of saving, or at least preserving, Cajun culture. The clips focus on an introduction to the Cajun dance steps (three and a half minutes at the start), on the Cajun Mardi Gras celebration (a two-minute pause during the jitterbug instruction), on Michaul's Restaurant (two minutes preceding the waltz instruction), on the Cajun people (two minutes before the two-step instruction), and the two-minute concluding segment, again promoting the restaurant. Also, each of the instruction segments is introduced with a header such as "The Waltz at Michaul's" and "The Two-Step at Michaul's," and one segment is devoted to the aforementioned "Michaul's Stomp." Finally, given that the instruction is situated in a group of dancers on the Michaul's restaurant dance floor (except for fourteen minutes of the jitterbug presentation by the Blanchards alone), all dancing appears as if the viewer were there in the restaurant, with two different bands playing for the different segments.

Like tape and CD recordings by Cajun musicians, these instructional tapes clearly participate as important supplements in the actual live dance/music dialogue in clubs, bars, and festivals. At the same time, they constitute documents that have resulted from the Cajun cultural renaissance of the last several decades. Clearly, the producers serve as proponents of Cajun dance expression in a sincere attempt to make this creative form available to as wide an audience as possible. The aspects of the explicit cultural frame detailed above emphasize the links between dance and Cajun heritage as well as the repeated key term common to all the tapes, "fun," as the all-important impetus for the commercial goals of each tape.

However, as I have suggested, these tapes also function in several ways as hybrid cultural practices. The tapes all assure a certain preservation and transmission of the current dance practices, and Michaul's might be commended in particular for disseminating additional steps with the "freeze" and the "stomp." Still, these initiatives serve to regularize difference and thus reflect the in-betweenness of the desire to celebrate and enhance the cultural heritage. That is, when this difference reverts to "tradition" through its transmission and regularization, as Homi Bhabha reminds us, an implicit "rite of power" is inevitably enacted (1994, 112). These entrepreneurs are joined by many other distinguished groups in "stag[ing] authenticity *in opposition to* external, often dominating alternatives" (Clifford, 1988, 12). The annual Lafayette Festivals Acadiens and the Mamou Cajun Music Festival (to name but two such events), the Eunice Liberty Theater and the adjoining Jean Lafitte National Park Cajun cultural exhibit, and the "living history" exhibits of Acadian Village and Vermilionville are all different initiatives meant to "preserve heritage" and to "stage authenticity" and thereby participate in the complex in-betweenness of cultural hybridity.[28]

The preceding analyses give a sense of the ways in which different forms of the visual medium—commercial films, documentaries, instructional tapes—contribute to the development of a collective feeling, both of identity and community, in the Cajun dance and music arena. These films and videos accomplish this both by facilitating the self-definition of this identity and community and by attracting non-Cajuns to participate in versions of this community's cultural practices. The commercial products such as the dance tapes also constitute important elements in the creation of the spaces of affects that relate to the Cajun dance and music arena. That is, they orient dancers generally to the live experience in the dance venues and especially to the steps that they would perform therein, thus functioning as important cultural markers that represent key facets of Cajun cultural practices. Moreover, these representations render this otherwise complex cultural context less difficult to grasp, less "exotic," and less "other."

However, as I suggested in the previous chapter, the cultural context of the Cajun dance and music arena is based on the imposition of various hybrid practices that fulfill a paradoxical function. Despite the clarifying or homogenizing efforts described above, these practices still render the context "strange"—linguistically, artistically, and even socioculturally—in relation to the dominant American culture. Yet these same practices also condone, implicitly or explicitly, the participation of cultural agents in the commercial and political strategies that characterize the dominant cultural formation. In terms of Cajun dance and music, this paradoxical cultural context most often passes unrecognized by the purists. Although these purists are reduced in number, they extol the possibility of maintaining "traditional" forms—for example, disdaining the jitterbug in preference to the two-step, or eschewing hybrid musical forms (the zydecajun of Wayne Toups early in his career is an obvious example). However, rather than seeing this hybrid in-betweenness as an absolute difference in relation to so-called tradition, I understand it precisely as that which gives Cajun and Creole dance and musical forms their distinction both as cultural practices and as multicultural modes of ethnic affirmation.[29]

The tendency toward excluding, implicitly or explicitly, such hybrid forms on the basis of so-called tradition participates in the concomitant debate outlined in chapter 1 regarding authenticity. The discussion of "authenticity as positionality"—regarding implicit inclusions and exclusions—arises both in terms of ethnic origins and in terms of Cajun music as well. Given these difficulties regarding authenticity, the proximity of other forms of dance and music expression—rock, rhythm and blues, country, and especially zydeco—to Cajun music and dance practices contributes immeasurably to the tensions about maintaining strict boundaries around would-be traditional cultural forms. Thus, in the next two chapters I consider two facets of the constructed nature of tradition and authenticity: in chapter 4, I address the music/dance polylogue in various dance locales that gives rise to the creation of different spaces of affects. Then, in chapter 5, I consider a number of problematic representations of Cajun cultural practices that effectively disenchant *les bons temps*—that is, those that force us to address the impact of social bias in 1990s Louisiana on Cajun folk practices.

4

Feeling the Event:

Spaces of Affects and the

Cajun Dance Arena

.
.
.

"Deez gurls ken dance." He was right. I was flat in the middle of a magic place . . . Whiskey River Landing on the levee of the Atchafalaya Swamp in sout Loosiana. The floor was givin' underneath the dancers. . . . They stood on their toes, rocked on their heels, they moved like water skippers on the top of a chocolate swamp. Pausing, sliding, setting, pirouetting, leaping from a starting block, breaking to a smooth stop, heaving to, boat-like against a floating pier. Then off again into the blur of circling bare legs, boot tops, and bons temps all in perfect rhythm to the beating of the bayou heart. . . . On that dance floor I felt a ripple in the universe, a time warp moment when the often unspectacular human race threw its head back and howled at the moon.—Baxter Black, "Cajun Dance"

As Baxter Black communicates poignantly in his words above, the *bons temps* that never cease to *rouler* in Louisiana are endowed with an enchantment that produces a sense of wonder, joy, and a righteous cause for celebration. At the same time, this enchantment can evolve into a form of illusion when the practices of celebration (dance and music especially) are delineated, implicitly and explicitly, in the too-exclusive terms of tradition and authenticity. In this chapter, I continue to view critically the disenchantment of *les bons temps* while also appreciating their enchantment in full measure, here in the context of dance and music practices and spaces.

In working to conceptualize these practices from a number of critical perspectives, I have approached the multifaceted elements of the dance and music event as constituting "spaces of affects."[1] A succinct way to describe spaces of affects is in terms of the "thisness" of the event, the immediacy at once of the "magic place" and the "time warp moment" to which Baxter Black refers. In order to discuss these spaces as they are constituted, night to night and site to site, as experiences of thisness, I have taken to conceptualizing them less in terms of the people who inhabit them than in spatial terms, which Gilles Deleuze and Félix Guattari call "haecceities"—that is, "longitude and latitude, . . . nothing but affects and local movements, differential speeds" (1987, 260). Although an apparently difficult term, "haecceities" quite simply designates an intersection, a conjunction of speed and affects that constitute the event. In this chapter I want to capture some senses of the thisness of spatial practices in the Cajun dance and music arena by developing my experience with different Cajun bands and in different audiences in an array of dance and music venues.[2] Because the terms deployed in this paragraph and chapter do require explanation, I would like to begin by describing a particular experience of thisness in a dance and music event that links the spatial, territorial, and affective concepts developed more fully in subsequent sections.

In early April 2001, at the Detroit Institute of Art's monthly First Friday event, the extremely productive and culturally important band Balfa Toujours played two sets in the wonderful setting of the institute's Diego Rivera Hall. Among the many visitors to the institute that evening was the disparate group of Cajun and zydeco dancers who have regularly danced together since November 2000 at the dance and music event organized by Gary Kaluzny and held monthly at the Ann Arbor Pittsfield Grange Hall. For the first of the two sets, the dance and music venue at the institute was ideal for dancing as well as for the interactions between dancers, musicians, and the many spectators. The floor of Rivera Hall is smooth marble broken only slightly by the Pewabic tile inset toward the middle of the floor, and the organizers had left a very large space open, without chairs, to accommodate the dancers. Hence, surrounded by the impressive murals, the crowd of spectators that filled the hall, and the distinctive musical sounds of Balfa Toujours, we dancers had the perfect conditions to experience the smoothness of relatively unimpeded dance movement, yet also within the particular limitations of the waltz, two-step, and jitterbug dance conventions. During the set, Balfa Toujours stopped the flow in order to explain the origins of their music and even to provide examples of special folk practices, such as the fiddlesticks tapped rhythmically by Kevin Wimmer on the strings of the fiddle played simultaneously by Dirk Powell. Also enhancing this extraordinarily enjoyable space of affect was the interaction of the band members—Christine Balfa with Powell and Wimmer—and the added attraction of the newest, and youngest, band member, Christine Balfa's cousin, Courtney Granger. Thus, the combination of setting, open dance space, crowd participation and responses to the dancers, and close interaction between dancers and musicians created something of a dream space of affect, a particular kind of thisness rarely experienced by many dancers.

Following the first set came a forty-five minute pause, and as time for the second set approached the previously open dance floor gradually became the site on which numerous families, parents with their children, settled down in order to watch the concert. All the dancers observed this development with considerable alarm, and even the emcee warned the spectators camped out on half the dance floor that they had best watch their fingers and toes as the dancers entered the space. At first, my partner and I found the dancing to be quite the opposite of what we had experienced during the first set, and the initial feeling of difficulty—of having to maneuver in a now cramped space bunched with the other dancers and bordered by sprawled and vulnerable bodies—seemed likely only to increase. Then, a number of parents quite sensibly opted to have their children stand up and dance among the Cajun-style dancers as a way to avoid accidents. However, the dancing of these several dozen boys and girls, nearly all preteens, resembled the spontaneous explosion of energy propelling small bodies—individually and in packs of four or five, some with parents, some on their own—and hurtling around the dance floor quite unpredictably. Again, my immediate response was to avoid these bodies, to continue to maneuver around them and even away from them, and to recapture the regularity of the regimented, rule-governed dance movement that I had enjoyed during the first set.

However, after one number that seemed more of an ordeal than a pleasure, I realized suddenly that the sense of ordeal came from *my own response* to the space of affects and not from the space itself, from the people there, nor above all, from the music. I quickly adapted my dance style to move within and through the helter-skelter melee of pulsating children. I thereby discovered entirely new ways to dance, first the waltz then the two-step, by flaunting and violating the dance-step conventions that I was accustomed to respect in the usually striated, hierarchized dance spaces and steps, as performed during the first set. Although the usual conventions are anything but unenjoyable, it took the uncommon ebullience of dancers completely unaccustomed to any such conventions to help us learn to follow their lead in a distinct becoming, both becoming-dance with the other moving bodies as well as becoming-music with the inspired musicians. In this way, we moved toward an in-between of different kinds of spaces, neither entirely rule governed, nor entirely free floating. By the end of the set, during the final numbers when most children had tired of dancing, the floor opened up much more, but the vibrations of their energy and example still remained on the floor with the dancers, musicians, and spectators in ways that were quite evident from the manner in which all participated in a collective assemblage of dance and music expression, in the special thisness of the event.

As we have seen in earlier chapters, the particular kind of event that I consider here may be situated sociohistorically: the Cajun music renaissance that developed slowly in the 1960s reached a crescendo in the mid-1980s and now has settled into continued development of Cajun cultural forms. Among the most important of these forms are the expansion of the repertoire of musical compositions, both old and new, and the maintenance of a limited number of dance steps, notably the Cajun waltz and two-step, to which has been added more recently an adaptation of the jitterbug to Cajun music (see Plater, Speyrer, and Speyrer 1993). Furthermore, the Balfa Toujours concert at the Detroit Institute of Arts is another important example of this development, both as a form of educational outreach beyond the border of Louisiana and as the continued growth of a particular band representing the best in the talent and enterprise that Louisiana Cajun music has to offer.

I propose to develop this reflection on the intersections and assemblages of dance movements and dancing bodies within Cajun dance and music spaces from three intersecting perspectives. First, I consider the sites in which the dance and music encounters occur in terms of territorialization, the music and the dance responses inciting different forms of flows and blockage within each venue and on each dance floor, whether smooth and opened to a broad range of possible modes of dance expression or striated and relatively locked into particular dance steps. The purpose of this consideration is to situate the thisness of the event in terms of different hierarchical limitations in the protocols of spatial practices in dance and music venues.

Second, I consider the thisness of the event from the perspective of the affective and corporeal investments in the dance and music event. On one hand, I want to conceptualize this event both as a kind of overcoding of individuals within a dance and music venue and as a movement away from such overcoding toward in-between forms of spatiality at the intersection of music and dance expressions. On the other hand, I want to consider the actual physical contact and sensory experience of dance and music as the very expression of this in-between and thisness of the event.

Third, I try to disturb the perhaps too precisely situated analysis that precedes by expanding the social field of Cajun dance and music practices in relation to Louisiana and by questioning the very distinction of "inside" and "outside." I understand the trajectory of this analysis, then, as moving from spaces of affects in territorial terms toward the affective assemblages of dancers, spectators, and musicians engaged together in multiple sensory experiences of music and dance, and then toward a disruption of the geographical specificity of the cultural practices as new modes of thisness are constituted in a broad array of venues.

Smooth and Striated Spaces

To begin my analysis, I wish first to account more precisely for the term spaces of affects by introducing the complicated and mixed senses in which Deleuze and Guattari distinguish different kinds of possibilities for spatial practices with the terms "smooth space" and "striated space" (1987, 474–500). Rather than posing these terms as yet another suspicious binary, Deleuze and Guattari present them as a complex intersection of elements that constitute the "event." On the couple-dominated social dance floor, whatever the cadence (i.e., the aural landscape to which one responds) or whatever dance steps are chosen, there exists only the in-between of interactions that inherently move between complete openness (smooth) and rule-governed limitations (striated)—that is, in various degrees of modulation between the smooth/striated poles. The relation of dance movement to spaces of affects is not fully striated— that is, not strictly hierarchized by customs and rules set in place, despite the implicit imposition of many of these depending on the particular venue. Nor is the relation entirely smooth—that is, allowing unfettered openness to free flows of movement or total improvisation, yet again depending on the venue. Rather, only passages and combinations of movement and rest between smooth and striated spaces emerge to animate the initially empty dance site. As Deleuze and Guattari insist, "What interests us in operations of striation and smoothing are precisely the passages or combinations: how the forces at work within space continually striate it, and how in the course of its striation it develops other forces and emits new smooth spaces" (500).

To animate these concepts in terms of the Cajun dance and music arena, I want to consider how the intersection of blockages and flows in music and dance venues (i.e., the movement and space in-between) comes about. To do this I will discuss several different modes of spatial practice in the dance and music exchange; before the band begins to play and dancers to dance, the empty space of a dance hall, club, or festival locale may seem to be the smoothest kind of space of all. Yet, without the interaction of dancers and musicians there is still no event nor space of affects other than one filled with simple anticipation. Beyond this nearly "zero degree" of the event, a particular form of striated space corresponds to the musical performance in a concert setting—that is, with the dancers' limited participation, if at all. In this venue, the event is determined solely by the order and succession of musical pieces (waltz in 3/4 time, two-step in 4/4), selected by the musicians who receive no dance response from the audience, which appreciates the musicians' performance usually passively other than through its applause.[3]

I have participated in a number of such events in which the renowned Cajun group BeauSoleil has performed. In all of these performances, usually outside Louisiana, the event mutated gradually toward increased audience (dancing) participation and thus toward different forms of mixture between striated and smooth spaces. The most striated by far occurred in the early 1990s at a BeauSoleil venue in the Ann Arbor, Michigan, club The Ark. Despite the band's repeated entreaties for some sort of active dance response, the lack of any space specifically for dancing dictated the audience's passive, seated appreciation of this music. The one couple who ventured into the aisle to dance was viewed by the audience of folk aficionados as breaking some sort of unspoken behavioral code through their gyrations and exertions. Hence, both the physical and affective determinations combined to inhibit any response outside fairly striated lines of comportment.[4]

On another, more recent occasion (summer 2000) in Detroit, Beau-Soleil limited the selection of tunes to their CD *Cajunization* (1999), on which they have an extremely eclectic mix of beats, many of which are not the usual Cajun waltz or two-step. The result was the emergence of a relatively smooth space in which free-form rock dancing dominated the dance floor during most numbers. In the few moments when BeauSoleil performed waltz or two-step compositions, a few couples responded on a relatively empty dance "floor" (the lawn in front of the stage) with either Cajun or zydeco steps.[5] As one of these dancers, I felt more awkward than pleased to have the floor nearly to myself and my partner. This discomfort arose partially for technical reasons—that is, the uneven, fur-rowed terrain over which we had to negotiate in order to dance. However, we also felt that without participating in a collective dance expression and response, we became just one more element in the concert-as-spectacle, in the relatively passive appreciation of the performance by the audience. Thus, despite the openness of the physical space itself for dancing, the event as spectacle remained striated within the audience's own passive parameters and through the overall minimal investment of affect and movement.

These two examples suggest how the development of spaces of affects in different dance and music venues can vary both as a result of a ten-dency toward more rigid delimitation of protocols and as an apparent smoothness, yet really without the interchange of dancers among them-selves as well as with the musicians. Fortunately, on many other occa-sions in which BeauSoleil has performed, especially in small festival settings, a wonderful coalescence of dancers has occurred in polylogue—with each other, with spectators, and with the band. The mix of dance styles in response to the band's own mix of musical compositions gradu-ally mutates into a dynamic event, the thisness of speed and affects conjoined. Indeed, the clearest example of how the dancer/musician/spectator polylogue can transform a striated dance site into a relatively smooth (i.e., mixed) space of affects occurred with BeauSoleil on a cold December evening in suburban Chicago in 1995.

When we arrived at Fitzgeralds' in Berwyn, we found a packed house with all the tables removed to create a dance floor. Yet the vast majority of patrons in attendance were there to participate as passive observers, onlookers with evidently little interest in yielding space for dance move-ment. Our apprehension at this Cajun music-in-concert setting was not unfamiliar because we had attended the BeauSoleil performance in Ann

Arbor mentioned above, among other concert settings. Indeed, on this December evening, during the band's unusually brief first set, we and the few scattered couples on the floor had to struggle to make room to dance, at times hurling our bodies against static onlookers. However, during the break, as the crowd thinned out, we conversed with the other dancers so that, during the second set, we were ready to coalesce with each other's movements and with the music. By exchanging partners and drawing in new partners from the crowd, we gradually gained ground both spatially and affectively, with nearly everyone in the audience either dancing or at least moving to the beat. BeauSoleil's second set lasted well over an hour, and when the band returned after the closing ovation they provided an exuberant forty-five-minute encore.[6]

This example helps us better to grasp the very nature of the dance and music event in terms of its thisness, which is not rigidly just "this" or "that" but in fact unfolds as a becoming, consisting, according to Deleuze and Guattari, "entirely of relations of movement and rest between molecules or particles, capacities to affect and be affected" (1987, 261). The dancing bodies of couples joined in counterclockwise and/or twirling movements can be conceptualized as "a mode of individuation very different from that of a person, subject, thing, or substance," specifically as conjoining through the participation of dancers, musicians, and spectators in a collective assemblage of the dance and music event, tending (however fleetingly) toward a thisness "which knows only speeds and affects" (261–62). Deleuze and Guattari do argue implicitly for the conjunction of this apparent dichotomy by insisting that "you will yield nothing to haecceities unless you realize that that is what you are, and that you are nothing but that" (262).[7]

In "yielding" to haecceities as we do, for example, each time that we step onto a dance floor, we thereby accede to a "becoming" ("longitude and latitude, a set of speeds and slownesses between unformed particles, a set of nonsubjectified affects" [1987, 262]). That is, the constitution of spaces of affects—these events, haecceities, becomings—occurs nonetheless as in-between modes of individuation through the movement and speed of the individuated aggregate in relation to the assemblage. What is of interest then, according to Deleuze and Guattari, is how "the plan(e)—life plan(e), writing plan(e), music plan(e)—," and I would add dance plan(e), "must necessarily fail for it is impossible to be faithful to it; but the failures are part of the plan(e) for the plan(e) expands or shrinks along with the dimension of that which it deploys in each instance" (269). That is, whatever the experience, its possibilities of expansion, quantitatively or qualitatively, are enhanced or limited at any given moment, and between moments, as that plane unfolds temporally and spatially. And yet, this "failure" is necessary in order to retain the bearing to which we have become accustomed, what Deleuze and Guattari call "a minimum of strata, a minimum of forms and functions, a minimal subject from which to extract materials, affects, and assemblages" (270).

Despite Deleuze and Guattari's insistence on the distinction of planes, I would argue that the intersections, mixtures, flows, and blockages that constitute the thisness of Cajun dance and music events create not so much a *failure* as a *complication* of the "individuated aggregate" in relation to the virtual yet real variation within the assemblage. For example, on occasion in certain dance and music venues, a partially striated dance response can develop when dancers perform the step to a slow two-step number called the "Cajun freeze"—that is, a line dance familiar to the country and western dance and music arena. I designate this step as partially striated because all of its performers uniformly follow the same step in nearly equidistant, rectangular formation on the dance floor.[8] When a sufficient number of performers dance this step together, they occupy so much floor space that performance of any other dance steps becomes impossible. Hence, the uniform and coordinated performance of this step results in partial or complete blockage of circular movement by couples who would otherwise perform the two-step or jitterbug.

However, a related kind of complication is more frequent, even quite common: when a sufficient number of dancers perform the jitterbug (i.e., couples in twirling formation, yet relatively fixed in place) they prevent two-step dancers from circulating around the dance floor. This complication can even give rise to tension and additional forms of striation. For example, in certain dance halls and local clubs (usually in rural Louisiana) that attract an older audience of dancers, the two-step is de rigueur as the dance response "appropriate" to songs of the 4/4 beat. In such settings, an intrepid jitterbug dancer is perceived simply as misunderstanding the implicit local codes or, more ominously, as being an unwanted intruder, and may sometimes be actively discouraged from practicing this step, usually by two-steppers who simply move through (or into) the steps of the twirling jitterbug dancers. I return briefly to this conflictual response in both of the following sections.

Most commonly, however, dancers form couples to waltz, two-step, and jitterbug as variable responses to the anticipated musical performance, while the musicians prepare in each dance venue to provide the musical style(s) that anticipate the physical—that is, performative—dance demands of the particular audience. This common anticipation of interchange prepares the differences in repetition that Deleuze and Guattari call "refrains" (*ritournelles*), which contribute to the event by enveloping the dance performance within the many musical elements that propel the haecceity: lyrics, rhythms, instrumentation, and vocal and musical interpretation. However, these refrains also correspond to the anticipation of the physical repetition of steps and movements through which the dancers' propulsion establishes a complex and shifting polylogue: within the couple, with other couple pairs, with the musicians, and even with spectators. It is precisely such variable experiences of speed and affects circulating intensely between musicians, dancers, and spectators that establish spaces of affects as an in-between complication of matter and forces.

Bodies in/and Sight, Sound, and Touch

The scene is a record store in New Orleans in the mid-1980s. I am flipping through the bins of vinyl, selecting the first of many Cajun albums I would eventually buy. Among the initial choices was one with a local Louisiana label, on the front cover of which was the sketch of a dancing figure holding an accordion in a sailor-type cap. This was Wayne Toups's first album, *ZydeCajun* (1986), and although I had never heard of him, the name "ZydeCajun" and the cover sketch beckoned to me, welcomed me somehow. It was one of my first and best purchases.

Switch to 1987 on a Thursday evening on Oak Street in New Orleans, the weekly Cajun dance night with Filé at the Maple Leaf. As I pay the cover, the doorman tells me, as a warning and almost with a sneer, "Filé isn't playing tonight. It's some guy named . . . Wayne Toups." Hearing this, I nearly leapt through the door onto the dance floor. Yet, despite the musical brilliance of the band's sets and Toups's virtuoso performance on the accordion, the collective mind-set of my fellow dancers seemed to match the doorman's disdain: ZydeCajun's music wasn't "traditional enough." Still, whether it was the traditional waltz and Toups composition "Mon Ami," or the cover version of Van Morrison's "Tupelo Honey," the performance by the dancing figure and his group worked for me just fine.

Switch again to other Thursday evenings in spring 1988, across the

Mississippi River at Algiers Point in the original Michaul's.[9] Trying to compete with Cajun night at the Maple Leaf, Michaul's owners brought in Wayne Toups and ZydeCajun for a series of weekly venues. On some nights the bar was full, while on many other Thursdays we were the only dancing couple, with Wayne Toups asking us between numbers, "What do you want to hear next?" Through this succession of Thursday evenings, we came to know the group's renditions of waltzes, fast two-steps, and occasional cover versions of non-Cajun songs, and with this intense engagement between our dance and ZydeCajun's music, we honed a dance response, a movement to and in-between the rhythms, words, and atmosphere unique to Toups's performance. And somehow, even without the exchange with other dancers, the jitterbug on that smooth tile floor could hardly have been more enjoyable with the band to ourselves.

Jump in time and space, nearly a decade later, to Dearborn, Michigan, and to Wayne Toups with a different set of musicians, a reconstituted ZydeCajun. The selection of compositions was geared to a non-Louisiana audience—that is, fast two-steps and some covers of popular songs as the majority of numbers. While the dance floor was filled with rock dancers who made the Cajun two-step and jitterbug nearly impossible, the floor remained empty for the rare waltzes. After a solo dance to the first waltz number, we were reluctant to become the lone waltzers yet again. On the third waltz, however, Toups invited us onto the floor to dance and to join the band, not just in its performance but in the exchange that constitutes the dance and music event. At the break, Toups joined us at the next table, and reminded us, "I've been knowing you for a long time."

My evocation of these temporal, spatial, and experiential scenes related to Wayne Toups and ZydeCajun is a way of forming instantaneous resonances with the thisness of the dance and music event by emphasizing diverse elements that create links between dancers and musicians. As I suggested above and elsewhere (Stivale 1998, 174–87), this interchange consists of a complex polylogue that moves beyond subjects into the thisness of the event, into the creation of affective becomings in the dance and music interchange. The reflection in the first section about spaces of affects provides the basis for examining other sorts of in-betweenness, which the instantaneous scenes above help to animate.

The interchange between musicians and dancers and spectators in complex forms of visual and aural interplay establishes the affective "rhythm" or "refrain" that underlies the event. Simultaneously, there is also the polylogue of the dancers between themselves responding to the refrain within the dancing couple, in relation to other couples, and even in relation to the spectators surrounding the dance floor. Intersecting these exchanges within the dance and music event is its own in-between relation to the broader dance and music arena, the sociocultural context that defines, constrains, and yet opens possibilities for the dance and music event at each venue. I propose here to reflect on this affective in-between through the rhythmic constitution of bodies within the simultaneously sensory and territorial field of the dance and music event.

To situate the processes of breaks and flows—the processes of becoming—in the dance and music event, we can try to conceptualize this movement in relation to fixed and coded subject positions—what Deleuze and Guattari call "faciality"—which are nonetheless always in a complex dance and music assemblage between musicians, dancers, and spectators. Bodies in motion, with their relative speeds and affective intensities, correspond to faciality in that this concept designates a decoding, then an overcoding, of individual bodily traits into something that Deleuze and Guattari designate as "the Face," a totalizing "screen with holes, the white wall/black hole, the abstract machine producing faciality" (1987, 170). The body parts, they maintain, can all become facialized, akin to a fetishism that overcodes the otherwise decoded body parts. Yet, Deleuze and Guattari argue further that humans must "escape the face"—that is, escape such corporeal overcoding—"by strange true becomings that get past the wall and get out of the black holes, that make *faciality traits* themselves finally elude the organization of the face" (171).

Like Baxter Black's description of Whiskey River Landing, Deleuze and Guattari's description of this disorganization of traits borders on the abstract and poetic, "freckles dashing toward the horizon, hair carried off by the wind, eyes you traverse instead of seeing yourself in or gazing into those glum face-to-face encounters between signifying subjectivities" (1987, 171). Yet, in the dance and music contexts, this description of speed and intensity of disorganized faciality traits seems quite clear. For, corresponding to this visual spatial coding is the background, or "landscape," that is the necessary correlate of this incessant mode of (dis)organization (172). Populated, say Deleuze and Guattari, "by a loved or dreamed-of face," landscapes develop "a face to come or already past" and constitute "not just a milieu but a deterritorialized world" (173), thus helping shift the body from an overcoded faciality toward connections of diverse strata beyond such overcoding. These traits can correspond to proprioceptive sensations, particularly of movement and relations of dimensions in space, that Deleuze and Guattari have related to the mother-child relationship.[10] Situating these sensations within a specific Cajun dance and music venue (e.g., with Wayne Toups at Michaul's) we were able to find a territory there, an abode, through the refrain. This experience was a becoming-music through the dance response, and "when the rhythm has expressiveness," as Deleuze and Guattari describe it (312–15), the complex polylogue of the dance and music event emerges to envelop all participants.

Moreover, the spaces of affects are a visual, aural, and tactile assemblage in which the dancing couple is but one constitutive element, contributing to the (dis)organization of the faciality traits on the landscape of the event. For example, when we dance in a crowd or, as in the scene above with Wayne Toups at Michaul's, in a relatively empty space, these sensations play an important role in our response to the music as well as in response to the bodies *and space* around us. Whereas at the BeauSoleil venue in Detroit in which we felt uncomfortable becoming dancers-as-spectacle, at Michaul's we counted ourselves lucky to have the band and the floor to ourselves. In the first case, there was little, if any, exchange with the band perched above the crowd on a stage erected for the occasion. Moreover, our dancing appeared out of place, *unheimlich*—uncanny, strange, and not at home—alongside the few dancers joining us on the fairground lawn. In the second case, even on the occasions when no other dancers were present, our dance expression was in constant exchange with the band, and the spectators in the bar recognized this exchange, as did we, as entirely in place, at home.[11]

Furthermore, when Wayne Toups asked us for our choice of music while dancing at Michaul's, or recognized our dancing in Dearborn years later, these forms of recognition were directed less toward individual dancers or to a particular couple than toward these faciality traits populating and creating the dance and music event, then mutating into the collective landscape of speed and affects in the polylogue between musicians, spectators, and dance partners. Bodies take shape and materiality in a collective assemblage of enunciation through the rhythms, patterns, movements, speeds, and intensities in which they engage on a dance floor, thereby producing the event of spaces of affects.

As with the territorializing spatial dyad considered in the first section, we find ourselves again located in between immanence and stratifica-tion, the movement toward relative deterritorialization and back that processes of coding and protocols impose on the dance floor. Just as in any creative enterprise and engagement of bodies within the speed and intensity of thisness, the movement in-between concerns a particular engagement in the polylogue of the dance and music assemblage. To situate this engagement within a social formation, Deleuze and Guattari suggest, "First see how it is stratified to the deeper assemblage within which we are held; gently tip the assemblage, making it pass over to the side of the plane of consistency" (1987, 161).

This is, of course, the hard part, but in the dance and music assem-blage the very creative movement of intensity and speed in dance can lift one toward this strategic shift of plane, however briefly it may happen. At any given moment in any given dance venue, the potential for this dy-namic is alive, the "connection of desires, conjunction of flows, con-tinuum of intensities" (161), in an active becoming with a partner, with a crowd, as event. We know these moments well—as whole evenings or festivals, or just sporadic moments at a dance and music venue—because it is in this way, insist Deleuze and Guattari, that you will have "con-structed your own little machine, ready when needed to be plugged into other collective machines" (161).

To extend my own "little machine" further, I have come to reflect on the dance and music event as a multisensory, or haptic, experience.[12] To describe this experience, I employ the neologism "hapticity" in a chemi-cal sense—that is, as the physical bonds created and ruptured in the sensory field as haptic event. Furthermore, I follow Jennifer Fisher in linking the haptic (or proximal sense) to the strictly visual and aural (or distal senses), and from this perspective I conjoin distal and haptic senses in order to extend faciality toward the full sensory dimension of experience. As Fisher argues: "Haptic perception can elucidate the ener-gies and volitions involved in sensing space: its temperature, presences, pressures and resonances. In this sense, it is the affective touch, a plane of feeling distinct from actual physical contact. And inside the skin, it is interoception, an aspect of the haptic sense, which perceives the visceral working and felt intensities of our interior bodies" (1997, 6).[13] Within the dance and music space, I wish to take note of the experiences of physical as well as interoceptive touch, of the aural and visual interplay, in which the dancers engage in their relation to the music performance.

Moreover, physical presence and even scent are crucial parts of the literally vital engagement of dancers and spectators in the dynamic spatio-temporal becoming on crowded Cajun dance floors, whether in waltz, two-step, or jitterbug.

The complex integration of sensory input—from the lead and follow through physical contact in conjunction with the musical beat—constitutes the fundamental elements of the dance movement both within the couple-unit and in relation to other couple-units, the spectators present, and the musicians themselves. Notably, in the waltz and two-step, the sole points of contact are, for the lead, right hand on the partner's lower back (waist level) and left hand in the partner's right; for the partner, the left hand on the lead's shoulder, and right hand in his/her left.[14] It is through these contact points that all signals are communicated within the couple, but as one dances with the same partner over time, an interoceptive sense develops in terms of the partner's body movement and weight shifts. This sense is beyond scent and feel, transmitted by contact of mutual care and attention to the spatial relations with other couples and spectators, and in relation to the performative progression of each tune toward its conclusion. For when the dancers become familiar with the tunes and especially with the musicians' particular interpretation of them, one can pace the sequence of steps and moves within a jitterbug number, for example, so that one has time to rest during the long numbers but also so that one can move faster and accelerate in pace toward the intensity of the musicians' finale of each number.

As may be apparent, physical movements can be limited on the dance floor most notably within a crowd of dancers, and this confluence of movement and speed creates the paradox of touch: touch between the couple is vital for successful dance movement, whereas touch between couples is strictly to be avoided. In fact, dancers need and deploy specific waltz and two-step steps in order to navigate on the floor to avoid collisions.[15] Moreover, in recent years one development is the importation to the waltz and two-step of upper body movements from the jitterbug and country-style two-step (e.g., twirls, turn-outs, extended arm positions, side-by-side steps). While often quite beautiful if performed well, these expansive movements can sometimes interrupt the smooth counter-clockwise flow of the waltz and two-step numbers, leading to varying degrees of difficulty for the dancers within certain venues who find their own dance movement significantly impeded.[16]

So far, I have not considered the Cajun jitterbug, but its introduction and practice on the two-step dance floor can create the territorial constraints and interruptions that I mentioned earlier: notably, if the regular counterclockwise flow of the two-step is to proceed unimpaired, then two-step couples must navigate with care when the spinning and rotating jitterbug dancers necessarily create blockages to the flowing two-step movement. Again, this clash of movement can cause fundamental tensions on the dance floor, as is momentarily evident in a very brief but significant moment of the final sequence in the documentary *J'ai Été au Bal* (Blank and Strachwitz, 1989a). During the supercharged performance of the Cajun standard "Allons à Lafayette" by Wayne Toups and ZydeCajun, among the many dancers shown is a couple consisting of two young women, clearly the best dancers on the floor. At one moment, as they complete a turn, the man in the couple next to them bumps into one of the two women, without acknowledging the contact with an apology. The attentive viewer will note that she instinctively turns her head to glare at him in a relatively good-natured fashion, and continues her next move unimpeded.[17]

This example brings me to the important matter, already discussed for the waltz and two-step, of the disposition of basic arm and body positions in the jitterbug. The fundamental points of contact are: first, hands joined lightly in the back and forth arm movements of the face-to-face basic step (the couple in the form of a moving parallelogram), a kind of dancers' home base from which all other jitterbug moves proceed; and, second, the side-by-side movements of the other basic step, a bouncing movement forward and back in which each dancer favors one leg over the other to create the effect to which some critics of the jitterbug attribute the name "crippled chicken step." The points of contact in the second jitterbug step shift from mere fingertip/hand touch as well as eye contact in the basic step, to hip and arm contact in different side-by-side moves, to hand and arm contact in over-the-shoulder and side-by-side twirls.[18]

I have developed this explanation not simply for the sake of completing the explanations I provide for the other two Cajun dance steps, the waltz and two-step, but because the Cajun jitterbug step has crucial importance for understanding hapticity in the dance and music event. For, in the give and take of the follow and lead within the couple, the lead must pay particular attention to the proximal movement of the other dancers in order to lead the partner smoothly and to achieve what I can only describe as "lift-off"—that is, that sense of movement and speed and of an instantaneous synch of thisness in the event. This careful attention is all the more important when, on a crowded dance floor, the lead must avoid moving the partner into physical harm. This statement may sound alarmist, possibly even silly, but in almost any crowded dance venue one finds ample reason for attentive care in relation to the movements of other dancers. Indeed, the lead must protect the partner, for example, by avoiding moves that might bring the partner into collision or contact with the moving arms and bodies of couples nearby. Because the decisions for leading the partner to the next move are both spontaneous and usually instantaneous, the haptic sense of the dance space is at once proprioceptive (toward movements and spatial relations) and interoceptive (toward internal possibilities for successive movements).

Similarly, the partner also must pay a particular kind of attention, not just to the proximity of other dancers to the lead (signaling with a firm hand pressure to the lead's shoulder if someone draws too near), but also to the manner in which other leads engage with their partners on the dance floor. The reason for this is quite simple. Because the custom in many Cajun dance venues is for men to invite to dance women other than their regular partners (if they are accompanied), each partner (usually a woman) needs to learn quickly if a particular man will lead her attentively or if his dance/lead style focuses on the "black hole" of himself—that is, without attending to the woman who must follow his movements. In other words, the exchange of lead and follow is a constant dialogue between partners, themselves in dialogue with other dancers often displaying disparate styles and choices of step. And to this, of course, we must add the aural and visual exchange between musicians and dancers, the music and beat enveloping, penetrating, and propelling the dance performers.

Throughout these exchanges and within this complex polylogue, the Spinozan question, "What can a body do?" comes fully into play.[19] For the very definition of haecceity—of a body's "longitude and latitude," as interpreted by Deleuze and Guattari—is directly linked respectively to relations of speed and slowness and to intensities that augment or diminish an individual's *puissance*—that is, intensive power of action (1987, 256–57). As an important component of the thisness of the event, hapticity allows us to conceptualize the direct engagement of bodies within the dance and music event, not in any absolute movement of flow but rather that of the relative shifts of territoriality mentioned above. The body's potential for becomings relates to the territorial concepts developed earlier, "a composition of speeds and affects involving entirely different individuals," say Deleuze and Guattari, "a symbiosis . . . in a matter that is no longer that of forms, in an affectability that is no longer that of subjects" (258). These elements are neglected traits of hapticity because they constitute an aggregate of sensations within the Cajun dance and music assemblage. Indeed, in order to discuss hapticity, we need to conceptualize these corporeal dynamics in terms of dance and music *atmospherics*, those diverse facets of the thisness of the event, as, according to Deleuze and Guattari, "a very singular individuation . . . a degree of heat, an intensity of white . . . as in certain white skies of a hot summer" (261).

In light of the necessarily concise animation of concepts in terms of dance movements presented here, I wish to conclude this section by summarizing the haptic atmospherics that constitute the thisness of the event: within the dancing couple exists the aural landscape, rhythm or beat, from which they gain propulsion. Depending on the dance step, they communicate through precise contact points—hand and body positions, subtle gestures of body weight and thrust, and eye contact (minimum for waltz and two-step; maximum for the jitterbug). Between the dancing couples in movement on the floor are the varieties of modes of leading and following and of relative movement and stasis. In contrast to the evident contact points within the couple, physical contact is rigorously avoided except accidentally between couples. Compared to some other contemporary forms of dance in which contact is frequent, even welcomed (e.g., mosh pits), this avoidance may seem excessive. However, with quick foot movements as well as arms and legs in motion depending on the dance step, dancers do risk injury, occasionally severe, and therefore the dance and music assemblage encompasses qualities of constant care and occasional pain.

Moreover, given that all of this movement entails considerable physical exertion, the results are predictable corporeal responses of sweat, dampness, scent, and fatigue. The latter response very frequently regulates the participation of dancers in each number, and hence the role of spectators (virtual dancers) in any dance and music venue is of utmost importance. Indeed, Deleuze insists that "the event is inseparable from *temps morts* [suspended moments] . . . [that are] in the event itself, it gives to the event its thickness [*épaisseur*]" (1995, 160; my translation). That is, the *temps morts* are the complementary face of the flow continuing from one song to the next because it is in this moment that socializing occurs where dancers can trade instructions on steps or simply recoup their energy.

The thisness of the event thus encompasses and is constituted by all participants, some of whom, even as nondancers, are drawn into the combinations of speed and affects to participate in a variety of corporeal expressions. Finally, the thisness of the event emerges through the constant exchange between dancers/spectators and the musicians who maintain the polylogue through musical expression.

In between Outside and Inside

These different reflections about limitations of touch and movement, potentials for speed and affects, and especially the in-between of becomings raise a number of questions. For example, with all my discussion regarding the in-between of the event, one might rightly ask, "Where is this in-between if the dance begins, say, at 8 p.m., then the doors close, and then the musicians and dancers go home at, say, midnight? How can we understand this dance and music event to settle easily into the concept of an in-between?" For dancers, this in-between is quite simple to understand: just because the venue ends, the dance itself does not stop. Ardent, devoted dancers of all sorts of styles—from country and square dance to tango and salsa—are ever on the lookout for the next venue as if the previous one had merely been interrupted. Indeed, it is easy to judge the extent to which the Cajun and zydeco dance and music arena extends through cyberconnections by observing the proliferation of Web sites announcing activities not just in Cajun music and dance but also for zydeco.[20]

However, we have glimpsed another manner in which the in-between of the dance and music arena continues—that is, in the disparaging reference by the doorman about Wayne Toups, mentioned in the scene at the Maple Leaf. This reference expresses the imbrication of musicians, dancers, and spectators within the sociocultural fold of preconceived ideas and preferences enveloping and intersecting the dance and music arena. This fold contributes to the myth of *les bons temps*, a myth that requires our attention both in terms of its disenchantment and in terms of appreciating the force of enchantment itself. I wish to conclude here by pointing to two ways in which this fold intersects, not as an "outside" (social field) versus a mythical "inside" (the dance and music venue), but rather as a layering and overlapping through which these distinctions intersect as a "doubling" of lines.[21]

For musicians, the selection of musical pieces from the Cajun music repertoire does much more than provide the aural landscape into and through which dancers and spectators flow. The sequence of selections and interpretations of those selections also provides an immediate form of recognition, even of self-recognition, for dancers and spectators, regarding the kind of musical style to which their dance response will adhere—"style" often designated as "traditional" or "progressive." Although this binary distinction is inadequate, it has served and still does serve as a crucial distinction for many dancers. Because a band's play list for a performance will usually alternate between the two dance beats—waltz to two-step/jitterbug and back to waltz—any deviation from the equal alternation serves to characterize the particular dance venue and performance: the more "traditional" would include a dominance of waltzes, while the more "progressive" would consist of a dominance of two-step/jitterbug numbers and often rock and rhythm and blues numbers adapted to the Cajun beat.

On the side of the dancers, the actual positions of physical bodies on the Cajun dance floor—the minimal points of contact in Cajun waltz, two-step, and jitterbug—recall the original courting function of many dancers in the early *bals de maison* and, later, in dance halls. In one extremely humorous intervention in *J'ai Été au Bal* (Blank and Strachwitz 1989b), Solange Marie Falcon speaks to the importance of this imposition of physical distance between the courting couple, and this strict convention of style remains in Cajun dance today. This convention also forms a strong stylistic distinction in contrast to the much closer, sometimes intimate, physical movements that can characterize the zydeco dance style. Hence, the style of waltz that a couple chooses (more or less flamboyant in mixing turns and other movement into the simple waltz flow), and especially the kinds of dance steps chosen in response to the faster 4/4 beat (two-step or jitterbug), tend to mark the particular dance venue and its possibilities for reconstitution of spaces of affects. That is, whatever the alternation of tunes by the musicians, the dancers engage in an array of complex spatial practices that deliberately create spaces of affects within the particular dance and music venue.

However, the recent development of Cajun dance styles—variations on the waltz and two-step mostly—raises other questions regarding limitations, usually imposed implicitly, within certain dance and music venues. I have previously discussed some of these differences, particularly as they relate to different locations (urban, rural) and kinds of venues (clubs, restaurants, festivals), and how in different venues one notes variable forms of allegiance between the fans and the musicians, with equally variable investments of affect through specific forms of dance expression (Stivale 1998, 182–84). I have referred above to some of these developments—for example, the expansive waltz and two-step movements and the occasional expectation on the part of dance partners for these "fancy" moves. Yet as Cajun music and dance have moved beyond the Acadiana region and the borders of Louisiana, the styles of dance have understandably evolved considerably as local groups of dancers learn to respond to the music however they can, from instructional videotapes, in group dance lessons, and through practice at a broad range of dance and music venues.

The perspectives on dance practices discussed in the previous section have an inherent bias toward a more conservative form of dance expression, and I made this choice both deliberately and naturally. That is, having learned to dance in Louisiana, I have come to understand and *to feel* the joy of performing a simple, gliding waltz and a fast, smooth two-step, and of leading my partner through these moves relatively devoid of elaborate flourishes. However, having by now danced increasingly in non-Louisiana venues, I have come to appreciate, especially for the intensity of spaces of affects, all kinds of dance expressions in response to Cajun music. For, if *les bons temps* are indeed going to roll, few if any limitations need be respected in dance expression except those that allow everyone to enjoy the dance and music flow. And this is as true of the music as it is of the dance forms, as Zachary Richard insists unambiguously: "There is no such thing as corrupting the tradition. . . . The end result of the worldwide recognition of Cajun music has been positive. The recognition has promoted the music to new audiences and generated interest in the phenomena locally" (qtd. in Caffery 2001b, 15).

Indeed, whatever the style, one can observe how couples on the dance floor reinitiate the polylogue as a song commences—joining hands, beginning to circulate and/or gyrate, depending on the step. This polylogue through movement helps us to conceptualize these changeable combinations as they develop toward a collective assemblage with its usual and frequent shifts into more distinct, individual parameters. A wide range of movements occur within this modulation, at once blockages and openings of flows in the reconstitution of landscapes within the time and space frame of a song. Alongside this flow and modulation, the haptic effects obtain in their elaborate complexity, within the couple and between couples, contributing to the dance assemblage. Beyond the dance floor, or just barely, the spectators participate as well, and to these intersections the musicians' beat is the driving motor while their performances respond to those of the dancers and spectators.

Enveloping and intersecting the haecceities of spaces of affects is the apparent "external world"—for example, the context of the venue (club, dance restaurant, festival), locale (city or country site), and geographical specificity (inside Louisiana or elsewhere—the United States, Canada, and beyond). Yet, no dance step nor musical selection is performed "inside" without relation to the sociocultural context and inherent limitations, and no aspect of this apparent external context determines or constrains absolutely, in any first or last instance, the performance flows that construct the dance and music arena. This is the sense in which the in-between of spaces of affects unfolds as a way to extend the elaborate and yet beautifully simple refrain, which Baxter Black describes as "a time warp moment when the often unspectacular human race threw its head back and howled at the moon."

5

Disenchanting *Les Bons Temps*

.
.
.

Is that what friendship is, harmony embracing even dissonance?
—Gilles Deleuze, *Negotiations*

The polylogue that defines the Cajun dance and music arena also characterizes the diverse attempts to recuperate the past and transport it into
the present. In chapter 3, I examined different ways in which filmmakers
sought to represent authentic Cajun identities and cultural practices in
the visual medium, and I considered the difficulties inherent to reconstructing memory as a sort of unity. As Gilles Deleuze points out quite
forcefully in discussing style (and nonstyle) in Proust, no privileged,
stable viewpoint is available for the interpretant, and the signs that we
would interpret resist totalization and remain necessarily in a fragmentary state. This is especially true in terms of the relation between past and
present, because the " 'effect' of explicative style," Deleuze argues, can
only be to produce "partial objects, . . . effects of resonance, and forced
movements. Such is the image as produced by style. This production in
the pure state is what we find in art, painting, literature, or music, *above
all music*" (2000, 167; emphasis added). As Allan Stoekl suggests in
juxtaposing Deleuze to Claude Lanzmann's film *Shoah*, "Deleuze forces
us to confront the question of transgression: the space of memory is not
one of a privileged sacred, but one of a violent, accursed sacred, one that
entails the sacrilegious and involuntary shock of a confrontation with a
fragmentary, obscene past" (1998, 81).

I raise this Deleuzian perspective and Stoekl's reflection about it in order to continue the task of disenchanting *les bons temps*. In chapter 4, I studied different aspects of the enchantment possible in the dance and music arena, and also the limitations inherent to the dance and music polylogue. I also raised the question of the necessary intersection of "inside" and "outside," neither one nor the other in a privileged position but, in fact, creating a fold or overlap such that both become indistinguishable. It is here that I wish to reconsider the sociocultural tensions that underlie *les bons temps*. The links already created between the self-representation of Cajun identities, the performance as event, and the territorial aspects of the Cajun dance and music arena provide the bases for considering how Cajun identity and authenticity are troubled both by linguistic isolation and by racial and social practices. In many instances, these practices constitute inherent attempts to protect the dance and music forms from intrusion by variously defined "others," some within Louisiana, others from beyond its borders.

This examination will also demonstrate the necessary and inevitable transgressive force that arises in confronting past and present, a force due both to the fragmentary elements of such remembrance and to the shock that many of these elements cause through their juxtaposition. For me, as a fan of Cajun dance and music and of Louisiana culture more generally, this chapter has been the most difficult to write. However, its composition has helped me comprehend the extent to which *all* American culture, past as well as present, is imbued with racist sentiments and exclusionary practices. In the context of the origins of American folk music, Ben Filene has skillfully and succinctly explained the fear of "racial degeneration" that motivated the defense by early folk song collectors of old-time culture and its authenticity. Filene insists that these folk enthusiasts' attitudes were not unusual in this era (late nineteenth and early twentieth century), but that what is significant "is that there was a racial undertone beneath the earliest self-conscious efforts to define America's folk song heritage" (2000, 25–26).

Thus, I believe that this disenchantment helps to open up new perspectives for better understanding of *les bons temps* and their force of enchantment beyond the unfortunate undertones as well as overt practices that remain prevalent in our own era. In the three sections that constitute this chapter, I follow the specific foci presented previously and thereby extend this disenchantment toward prevalent mythologies of identity and authenticity: first, in the lyrics and instrumentation of the

Cajun music repertoire; second, in statements and images about race relations made in selected documentaries; and third, in particular practices followed in various dance and music venues.

Lyrics and Instrumentation

Although I have already examined the development of *(dé)paysement* and of a rooted errantry as distinct thematics within the Cajun music repertoire, the question of tradition and authenticity remains extremely vexed given the evident origins of many of the songs that constitute this repertoire. In her study *Cajun Music: A Reflection of a People* (1984), Ann Savoy is quite clear about the paradox between original songs that came to Louisiana with the Acadians in the 1760s and songs of the contemporary repertoire: "These [original] ballads are not widely performed today, but are being sought out and revived by folk musicologists and dedicated young musicians" (13). In fact, the oldest songs were fiddle tunes "full of half tones and complicated note structures that were largely lost after the accordion gained popularity" in the 1920s (14). In other words, one instrument associated with "traditional" Cajun music, the accordion, caused the impoverishment of the repertoire by blocking the performance of more traditional tunes created by an instrument used even earlier, the fiddle.

Still, as Ann Savoy notes, "many beautiful new tunes were inspired by the accordion, and this new accordion era [in the 1920s and early 1930s] perhaps defines what many people today consider to be traditional Cajun music" (1984, 14). The pioneers of this new era were the black accordion player Amédé Ardoin and the French Cajun fiddler Dennis McGee, both of whom, says Savoy, "laid the ground work for many of the greatest players that followed" (14). She also cites the often-neglected Amédé Breaux as another important influence on later generations (80–81). However, this "golden accordion era" was actually quite short-lived, "swept away in around 1934 when the discovery of oil brought an influx of hillbilly music into Louisiana" (15). Whereas the string bands reigned through World War II with the fiddle regaining its place as the lead instrument in Cajun music, the accordion returned after World War II thanks to the inspired music of Iry LeJeune, Lawrence Walker, and Nathan Abshire. All of these accordionists provided a distinct sound that significantly corresponded to the growth of Cajun identity and pride that emerged increasingly following the return of Cajun GIs to Louisiana after World War II.

Thus, the tunes now performed in the Cajun clubs, restaurants, and festivals are adaptations of older tunes from earlier in the century with the added contribution of occasional new compositions, all generally based on the traditional, paradoxical thematics of *les bons temps* and pain, loss of love being the most common theme. In his overview of Cajun music, Barry Jean Ancelet (1989a) traces many of the early songs that reflect the settlers' European origins, their pastimes as drinkers and travelers, and also dance tunes (called *reels à bouche*) meant to be hummed—hence revealing the oral tradition of many of these songs (1989a, 3–8). What Ancelet barely touches on in this brief study, however, and what is of particular interest for claims of identity and authenticity, are the intersections between the music of the French Cajuns and the forms and lyrics of the indigenous Afro-Caribbean population in southern Louisiana, the so-called black Creoles.

Although evidence of these influences is amply available in many of the interviews with Cajun musicians that Ann Savoy provides, she indicates in one chapter, a "Brief History of Old Time Creole Music and Modern Zydeco and Its Instrumentation," that the poverty of Louisiana blacks in the nineteenth century and into the twentieth actually prevented them from owning instruments (1984, 304–6). Thus, early Creole music is truly an oral tradition with syncopation and rhythm provided by foot stomping and other forms of percussion (e.g., spoons) that historians trace back to African and Caribbean roots.

The selections comprising *Louisiana Cajun and Creole Music, 1934: The Lomax Recordings* (Doucet and Ancelet 1987), from which Ancelet (1989a) derives many of his references, provide examples of different genres of early Cajun music as well as songs of the tradition of "zarico, juré and the blues" (Doucet and Ancelet 1987, side four). Just as Cajun music suggests the strong influence of the black Creole tradition, the lyrics as well as the forms of tunes in the Creole selections provide clues to the important influence of the Afro-Caribbean tradition of shouted music (known as *juré*) for Cajun music as well as for the most recent Creole musical form, zydeco.[1]

My purpose in discussing these origins and intersections is to emphasize how difficult any particular claims of distinct identity and authenticity are in terms of the Cajun music repertoire. That is, the earliest tunes necessarily include Creole lyrics and forms, and based on this tradition it is as traditional to sing without instrumentation at all and with improvised lyrics evoking themes of poverty as it is to play tunes with accordion, fiddle, guitar, and triangle about one's loneliness or lost love. Furthermore, these comments on Cajun and Creole musical origins and intersections help establish a complementary point, the necessity for extreme prudence in appreciating and explaining the lyrics of songs that come from the mixed French Acadian/Afro-Caribbean origins. One particular song, attributed to the Cajun accordionist Nathan Abshire, called "Pinegrove Blues," allows me both to emphasize this need for prudence and to underscore the complexity of the issues of identity and authenticity as expressed in musical lyrics.

The facts about this song are quite clear: influenced by the Creole blues tradition, and particularly by Amédé Ardoin (see Ancelet 1999, 102), Abshire adapted the Creole song "Ma Négresse" (see Nyhan, Rollins, and Babb 1997, 23) with a new title corresponding to the kind of blues titles that Abshire tended to give to many of his songs.[2] The form of this song is a slower version of the two-voiced *juré* tune recorded by Lomax, that is, a conversation between the singer and his "woman," addressed as "ma négresse" (literally, "negress," but sometimes translated familiarly as "honey" or "sugar").

Pinegrove Blues

Voice 1: Hé, let's go. Ho!
Hé, négresse!

                             Voice 2: Quoi tu veux, Nathan?

Voice 1: Ayoù toi, t'as été hier au soir,
ma négresse?

                             Voice 2: J'ai été au bal, nègre.

Voice 1: Hé, négresse!

                             Voice 2: Quoi tu veux encore,
cher?

Voice 1: Ayoù toi, t'as été hier au soir,
ma négresse?

                             Voice 2: J'ai été au bal, cher. Je
me suis soûlée.

Voice 1: T'as arrivé à ce matin,
Le soleil était après se lever.
Ça me fait de la peine pour toi.

Voice 1: Hé, négresse!

> Voice 2: Quoi tu veux encore,
> Nathan?

Voice 1: Ayoù toi, t'as passé hier au soir,
ma négresse?
(Je m'ennuie de toi.)

> Voice 2: J'ai passé dans la barri-
> ère. J'étais après me sauver.

Voice 1: Hé, négresse!

> Voice 2: Quoi tu veux encore,
> Nathan?

Voice 1: Ayoù toi, t'as passé hier au soir,
ma négresse?
(Je m'ennuie de toi.)

> Voice 2: J'ai passé dans la barri-
> ère. J'étais après me sauver du
> gros nègre.

Voice 1: T'as arrivé ce matin,
Ta robe était tout déchirée.
Ça me fait de la peine pour toi.

Voice 1: [Hey, negresse!

> Voice 2: What do you want,
> Nathan?

Voice 1: Where did you go last night,
my negresse?

> Voice 2: I went to the dance,
> dear.

Voice 1: Hey, negresse!

> Voice 2: What do you want
> again, dear?

Voice 1: Where did you go last night,
my negresse?

> Voice 2: I went to the dance,
> dear, and got drunk.

Voice 1: You came in this morning,
The sun was just rising.
I felt sorry for you.

Voice 1: Hey, negresse!

 Voice 2: What do you want again,
 Nathan?

Voice 1: Where did you pass last night,
my negresse?
(I'm lonely for you.)

 Voice 2: I passed through a
 fence. I was running away.

Voice 1: Hey, negresse!

 Voice 2: What do you want again,
 Nathan?

Voice 1: Where did you pass last night,
my negresse?
(I'm lonely for you.)

 Voice 2: I passed through a
 fence. I was running from the
 big Negro man.

Voice 1: You came in this morning,
Your dress was all torn.
I felt sorry for you.]
(Abshire 1986)[3]

In this transcription and translation (presumably by Barry Jean Ance-let, who is credited with this work in the liner notes), the term *négresse* simply goes untranslated, while *nègre*, with reference to the singer, is equivalent to the familiar *cher* (dear one). With reference to someone else, however, *nègre* takes a less familiar and decidedly stronger, possibly pejorative, significance, as in the line "me sauver du gros nègre" (save myself from the big Negro). Granted, this rendition emphasizes much less the response lyrics than the main vocal part, but the shift in narrative through chanted dialogue is quite remarkable—from the woman's simple statement of getting drunk the previous night to the more ominous avowal of having escaped from the *gros nègre*. Equally remarkable is that one rarely ever hears this version of the song or reads it so transcribed. Indeed, for his brief study of Cajun music (1989a), Ancelet chose to transcribe a different version, from Abshire's earlier *Pine Grove Blues* album (1979), which omits all lyrics that would require translation and transcription of the double use of the term *nègre*.

With its plaintive chant and distinctive lyrics as back-and-forth dialogue, this song has become a standard of the Cajun music repertoire and is notably featured as the opening song sung by Dennis Quaid, Dewey Balfa, and friends in the *bal de maison* scene of *The Big Easy*, which I discussed in chapter 3. Despite its prominence or perhaps because of it, the song has required that certain musicians take pains to revise the lyrics and even the titles in order to include it in their individual repertoire, and certainly to present its transcription and translation with the recordings. For example, the first album by Filé, *Cajun Dance Band* (1987), includes a wonderful two-step version of "Pine Grove Blues," and the album sleeve provides lyrics and translations of all the songs, prepared by Mrs. Catherine Blanchet. The lyrics of this version include both the repeated cry, "Hey, hey, négresse," translated as "Hey, hey, honey!," and the reply "Quoi tu veux, mon nègre?" translated as "What do you want, my man?" This version also omits any reference to the woman's running through the fence or running from anyone. Moreover, the transcription omits a word (mistakenly or deliberately is not clear), *me*, from the refrain, "Ça me fait de la peine pour toi," and hence creates a new translation, "That makes trouble for you."

Following these transcribed and translated lyrics, Mrs. Blanchet's additional notes state: "Also known as *Ma Négresse*, this song was written or popularized by Nathan Abshire, the legendary accordionist. It was popular in the late forties and early fifties, and sung to me by school children who had learned it on the radio." Then she adds: "The terms 'nègre' and 'négresse', which literally mean Negro and Negress, are terms of endearment and familiarity among the Cajuns, who seem never to have had racial hangups." While I will return to this generalization later, I should point out here an additional note that Mrs. Blanchet provides after the album's final song, "T'en As Eu, T'en Auras Plus": "The term 'nègre' [included in this song] is here used as a term of affection or intimacy, not as a description of a member of the Negro race. It is almost impossible to translate the exact shade of meaning, especially as it differs in different circumstances" (qtd. in Filé 1987).

Other than the rather astonishing exaggeration about no "racial hangups," Mrs. Blanchet's explanations are quite accurate, at least for this version of "Pinegrove Blues" and for the familiar use of *nègre* more generally. Indeed, one need only consult the lyrics of several songs in Ann Savoy's *Cajun Music* to find frequent use of the word *nègre* as a familiar reference.[4] Moreover, not only has "Ma Négresse" been recorded by a number of Cajun and zydeco artists (e.g., Clifton Chenier, Rockin' Dopsie, John Delafose, Waylon Thibodeaux), a variant translation, but a different composition, is also an old blues number titled "Black Gal," adapted by Clifton Chenier and appearing on three of his albums.[5]

Besides pointing to the discrepancies between presentation of different versions of "Pinegrove Blues," I wish to suggest that this very discrepancy underscores the marked tension about race that traverses Cajun dance and music practices.[6] In adapting the Creole song "Ma Négresse," Abshire followed the time-honored practice of adapting an older Cajun and Creole song, which Ann Savoy documents in *Cajun Music* (1984). However, other musicians who selected the same song for their repertoire have clearly avoided these lyrics altogether through further adaptation. Notably, on Wayne Toups's second album, *Johnnie Can't Dance*, the longest song is a bluesy adaptation of "Pinegrove Blues" in which "ma négresse" is replaced with the words (and the new title), "ma jolie" (My pretty) (1988). Yet another adaptation, by the zydeco singer Buckwheat Zydeco (Stanley Dural), changes the title to "Ma 'Tit [*sic*] Fille" (My little girl) (1987), which is also included in the soundtrack to *The Big Easy* (although omitted from the film itself). While neither of these albums includes transcriptions or translations, the lyrics correspond to the simpler version selected by Ancelet (1989a) and Filé (1987).

One can only wonder what the reasons are for these particular lyrical modifications. An obvious speculation is that, in seeking the widest distribution possible for their albums—particularly for Buckwheat Zydeco, whose albums (for example, 1987 and 1999) have increasingly sought crossover potential with his zydeco-style covers of songs as diverse as "Hey, Joe," "Time Is Tight," and "On a Night Like This"—these artists took no chances in choosing to include this song. Given the many precedents for adapting standards, they thus modified the song further from its original adaptation of an even earlier form. In Toups's case, he transformed the Abshire adaptation into a slow blues song sung in French, thereby following his own consistent practice of trying to make the Cajun repertoire more accessible to the younger generation, while respecting his Cajun French origins.

My selection of this example may well appear to split hairs in a repertoire noted predominantly for ballads of heartache and lost love, drinking tales, and two-steps that celebrate the dancing, music, and courting rituals of Cajun culture. However, as such a prominent tune, arguably third only to "Jolie Blonde" and "La Chanson de Mardi Gras" as a traditional Cajun song, "Pinegrove Blues" has caused different artists and archivists varying degrees of difficulty in rendering it both in music and in print. Although such difficulty and variations are not uncommon for a musical repertoire that has until quite recently been passed on entirely as an oral tradition, I believe that this example points to tensions prevalent in other forms of representation of tradition and authenticity in Cajun folk practices.

Statements and Images of Race: Cajun and Zydeco

To the Cajun and Creole musical repertoire we must add the growing body of visual documentation that has been generated since the 1980s about Cajun and Creole dance and music cultures. While I have already considered in chapter 3 different aspects of authenticity and tradition in three visual genres, I return here specifically to two documentaries on Cajun dance and music as the context of race relates to the many intersections of Cajun and Creole music.

In the previous section, I followed Cajun historians in noting that the growth of these musical forms are inextricably linked: not only was the proximity of French Cajun and Afro-Caribbean Creole cultures an important factor from the eighteenth century onward, but also the influence of remarkable Creole musicians has been crucial both for the development of Cajun accordion and fiddle styles and for the development of compositions and genres in the Cajun music repertoire. In light of these important intersections, I propose to consider how seamlessly the history of this development is rendered in the foremost documentary, the film *J'ai Été au Bal (I Went to the Dance): The Cajun and Zydeco Music of Louisiana* (Blank and Strachwitz 1989a), and to contrast this development to the more nuanced emphasis on these relations in Alan Lomax's *Cajun Country: Don't Drop the Potato* (1990).

As I indicate in chapter 3, *J'ai Été au Bal* is a remarkable document of musical and cultural history, but a careful examination of its narrative strategy reveals some telling details. What follows is an outline of the narrative sequence of *J'ai Été au Bal*, and I particularly wish to emphasize important aspects that relate to the intersection of Cajun and Creole music in this film:

J'ai Été au Bal (approximately 82 minutes total, plus credits)
Introduction (9 minutes): different situating views of Cajun locales

Segment 1 (16 minutes): development of Cajun and Creole instrumentation and music [8 minutes on the role of the fiddle plus 8 minutes on the role of the accordion]

Segment 2 (20 minutes): development of French Cajun music I (1920s–1950s) [final 3-minute section on the impact of Iry LeJeune]

Interlude (6 minutes): "parallel story" of the development of zydeco

Segment 3 (18 minutes): development of French Cajun music II (1950s–1980s)

Segment 4 (13 minutes): development of zydeco (1970s–1980s) [final 3-minute section as segue from zydeco to Wayne Toups and Zyde-Cajun]

The nine-minute introductory section consists of different situating views of Cajun dance and music locations in rural southwestern Louisiana, some Cajun humor (with Marc Savoy telling a joke), and a map of the "Cajun belt" in southern Louisiana. These elements are followed immediately by the zydeco musician Queen Ida, who explains how Louisiana music has now come out from "behind the iron curtain" to national prominence. A brief transitional segment follows in which successive screens of text overlay the visual background of Michael Doucet, one of the film's narrators, paddling a pirogue in the swamps. These successive texts succinctly summarize the original settling of the Acadians in Louisiana, and the final text states: "There they mingled with Free Men of Color, Native Americans, and other French and European settlers, creating the unique Cajun and black Creole traditions that exist today."

In the first eight minutes of the first segment, Michael Doucet discusses the role of the fiddle in Cajun music, contrasting the Celtic origins of the Acadian fiddle music with the Afro-Caribbean origins of the Creole fiddle, with Canray Fontenot singing "Lorita" to provide the sharp contrast. In voice-over narration, Barry Jean Ancelet insists that it is due to the Afro-Caribbean influence that Cajun music sounds nothing like Acadian music, and this dual Cajun/Creole emphasis continues, first with a brief performance by and interview with the elderly Cajun fiddler Dennis McGee, then with a reference to his association with the Creole musician Amédé Ardoin. Following still shots and early recordings of Ardoin singing is a brief accordion performance by his descendent, Bois Sec Ardoin, accompanied by a fiddle and percussion on a cardboard box. This performance allows the filmmakers to enter the second part of this segment, eight minutes devoted to the role of the accordion and culminating with shots of Nathan Abshire in performance.

Then, a second segment commences, approximately twenty minutes devoted entirely to the development of French Cajun music, especially emphasizing the family and social relations that were the necessary counterpart earlier in the century of the performance of music and dancing at the different *bals* where the Cajun families mingled and young men and women courted under the watchful eye of the elders.[7] The segment's second section traces the Americanization of Cajun culture, the impact of the string bands on Cajun music in the 1930s, and then the slow revival following World War II of Cajun accordion music. This revival is attributed in a three-minute section to accordionist Iry LeJeune, and the segment ends with the evident turning point of the film, shots of newspaper clippings from 1955 announcing LeJeune's death in an automobile accident.

Although the narrators then pick up the "parallel story" of the development of zydeco, this story is really only a six-minute interlude devoted to the important role for Creole music played by Clifton Chenier. The narration quickly returns to the French Cajun story in an eighteen-minute segment on the successive roles played by D. L. Menard, Belton Richard, the advent of rock and roll and swamp pop, and finally Dewey Balfa, the "cultural missionary" of Cajun music in the 1960s, who is depicted in numerous shots of his performances with his brothers at the Festivals Acadiens that began in the mid-1970s. His impact on the younger generation—that is, the Cajun baby boomers—is the focus of the final part of this segment, with performances by Michael Doucet and Beau-Soleil at Mulate's, the famed Cajun restaurant in Breaux Bridge, and then by Paul Daigle and his band Cajun Gold at a rival restaurant, Belizaire's, in Crowley.

Although the opening segment (following the introduction) did emphasize the important intersection of Cajun and Creole music, at the three-quarter mark of the film the Creole tradition has received a mere six-minute segment in the center of the film. Hence, the narration shifts to zydeco musicians in the penultimate thirteen-minute segment. The emphasis here is on the movement between older and younger generations, and the final segue moves from the successful zydeco hit by Rockin' Sidney, "Don't Mess with My Toot-Toot," to the concluding mix of Cajun and zydeco musical traditions in the final performance, by

Wayne Toups with his band ZydeCajun. Although Toups is certainly not the only representative of such a fusion at the time of this film (late 1980s), his showmanship clearly stood out as an evident contrast with the more sedentary style of "old-timey" performances.

I have outlined here the narrative strategy of this documentary in considerable detail in order to be careful about the contrast I now wish to make with the Lomax film *Cajun Country*. In the previous section, I cited a comment in the Filé album notes about Cajuns "seem[ing] never to have had racial hangups," and judging from *J'ai Été au Bal* this statement could be the documentary's epigraph. This implicit message is all the more peculiar given that the film's final credits begin with the statement that the film was "inspired by Ann Allen Savoy's volume, *Cajun Music: A Reflection of a People*," in which several musicians offer stunning testimony to the extremely difficult circumstances of the Creole musicians in relation to the white society.[8]

The narrators of *J'ai Été au Bal* hint at none of these difficult conditions, and as one begins watching Lomax's *Cajun Country*, it would appear that a seamless presentation of the relationship of Cajun to Creole culture operates in this documentary as well. I provide here the sequences of the film's narrative development:

> *Cajun Country: Don't Drop the Potato* (approximately 56 minutes total, plus credits)
>
> Introduction (4 minutes): different situating views of Cajun and Creole music and dance [Lomax's anecdote about the expression *lâche pas la patate*]
>
> Segment 1 (7 minutes): views of Cajun Mardi Gras *courir*, then a Creole trail ride
>
> Segment 2 (10 minutes): French and Acadian origins of Cajun country and of Cajun music [final brief section with a Cajun and Creole crowd at a local racetrack]
>
> Segment 3 (5 minutes): African and Caribbean origins of Creole culture
>
> Segment 4 (10 minutes): French Cajun culture and music; women's condition; society and dance culture
>
> Segment 5 (8 minutes): post–Civil War violence, racial attitudes [5-minute section on the music and fate of Amédé Ardoin]
>
> Segment 6 (5 minutes): development of Cajun music, cultural conflicts

Segment 7 (5 minutes): revival of Cajun culture

Segment 8 (2 minutes): conclusion: Houma indians/Cajun Mardi Gras

After a brief introductory segment and the successive images of the raucous Cajun Mardi Gras ride, the *courir de Mardi Gras*,[9] Lomax presents the separate Creole Mardi Gras ride which places an emphasis on community—of men, women, and children together for music and food. Without commentary, Lomax passes to the French origins of Cajun society and interweaves the growth of the musical tradition with the social and economic bases, notably ranching cattle and horses. This development brings Lomax to a gathering of blacks and whites at a racetrack at the end of segment 2. While commenting on the Cajun penchant for gambling as well as on the general harmony of this community, Lomax observes to those assembled there that "this race stuff never did work"; that is, it was never important for these people of mixed heritage and intertwined destinies. While one might be tempted to conclude from this comment that, like the narrators of *J'ai Été au Bal*, Lomax seeks to develop a seamless view of the cultural intersection of these ethnic groups, his own history as a folklorist speaks forcefully against such a conclusion (see Filene 2000, 47–75, 139–82).

Furthermore, any such impression is quickly dispelled in the subsequent segments where Lomax starkly contrasts the impoverished roots in slavery of the Afro-Caribbean music of Louisiana with the more privileged socioeconomic status of the Cajuns. He interviews several Cajuns about the extraordinarily difficult circumstances for women who, once married, were usually left alone in the desolate rural homes to give birth to and raise huge families.[10] Then, Lomax introduces another subject rarely discussed, the violent attitudes and behavior that developed after the Civil War among whites as well as between whites and blacks. Indeed, as historian Carl Brasseaux has noted (1992, 74–88), the fortunes of Cajun society shifted dramatically for the worse after this conflict, and impoverished and déclassé Cajuns as well as other poor whites could not abide the freedoms accorded to blacks under Reconstruction. Through a combination of images and interviews, Lomax is able to evoke the definite shift of attitude, and one Creole interlocutor is outspoken in explaining that blacks simply were discouraged and forcibly prevented from seeking any kind of higher position or self-improvement.

It is within this context that Lomax introduces what he calls "the tragic story" of Amédé Ardoin. Lomax first establishes Ardoin's importance for Cajun and Creole music and then emphasizes his precarious existence playing white dances for money but always running the risk of being attacked by drunken rowdies. Lomax enlists testimony from Canray Fontenot and Wade Frugé to recount how Ardoin sought to earn higher pay performing for white dance venues, always under the patronage of the venue's owner. As constructed by Lomax, the sad tale of Ardoin's demise culminates in a crucial, near fatal moment when he "crossed the line." Having accepted a handkerchief from a white woman to wipe his brow, Ardoin was beaten senseless following the dance, run over by a Model-T, and left physically, then mentally, unable to continue performing. Ardoin died in or near an asylum in central Louisiana, never having regained an ability to perform. This segment is skillfully edited and extraordinarily moving, and constitutes a moment of stark, ugly truth about life in southern Louisiana in the 1930s.

Just as the tragic death of Cajun musician Iry LeJeune in an auto accident is the central turning point of *J'ai Été au Bal*, the demise of Amédé Ardoin is an emphatic statement in *Cajun Country*. But, we must recall that in *J'ai Été au Bal*, after discussing the importance of the collaboration of Amédé Ardoin and Dennis McGee, Michael Doucet says in a voice-over that what these musicians played together formed the very basis of Cajun music today. That is, the many tunes that now constitute the Cajun music repertoire are derived from their early work together on accordion and fiddle, just before the advent of the string band era of the 1930s. Yet, no mention is made of Ardoin's circumstances or fate in *J'ai Été au Bal*, whereas Iry LeJeune's tragic car accident is highlighted dramatically and visually. Although LeJeune certainly was important for having reintroduced the accordion into Cajun music in the 1950s, Michael Tisserand insists that "the celebrated return of the accordion into contemporary Cajun music was largely due to LeJeune's version of Ardoin tunes" that LeJeune heard on his uncle's 78 RPM recordings of Ardoin (1998, 65).

Besides serving for Lomax as a tale of the stark racial tensions in southern Louisiana, the Ardoin segment also provides a bridge toward understanding other forms of strife in Cajun culture. Through successive interviews, Lomax links the tragic tone of Cajun singing not just to the traditional theme of lost love but also to economic realities, particularly the homogenizing impact of Americanization on Cajun French language and culture. Various interlocutors, Cajun and Creole, attest to having been persecuted in the school yard for speaking French, and an interview with several Houma indians attests to the discrimination that they underwent throughout this century. Hence, within this context of social dislocation and cultural annihilation, Lomax ably valorizes different efforts to affirm the importance of Cajun language and culture.[11] While Lomax provides images in the penultimate segment showing the positive results of the Cajun renaissance that one interlocutor calls the "Cajun craze" in the 1980s, he also ends with a counterpoint to this celebratory tone: he returns to the Houma indians who insist that all this growth and celebration of culture is at the price of destroying the environment of the Louisiana wetlands, suggesting that not all Louisiana natives, least of all the Creoles, are included in the renaissance.

Through comparative analysis of these two documentaries, I argue that their different modes of construction raise a number of problematic questions regarding tradition and authenticity. Certainly, matters of film length, available footage, and narrative development must weigh into a film's final production, but such considerations are always closely linked to the need for fair and complete presentation of historical events. In these two documentaries, the filmmakers made evident choices to adopt particular focal emphases, and viewers must judge for themselves which emphasis most faithfully portrays the historical and social development depicted.

This question of representation is all the more unsettling because one need only look at Les Blank's filmography to know that he is highly aware of the importance and complexity of Creole culture, notably *Dry Wood* (1973a; on Bois Sec Ardoin and Canray Fontenot), *Hot Pepper* (1973b; on Clifton Chenier), and *Yum, Yum, Yum!* (1990; on Cajun and Creole cooking). Still, as I have suggested here and in chapter 3, the affirmation of any particular "identity" is necessarily bolstered by the mode of constructing such sociocultural representations, and *les bons temps* themselves only retain their happy aura through the apparent validation that these representations authorize.

Les Bons Temps Otherwise: Limitations and Exclusions

The different, almost fleeting, references in Lomax's *Cajun Country* to outsiders and to Americanization point to an important aspect of the racial issues to which I have referred. These issues are, in fact, but one prevalent manifestation of a more general tension between sporadic local practices within the Cajun dance and music arena and its "other(s)" in southern Louisiana. That is, these "others" are not located in some distant foreign location but are rather neighbors, and their practices are within plain sight, hearing, and feeling. Just as *les bons temps* may not always be joyful and celebratory, as we have seen, the different sites, spaces, and cultural practices that I have studied in this and previous chapters are not devoid of various forms of territorializing limitations and exclusions. I consider here three sets of practices related to the Cajun dance and music arena that particularly lend themselves to disenchanting *les bons temps*.

The first set of practices concerns the musical interpretation of Cajun music. As I mentioned earlier, in chapter 3 especially, certain styles reflect a so-called traditional mode of interpretation. Despite different variations on such tradition, a viable definition would be those interpretive practices that include (and thus exclude) certain instruments, rhythms, and kinds of vocalization. For example, whereas Dewey Balfa was always associated with a more traditional style of interpreting the music repertoire, the talented accordionist Wayne Toups in the mid-1980s shocked the Cajun music scene with his rocked-up and bluesy interpretations of standard songs. Besides his lively performance and passionate vocalizations, Toups's band, ZydeCajun, did not include the traditional fiddle and minimal percussion, but rather substituted these with an electric guitar, electric piano, and full drum kit. Indeed, with the band's very name, Toups emphasized the bridge that he wanted to make between Cajun music, with its often quite staid and constrained style, and zydeco, with its lively, blues-based renditions of many of the very same compositions as in the Cajun repertoire.

Toups's story is by now quite well known, his music having entered into the mainstream of the broadened Cajun music arena thanks, in large part, to Toups's own desire to return to his Cajun roots. However, what has become acceptable in Cajun musical interpretations certainly has evolved considerably as well over the past two decades. One would think, therefore, that the time had come in which any sort of musical interpretation would be admissible in this arena. Regrettably, the story of Horace Trahan suggests precisely the contrary and shows in stark terms how the perceived betrayal of one's roots can have unforeseen consequences.

Trahan's tale begins in glory, with the talented young accordionist's music closely linked to the traditional Cajun style. At age nineteen, he released his first CD, *Ossun Blues* on Swallow Records (1996), with the significant claim in the subtitle, "Authentic Cajun French Music." Attesting to this claim were the musicians accompanying him—no less than D. L. Menard on guitar, Terry Huval (of the Cajun band Jambalaya) on fiddle, Stacey Huval on triangle, and on certain selections, Christine Balfa, Kevin Wimmer, and Dirk Powell (guitar, fiddle, and fiddle, respectively; all members of the Cajun band Balfa Toujours), and Nelda Balfa (triangle; an original member of Balfa Toujours [see 1993], occasionally appearing on later recordings [see 1998]).

To this musical authentication by association, I should add the CD's liner notes, written by Barry Jean Ancelet, which begin with the important imprimatur: "Horace Trahan is the genuine article, reminiscent of Iry LeJeune in more than repertoire and style" (Trahan 1996). Ancelet explains Trahan's musical apprenticeship on the accordion with Zachary Richard's own mentor, Trahan's cousin Félix Richard. We also discover in these notes that as Trahan learned his instrument, he insisted on speaking only French with his family and friends. Says Ancelet, "he grew increasingly aware of the importance of preserving the language to preserve the cultural expression it represents." Acting on a tip from a staff member at the Jean Lafitte Acadian Culture Center in Eunice, Ancelet, acting as emcee of the weekly *Rendez-Vous des Cajuns* radio show broadcast live from the Eunice Liberty Theater, invited Trahan from the audience to play a tune on his accordion, following which "the crowd rose in a spontaneous standing ovation as he ended the song. . . . It was one of those magic moments filled with beauty and hope." Concluding his notes with thoughts on Trahan's sincere devotion to Cajun music and his heritage, Ancelet says, "Horace Trahan may be Cajun music's best hope for the future, ironically because he is so firmly rooted in the past." This best hope was officially crowned during the Cajun French Music Association's 1997 *Le Cajun* award ceremony, where Trahan was named accordionist of the year and *Ossun Blues* recognized as the best first album / CD by a band.[12]

What, then, happened between Trahan's first CD and the second, released in 2000, that would allow Herman Fuselier to report that, "in some people's eyes, Horace Trahan is the Great White Hope Gone Bad" (2000, 51)? Nothing less than Trahan's significant change in musical direction, toward a determined mix of Cajun music with zydeco, titled *Get on Board*. His new band, the New Ossun Express, includes none of the Cajun luminaries on the first CD, and the instruments and interpretive lineup—guitar (Paul [Slim] Washington), scrubboard (John [the Sheriff] Best), bass (Daniel Gaspard), drums (Paul [Bird] Delafoss), and accordion (Horace Trahan)—reflect a considerable shift to an entirely different orientation, a differently conceived "genuine article." Also absent from the second CD are any notes authoritatively endorsing this new direction, and the label is no longer the well-known Swallow Records but the local Zydeco Hound Records, produced by Fred Charlie. Still, the cover notes provided are a wonderful, if terse, statement of inclusion: "Here is a real Louisiana music treat. This group has a wide range of musical experience. Their background takes them through traditional Cajun, Creole, Zydeco and Blues music. So Get On Board The New Ossun Express where every one is welcome and sure to have a good time" (Trahan 2000).

So why "the Great White Hope Gone Bad"? Because, as Fuselier reports, Trahan's decision to pursue this new direction "has the purists keeling over," with Trahan now "learning [that] the cultural hype of *joie de vivre* and 'Laissez les bons temps rouler' often ring hollow" (2000, 51). The backlash occurred, quite simply and depressingly, as a result of Trahan's performance of zydeco, especially in a mixed-race band. Trahan recounted to Fuselier that during the CFMA *Le Cajun* ceremonies in 2000, someone commented derisively to Trahan about his plans to get married. As recounted by Trahan, one individual said of his fiancée, " 'I heard she was short and black,' " and Trahan concluded: " 'I could tell where he was going. He was just trying to be ugly' " (qtd. in Fuselier 2000, 51). Judging from this CD, Trahan has clearly not let the negative reaction deter him from pursuing zydeco while also performing standards by Iry LeJeune and Dewey Balfa. Nonetheless, it would appear that if one starts out with a hybrid Cajun musical style, as did Wayne Toups, only to return to one's roots, then a musician could be forgiven, especially if he has developed the following that Toups has over a substantial career. As a relative newcomer, Trahan took the opposite path, for which he has had to endure some painful experiences in the not so *bons temps*. The release of another CD with a similar forthright Cajun and zydeco mix, *Reach Out and Touch a Hand* (2001), suggests that this experience has fortified rather than weakened his resolve and direction.

The second site of these practices is highlighted in complementary seg-ments during the first part of Lomax's *Cajun Country*—that is, the distinct practices of Cajun and Creole Mardi Gras rides, the *courir de Mardi Gras*, celebrated in the oft-recorded standard "La Chanson de Mardi Gras." The continued racial separation of these rides the morning of Fat Tuesday provides an implicit statement about the separate status of these parallel cultures in southern Louisiana. The raucous cowboy culture of the Cajun *courir* relies on a male-dominated and socially insular structure, guarded by local rules of inclusion and exclusion and held in check during the event by the *capitaine* of the annual ride. Of course, much like the fabled New Orleans Mardi Gras festivities, the *courir de Mardi Gras* is steeped in particular sorts of tradition, and so, by dint of its very exceptional nature, this event might seem to be a poor example for "disenchantment." How-ever, I argue that this exceptional event confirms the rule of cultural separation, indicated by Lomax in the distinct cultural emphasis that he places on the Creole *courir de Mardi Gras*. Even though there are examples of border crossings in some Creole Mardi Gras performances, the impor-tant issue, says Marcia Gaudet, is "how African American/ Creole cul-tural groups have asserted their own separate identity through the forms and expressive styles of their performance" (2001, 172). In fact, these groups are compelled to assert their cultural pride as a marginalized group faced with the dominant regional image of Mardi Gras tradition in the Cajun community.

While evidence of the separatist rule is scarce, this scarcity is hardly surprising given the tight links between the tourist industry in southern Louisiana and the local media. However, this separatist rule did find an unfortunate confirmation during the 1995 local Cajun *courir* in Eunice: despite an open invitation to visitors to participate in the *courir*, even without a horse (flatbed pickup trucks were included), the Eunice Mardi Gras Association refused participation to an African American man. The grounds for this refusal were the assertion that "the association could not guarantee the safety of a black man," the association's president fearing that the "rambunctious" Mardi Gras riders "would get out of hand . . . [and] would harm" this individual (Turk 1995, 16). Although this unfor-tunate event no doubt was an exception to the Eunice community's concerted efforts over the past decade and a half to celebrate Cajun and Creole cultures in a number of lasting ways, the exclusion underscores the racial tensions that were apparent as recently as the mid-1990s.

Michael Tisserand amply documents in his book *The Kingdom of Zydeco* a detail that Lomax does not mention in his documentary regarding the Creole *courir*, that "the [Creole] trail ride has become the movable focal point of the current revival in zydeco" (1998, 257). Tisserand argues that this recurring event constitutes a "revival movement [that] took its current shape over the past twenty years, but its roots can be found in the neighborhood *boucherie*, a nineteenth- and early-twentieth-century social tradition that was once even more important to the survival of the community than the weekly house dance" (1998, 257). In contrast to the Cajun *courirs de Mardi Gras*, the trail rides are frequent throughout the year and are open to newcomers although, says Tisserand, "[they] don't advertise for [new visitors], and you have to know where to look" (1998, 258). Thus, the differences in these social and cultural practices point to different conceptions of identity and relations to "other(s)" that extend well beyond the events of traditional *courirs* and trail rides.[13]

To these movable celebrations, we should also link the dance practices at different kinds of Cajun music venues. As I mentioned in chapter 4, the loci of these events vary as well, notably between rural and urban clubs, between rural clubs themselves, and between Cajun and zydeco venues. In all cases, these differences concern a distinct contrast between openness to "other(s)"—variably defined in terms of race, gender, and social class—and insular, even xenophobic intolerance of "other(s)" manifested in subtle and sometimes not so subtle ways. Again, testimony of such exclusion due to interracial conflict is rare, but Tisserand discusses the issues of dance-hall discrimination quite candidly, and he attributes the heightened awareness of the racial tensions to the new economic tourism boom in rural Louisiana. Tisserand states that the Breaux Bridge dance club La Poussière "allegedly refused entrance to a black patron. According to case documents, a club employee told a black tourist that the traditional Saturday dance was a private party, and turned her away" (1998, 6). The tourist who was refused entrance happened to be a federal prosecutor from Chicago, and a member of her party, a white civil rights prosecutor, returned to the club later, where she (the white prosecutor) reportedly was told that the original refusal to her friend occurred because the friend was black. A federal investigation ensued, and as a result the club was required to post a sign with an explicit welcome to all visitors. However, Tisserand correctly sums up the heart of this debate— "the problem of music, dance, and identity"—and quotes a local informant on the matter: " 'All the coloreds got their own clubs, and the whites got their own clubs,' explained one white patron of La Poussière to the *New York Times*. 'And the coloreds don't dance the way the whites do' " (6).

Through my travels to festivals and clubs in rural and urban Louisiana, I can attest, if only anecdotally, to different experiences and observations of these practices. During my one visit to La Poussière, shortly after the events recounted by Tisserand, I discovered that the problem is not only one of race but of *any* other from outside the community. Perhaps the earlier incident had made the local patrons particularly sensitive to attendance by any apparent tourist at their Saturday night dance. Of course, I had no trouble entering the club and was made quite welcome at the bar. Once friends of mine from New Orleans arrived, we took our place at one of the empty tables close to the dance floor. What was troubling for us, first, was that we found none of the usual cordiality and hospitality so prevalent at many other Cajun dance and music venues in and around Lafayette and in New Orleans. Moreover, several of us simply had difficulty making our way around the dance floor, particularly during the two-steps. Although no one in our group had the cheek to dance the jitterbug on what was clearly a two-step dance floor, while dancing we felt as if there simply was not enough space on the floor for anyone who did not "belong there." This feeling became most noticeable to me when, during one two-step number, I received a solid hip-check by the man in a couple passing on my left that sent my partner and me careening into the tables. Later in the evening this occurred again, and although I was by then prepared for body-contact Cajun dancing, this exchange communicated much more than words ever could.

My experience and that of the tourists from Chicago recounted by Tisserand hardly constitute anything more than examples of local exceptions to the general rule of hospitality that one finds in most locations. Yet, the example of the Chicago tourist suggests the extent to which that hospitality may be specific to race. For me, one particular experience at the 1993 Mamou Cajun Music Festival, unrelated to race issues, showed how an apparently open two-day celebration of Cajun music and culture actually was carefully constructed to maintain a facade of authenticity for visitors and tourists from both near and far away. While there is no question that this particular festival and others like it help the local community affirm its identity, this affirmation comes at the cost of keeping local tensions in check, particularly for those locals who do not share or even care about the traditions that such events are meant to affirm.

Whereas previous Mamou festivals had been held in a local warehouse so that the event could go on even during a storm, this particular festival was held in a lovely park on the east side of town. Around mid-afternoon, the sky began to turn an odd shade of blue-green, and when a gust of wind suddenly blew through the trees, nearly three hundred folding chairs snapped shut in close-order drill as the participants fled for their vehicles. The downpour and then drizzle lasted for several hours, and although recordings could still be played through the plastic-covered sound system, the bands did not return to the stage until early evening. In the meantime, with the tourists departed and the rain only a minor nuisance, the organizers decided to continue with the different contests that had been planned, including nail driving, log cutting, and arm wrestling, among other feats, both men's and women's. Whereas I normally would have been dancing, I now observed these events closely and began to understand the extent to which they served in some ways as a safety valve for ongoing local rivalries. Although not condoned by the events' organizer, betting flourished all around the tables, particularly during the arm wrestling. At one point, aware of my "foreign" presence, the organizer warned the participants, "Pay attention, y'all, be careful. There are still tourists here." Thus, during these few hours, the local inhabitants, nearly the only festival participants left after the lengthy storm, took over and played out many local rivalries and dramas with the festival setting as the exceptional pretext and context for their interplay. These exchanges revealed the backstage scaffolding, as it were, to the careful annual construction and management of the local cultural event.

These attitudes and practices relate directly to a third focus, which brings us back to the vexed questions of tradition and authenticity in terms of dance and music practices, with the Mamou Cajun Music Festival providing a case in point. Having started for many years on Friday evening and continuing all day Saturday, this festival is special for the organizers' insistence that the musical groups invited to play respect the traditional line both in songs selected and in their interpretations. The significance of this question became apparent at the same (1993) festival discussed above, at a moment earlier in that Saturday afternoon during the performance of a group called, appropriately, Mamou. Although I had never heard the group before, one acquaintance told me that the group had a reputation for a repertoire that included more country rock songs than the traditional Cajun repertoire. This distinction seemed important to me only to the extent that I could or could not dance to a song, depending on its beat. However, the organizers saw matters differently because after the first few bars of one song, titled (I learned later) "Opelousas Sosthene," the band had to stop playing and start up another song because the organizers considered "Opelousas Sosthene" to be outside the traditional Cajun repertoire.

I mentioned above that dance steps also are subject to close scrutiny depending on the local venue, and in chapter 4 I described how the dance flow can be significantly impeded during both waltzes and two-steps when dancers fall out of synch with that flow, either through awkward or misplaced steps or, more commonly, through different combinations of twirls and turns. However, in some dance and music settings, an entire set of protocols may obtain for different social groups in particular venues. The most blatant example of such protocols were those that were "legislated" by a local chapter of the Cajun-French Music Association (CFMA) in the early 1990s. Uniting ten chapters from different urban and rural locations in southern Louisiana and southern Texas (known familiarly as "Cajun Lapland," where Cajun country "laps" over into Texas), the CFMA organization has allowed each chapter to create its own rules regarding different sorts of dance etiquette. In this context, one chapter took issue with its members—especially those wearing the "colors" of the CFMA—dancing the Cajun jitterbug to two-step numbers.[14] Hence, the chapter chose to ban the performance of this step, referred to also as "the jig," by chapter members because the step failed to meet sufficient standards of tradition imposed by the particular chapter.[15] Although this ban was quickly rescinded, the prejudice against the dance step imported from outside corresponds quite precisely to the different examples of rigid and tenacious exclusion of whatever appears to threaten the known, the familiar, and the traditional.

Although admittedly an exception both to the rules and practices of most other CFMA chapters, the preceding example still points to the importance for many Louisianans, some not even Cajun but so-called Cajuns-by-choice, of maintaining a sense and practice of tradition and authenticity in relation to the perceived excesses of the innovative, laissez-faire, and *les bons temps rouler* prevalent in the music of many Cajun and zydeco musicians. However, these practices of exclusion and inclusion work in both directions because one can also be too traditional in a given dance and music venue, particularly at festivals and clubs outside Louisiana. At some of these venues, dance protocols that are commonplace in Louisiana—whether traditional or progressive—simply are unknown, and dancers of Cajun or zydeco steps find themselves to be uncomfortable showoffs or, in compact and static rock and roll crowds, simply unable to dance at all.

Clearly, the preceding practices that territorialize Cajun dance and music along the particular lines of tradition and authenticity are consistent with the different manifestations of constructing identity that I have examined throughout this study. In the end, however, the particularities of Cajun dance and music practices and the concomitant constructions of identity and authenticity suggest their intersection with broader, possibly even global, practices of self-representation and commemoration. It is perhaps not at all coincidental that the Cajun cultural renaissance, begun in the 1960s following the success of Cajun music at the Newport Folk Festival, occurred at a time of what John Gillis has called "a new iconoclasm" in commemorative activities. The task of this new iconoclasm, Gillis argues, "became one of finding usable pasts capable of serving the heterogeneity of new groups that had become active on the national and international stage" (19). He points to outright opposition on national and international levels similar to those I have emphasized for Cajun culture, between proponents of the national "heritages" and reformers who promote "desacralizing the nation-state" and democratizing memory (19). As David Lowenthal has argued, "to serve as a collective symbol, heritage must be widely accepted by insiders, yet inaccessible to outsiders, . . . def[ying] empirical analysis; it features fantasy, invention, mystery, error" (1994, 49). As should be evident from the preceding chapters, although the Cajun heritage is, in fact, increasingly accessible to outsiders through tourism (in Louisiana), through ongoing Web site development, and through homegrown bands and dance events around the globe, the different emphases on this heritage have fostered modes of fabulation that reveal tensions still evident in Cajun and Creole cultures.

The extremes of these positions are the topics of daily headlines and news reports of struggles between national groups across the globe. Hence, while the stakes for local practices such as those in the Cajun dance and music arena are no less vital, the means to cordon off difference and "other(s)" tend to be more subtle, if persistent, often requiring rearguard actions that reveal the stubborn entrenchment of local attitudes. However it is waged, subtly or blatantly, this struggle still corresponds to the tactics of a "disciplinary society," still ruling by "order words" (*mots d'ordre*) such as "tradition" and "authenticity." The function of this disciplinary power, says Deleuze, "fashions those over whom it's exerted into a body of people and molds the individuality of each member of that body" (1995, 179–80). In this sense, the construction of identity and authenticity in the Cajun dance arena is part of national, even international, investment in defining and discovering a past. The question, indeed the heart, of the struggle is whether or not possible futures will also be permitted to break through as an active and vital part of this very process of definition and discovery. Despite certain practices uncovered in this disenchantment of *les bons temps* that suggest the tenacity of exclusion and limitation, I turn in chapter 6 to a number of contemporary initiatives that raise great hopes for future cultural growth and expansion beyond the boundaries inherited from earlier centuries.

6

Laissez les Bons Temps Rouler,
or, Death and Life in the
Cajun Dance Arena

.

.

.

I have a song that automatically reminds me of [my father] and sometimes when I hear it by accident I imagine that it secretly means he is thinking of me right then and the song is the sign of it. Sometimes it comes on the radio while we are eating dinner and I feel like I am seeing something in the room that no one else can see. Do you think it's possible that a song could be a message from someone?—Lynda Barry, *The Good Times Are Killing Me*

The title of this final chapter contains phrases and juxtapositions that require some explanation by way of introduction. The easiest part is apparently the French for "let the good times roll," which has served as the vehicle for examining its mythological and enchanting valences throughout this study. As we have seen, this phrase also encompasses the opposite experience, and hence both joy and pain, summed up by Lynda Barry's use of Nathan Abshire's great title, "The Good Times Are Killing Me." As for the emphasis on death in this title, and also its juxtaposition to life, it is out of the painful and harsh experiences of separation and death that, in a number of ways, has come new life, renaissance, in the Cajun dance and music arena.

Indeed, the performative thrust of Cajun dance and music culture has been the motor that has driven the cultural movement known as the Cajun cultural renaissance. As any number of Cajun spokespersons and performers have insisted, despite the pain of the Cajun heritage that many Cajuns refuse to forget, the joy of life and hope for the present and future can still be fostered. As I suggested in chapter 2, Zachary Richard clearly finds his 1976 song of protest, "Réveille," to maintain its currency today because he chose to include it on the French-language CD that ended the first twenty-five years of his career (Richard 2000b) and then on the CD *Coeur Fidèle* (2000c) that begins the next twenty-five years. This evocation of painful memory in Cajun music, in Richard's song "Réveille" and in much of the repertoire generally, emphasizes the past and its pain that will never go away but that musicians can recall while also expressing joy in the present and hope for the future. This dual quality and strategy are summed up wonderfully, but also in a subtly complex way, by the expression *laissez les bons temps rouler*.

To conclude this study, I would like to discuss certain cultural practices that suggest the forward movement of this culture, particularly some of the directions taken by Cajun artists in their music. I wish to focus here on three complementary aspects of recent developments in Cajun music: first, the emergence of Cajun groups consisting of women musicians; second, the growth and prominence of an exciting array of budding teen and even preteen Cajun musicians; and, third, the move among the rising generation of Cajun and zydeco artists to bridge the historical separation between their overlapping cultures through continuing collaborative projects.

Although one woman, Cleoma Falcon, stands at the threshold of Cajun music in the 1920s and 1930s, having recorded "Allons à Lafayette" with her husband Joe, this example is the exception that confirms the general rule of the exclusion of women from the limelight. In *J'ai Été au Bal* (Blank and Strachwitz 1989a), Solange Falcon testifies to the difficulty for women to appear on the bandstand—one could do so only with one's family and even then one ran the risk of appearing cheap. However, one tradition dominated by women was that of the "home song." Barry Jean Ancelet devotes a chapter to the home song in his recently updated *Cajun and Creole Music Makers* (1999), and Marce Lacouture (2000) has begun to revive the tradition with her musical renditions.

Ann Savoy is another pioneer, and not only as a performer in the Savoy-Doucet Band. More recently, she has undertaken a CD project to showcase Cajun music performed by musicians outside Acadiana (A. Savoy 2002; see Fuller 2001c; Willging 2002). And, of course, she is the author of the groundbreaking collection of Cajun and zydeco lyrics and accompanying interviews to which I have referred throughout this study,

Cajun Music: A Reflection of a People (1984). Based on the lyrics collected by Savoy, Laura Westbrook has developed a typology of the way that women are depicted in Cajun music, and she draws the conclusion that, "women [in these songs], although young and often small when they reach the marriageable age, are nevertheless dangerous and a potential cause of misery to men. Young, small, ill, or even dead women are idealized, perhaps because they seem the least likely to thwart their men" (1997). Moreover, the songs in this sample of the Cajun music repertoire work to reinforce the status quo in Cajun society, says Westbrook, by implicitly chastising a woman who would dare to step out of a traditional role.

That women musicians are now stepping forward to make their voices heard, both in Cajun music and in zydeco, is long overdue. Although there has been some female presence in zydeco for quite some time (Queen Ida Guillory comes to mind and, more recently, Rosie Ledet), women musicians have been slow to take their place in Cajun music. A few women have, of course, performed in different Cajun bands, and Sheryl Cormier stands out as the lone female Cajun accordion player who fronts her own band, Cajun Sounds (Nyhan, Rollins, and Babb 1997, 57–58; Cormier 1992). Over the past decade, however, women have started to gain a larger presence in Cajun music, and I point to three groups as evidence of this: first is Kristi Guillory and her group, Réveille (a name reminiscent, of course, of Zachary Richard's anthem and song of protest). In 1995, Guillory recorded an album with Bill Grass, titled *Réveille*, that included a set of songs from the traditional repertoire. The following year, her CD *La Dance des Ancêtres* (Dance of the ancestors) (1996) was released, with half of the songs as new compositions by Guillory herself. Whereas the earlier release still has the woman musician and singer performing songs composed entirely from the male perspective, the more recent release provides Guillory the opportunity to express her own viewpoint and affirm a certain desire for experimentation (see Spell-Johnson 1997, 30)—reverence for elders, desire for love, loneliness on the music circuit, and pride of being Cajun and from rural Louisiana. Still, one finds juxtaposed with these original songs several others that correspond to the traditional stereotype, one depicting a woman cruelly rejecting her husband (Belton Richard's "Je Peux Pas Retourner") and the Clifton Chenier blues song "Lucille" ("O Lucille, you made me cry / You left me to go away / You made me love you / You made me suffer / O Lucille, you left me to go away").

The second example is the pair of recordings from the Magnolia Sisters. On their first release, *Prends Courage* (Have courage) (1995), Ann Savoy teams with Jane Vidrine, and they are accompanied by "guest sisters" Deborah Helen Viator, Tina Pilione, and Lisa McCauley. In many ways, this recording is a wonderful initiative to revive songs from the repertoire and recast them in the two- and three-voiced harmonies between Savoy, Vidrine, and Viator. Furthermore, in the CD liner notes, they state that, "the pieces [recorded here] are a departure from the Cajun dance hall repertoire we play with our husbands. These songs speak to us as women and have created a bond of friendship between us. It is our pleasure to play them for you as we have shared them together." Among these songs are arrangements by the group members of traditional songs and also new renditions of songs previously recorded by women musicians (e.g., Cleoma Falcon and Yvonne LaFleur). One other aspect of this recording is noteworthy: the women on this album also share origins outside Louisiana. "We have each found Louisiana to be eye-opening in both musical and personal ways," and hence the recording is offered as an homage to the Cajun musicians that they have come to venerate.

The second Magnolia Sisters recording, *Chers Amis* (Dear friends) (2000), includes a different lineup of women musicians: the original members—Ann Savoy, Jane Vidrine, and Tina Pilione—are joined by Christine Balfa and Lisa Trahan Reed, the latter two being native Louisianans (Christine Balfa is the daughter of the renowned musician Dewey Balfa). As on the previous recording, the group members reprise songs by Creole as well as Cajun artists and record two songs by Cleoma Falcon, as much as an homage to her pioneering role as a professional musician in the early twentieth century as an opportunity to record songs rarely interpreted.

Although Christine Balfa participates in this important women's group, she is the lead figure in her own group, Balfa Toujours, which has continued the tradition of Dewey Balfa and which serves as my third example. The first album, *Pop, Tu Me Parles Toujours* (Dad, you still are speaking to me) (1993), appeared a year after Balfa's death, and unites sisters Christine and Nelda with three other musicians, Dirk Powell (Christine Balfa's husband), Kevin Wimmer, and, until 1999, Peter Schwarz, who was followed by Courtney Granger. Since their 1993 debut, Balfa Toujours, with different guest musicians, has recorded four more albums, three in the studio (1995, 1996, and 1998) along with a superb live CD set at the Whiskey River Landing near Breaux Bridge

(2000). Given the relations between past and present explicit in all of these recordings, the younger generation of musicians (all of whom were in their twenties during the 1990s) truly accepted the privilege of passing their gift and heritage on to the next generation. As Christine Balfa explains the group's popularity, "I think the appeal (of Cajun music) is in community. . . . People are attracted to that because we have that feeling. We have that warmth" (qtd. in Bier 1999, 33).

This movement from one generation to the next has had its most startling and promising manifestation at the end of the 1990s with the release of seven CDs recorded by young musicians. These recordings range from one by the (then) "elderly" sixteen-year-old Courtney Granger (1999) (who was then promoted to membership in Balfa Toujours) to the seven-year-old child prodigy accordionist Hunter Hayes (2000). Between these two extremes are recordings by Kaleb Trahan (age twelve in 1999), Matthew Courville (age ten in 1999), and La Bande Feufollet, which includes six children between ages nine and fourteen (in 1999). The sixth recording is by Moise and Alida Viator, whose mother, Deborah Helen Viator, was one of the "guest sisters" on the first Magnolia Sisters CD. Although no ages are provided in the notes to the Viators' CD, the Louisiana State University–Eunice Web site profile of contemporary musicians indicates that, in 1999, they were age eighteen and fifteen, respectively.[1] The style of the Viators goes back to the most basic, and the twenty compositions are a mix of Cajun and Creole standards (many rearranged) as well as original compositions by several of the musicians who appear on the CD.

I should mention that these are not the first children and teenagers to perform Cajun music. Besides Steve Riley as a prominent predecessor, there is the Cajun accordionist Roddie Romero (now playing electric guitar with Steve Riley and the Mamou Playboys). Romero's budding career started at age nine, and by age sixteen his performances in local bars and lounges provided the occasion, in July 1992, for the Louisiana state legislature to intervene by passing an exemption, called "the Roddie Romero bill," to allow Romero and other minors to play in businesses that sell alcohol. Romero discovered, however, that Cajun music purists did not support his use of the zydeco-style (piano) accordion in his interpretations of Cajun and non-Cajun music. Although Romero argues that he is a Cajun musician—"That's who I am and where my music comes from"—he also has insisted that he is not afraid to move beyond this strict boundary by experimenting with his music (Spell-Johnson 1997, 30).

The links of family and generation are evident in different ways on all of the recordings mentioned above: Courtney Granger's CD, for which he composed two pieces, is entitled *Un Bal Chez Balfa* (A dance at the Balfas' place) (1999), and given that Granger is Dewey Balfa's nephew, and hence cousin of the Balfa Toujours's Christine Balfa, his lineage and selection of recordings fall into the well-respected instrumental and lyrical tradition of the Balfas. On the *La Bande Feufollet* CD (1999), eleven-year-old Chris Stafford composed three pieces, which were produced by Mamou Playboys leader Steve Riley, who also produced La Bande Feufollet's second release (2001). Matthew Courville's father not only produced his CD but also cowrote the song dedicated to Matthew's grandfather that gives the CD its title *Avec un Coeur pour Mon Pa Pa* (With love for my granddad) (1999). Kaleb Trahan foregrounds lineage with his CD title *The Next Generation . . . It's in My Blood* (1999), produced by his father, Keith. And last but not least, the accordionist Hunter Hayes offers on his *De Mes Yeux / Through My Eyes* (2000) an amazingly eclectic group of selections ranging from many standards rendered in a style eerily reminiscent of Wayne Toups to zydeco tunes and even to two original compositions: "Six Years Old" (rendered as a slow, country blues tune with slide guitar) and "Malfunction" (a tale of heartbreak and betrayal).

In most other contexts, this promotion of children into a particular music industry might seem somewhat opportunistic on the part of parents apparently eager to see their children achieve some level of recognition in the entertainment world. The history of Cajun music has shown clearly, however, that few if any recordings in Cajun French are likely to become a runaway success anywhere except Québec and possibly France. Moreover, while a successful recording career might well begin in such a modest fashion, of greater significance is the fact that Cajun French is in danger of extinction precisely due to the the lack of transmission from one generation to the next and to lack of practice actively within the cultural context. This situation thus explains the particular importance of these children continuing the musical and linguistic tradition, a trend that has not abated: yet another youth band, Les Jeunes Cajuns, has appeared with a CD entitled *Notre Manière* (Our way) (2001), and La Bande Feufollet has been a prominently featured group at local venues in Louisiana, including the 2001 New Orleans Jazz and Heritage Festival, and a second CD was released on their own label the same year (2001; see Caffrey 2001e). At the 2002 New Orleans Festival, La Bande Feufollet again performed, as did Hunter Hayes and a broad array of the adult Cajun and Creole musicians.

Other grassroots initiatives merit our attention in this context. The CODOFIL organization (Commission on the Development of French in Louisiana) has struggled for decades to stimulate French language and cultural development in southern Louisiana (Ancelet 1988). Another important project that I noted earlier, Action Cadienne led by Zachary Richard, seeks to introduce Cajun French language into daily life at all levels, particularly in the elementary schools (see Caffery 2000). Moreover, it was Action Cadienne's initiative to seek the funding necessary from the Louisiana Department of Culture, Recreation, and Tourism in order to produce the superb documentary of the Cajun people *Against the Tide* (1999), which was the second-place winner in the National Educational Telecommunications Association Awards ("LPB Shows" 2001). Action Cadienne is complemented by a more recent initiative, the Louisiana Folk Roots organization, which began in 2000 under the leadership of Christine Balfa. This nonprofit organization is dedicated, according to the mission statement, "to nurturing the unique folkways and cultural resources that are of such legendary abundance in Louisiana."[2] Since 2000, Louisiana Folk Roots has sponsored weekly Cajun and Creole music jam sessions and crafts lessons, as well as an annual week-long Cajun and Creole heritage workshop. This workshop was expanded in 2001 as the Dewey Balfa Cajun-Creole Heritage Week, which brought together Cajun and Creole bands in a combined celebration of heritage (Caffrey 2001c). Furthermore, along with the heritage week programs one must take note of the current transformation of the live music scene in Acadiana, with a number of new clubs and art houses opening in the Lafayette region (Fuller 2001a).

Finally, one additional hopeful sign that speaks to the joyful prospects for *les bons temps* in this century lies in the growing intersection of the two musical forms, Cajun music and zydeco. I have already mentioned in chapter 5 the bold decision by Horace Trahan to shift from a publicly acclaimed Cajun style to a forthright mix of Cajun with zydeco. Judging from his continued musical production in this direction (see Trahan 2001), we must conclude that Trahan's musical exploration is quite sincere. A local effort that could have global consequences has recently been undertaken on behalf of the entire Louisiana musical community by zydeco musician Terrance Simien and his wife Cynthia. Their ambitious goal is to establish a separate category for Cajun and zydeco within the Grammy award categories (Caffrey 2001g).

Another example of this sociocultural overlap is the compilation CD issued by Rounder Records, *Allons en Louisiane* (1999), which includes not only fifteen tracks of Cajun music and zydeco on one disc, but also a video CD that provides an overview of southern Louisiana culture while giving equal place to Cajun and Creole musicians and cultural activities. Tensions and exclusions do still exist between a few die-hard Cajun music purists who reject the fusion of Cajun with zydeco, a fusion that Wayne Toups announced nearly two decades earlier with his group, ZydeCajun, and that has continued ever since.[3] However, while these tensions will never disappear entirely, the Rounder compilation and video CD emphasize materially the many ongoing initiatives and cultural collaborations that Mark Mattern calls the "lively cross-fertilization" (1998, 111) and that has acquired new vigor in recent years.

A manifestation of this crossover between heretofore geographically proximate but culturally distant traditions has occurred in the continuing musical collaboration between musicians of different races and musical backgrounds. Already in the 1980s, BeauSoleil collaborated with Canray Fontenot on one album (1989b), and the group has also helped to develop public workshops on Cajun and Creole instrumentation—for example, at the Festivals Acadiens. Among other collaborations is the fortuitous meeting in 1998 of two generations, two families, and two races when Balfa Toujours and Steve Riley recorded an album, titled *Allons Danser*, with the Creole elder musician Bois Sec Ardoin. The same year, Balfa Toujours's Christine Balfa and Dirk Powell as well as Steve Riley appeared on Geno Delafose's *La Chanson Perdue* (The lost song) (1998), and Delafose appears as drummer for three songs on Balfa Toujours's *Live at Whiskey River Landing* (2000). The final album by zydeco pioneer Boozoo Chavis, who died in 2001, places musicians David Greely (of the Mamou Playboys), Sonny Landreth, and Scott Billington alongside Chavis and his sons. Dirk Powell expresses the significance of these different moments of convergence quite succinctly in the liner notes to *Allons Danser* (1998):

> Perhaps most importantly [this project] is Bois Sec's first studio session in twenty years. It is also a chance to capture the fun we've

had over the years playing together at various parties, visits and festivals. And it is yet another chapter in the interaction between the Ardoin and Balfa families. It looks back, we hope, to an era when Creole and Cajun music were not so separate. Likewise, we hope it looks forward to an era of Cajun/Creole unity and pride. Mostly, it is centered on the here and now, music from our souls to yours.

It is no coincidence that these initiatives—Delafose's *La Chanson Perdue*, Balfa Toujours's *Live at Whiskey River Landing*, Ardoin's *Allons Danser*, the compilation *Allons en Louisiane*, and the Boozoo Chavis album—are all recorded on the Rounder Record label. Thanks to the attention of producers like Scott Billington at Rounder and Floyd Soileau at Swallow Records, artists of distinct yet conjoined traditions can be made available on the record market. And despite their likely commercial motivations, these initiatives clearly show how a group of talented and enthusiastic Cajun and Creole artists, young and old alike, can continue to make a difference. This work, along with other cultural initiatives (such as those of the late 1980s that established the Liberty Theater and the adjoining cultural center under the auspices of Jean Lafitte National Park) suggests that hope for the proliferation of francophone culture in Louisiana lies in the efforts made by members of successive generations and different yet related ethnic backgrounds to reconceptualize new becomings through musical and dance expression.

To conclude, I again evoke the power of the order words "tradition" and "authenticity," which can serve to regulate individuality and, potentially, to exclude individuals or activities failing to adhere to the constructed version of particular cultural practices. Order words can set forth a form of judgment in this way, implying "a death sentence, even if it has been considerably softened, becoming symbolic, initiatory, temporary" (Deleuze and Guattari 1987, 107). Yet, the implied expression of a death sentence is but one aspect of the order word. The other aspect is what Deleuze and Guattari compare "to a warning cry or a message to flee," a mode of transformation corresponding to the particular order words that have animated this study, *laissez les bons temps rouler*. Depending on how this imperative is exploited, it too can hold the exclusive judgment and death sentence of the strict regard for authenticity and tradition. But the same expression can also be understood as a supple and smooth manifestation of authenticity and tradition, and *les bons temps* can thereby evoke a call toward movements and metamorphoses such as those I have outlined in this chapter. Rather than bind Cajun cultural practices within strict forms of limitation and exclusion, these initiatives move *les bons temps* toward a "flight from contours in favor of fluid forces, flows, air, light, and matter" so that "life must answer the answer of death, not by fleeing, but by making flight act and create" (Deleuze and Guattari 1987, 109–10).

Thus, the musicians and composers who have established the bases for Cajun and Creole musical expression continue to make common cause with the younger generations who seek to extend this heritage. Their efforts, those of the cultural folklorists who support them in Louisiana, as well as additional initiatives by musicians, dancers, and fans inside and outside Louisiana all combine to create a network of exchange and polylogue that demonstrates the possibility of maintaining the vitality of these cultural practices for generations to come. However we might qualify the operative expression of the spirit of Louisiana, then, we can find ample reason to respect the imperative *laissez les bons temps rouler* as a forceful affirmation of creativity and life.

NOTES

Introduction: "The Good Times Are Killing Me"

1 In adopting and adapting the term "dance arena" from Hazzard-Gordon (1990), I employ it to refer to the assemblage of sociocultural practices that constitute Cajun dance and music representations. I will use the term "venue" to refer to the individual events in which Cajun dance and music are performed.

2 Jason Berry (2000) describes this "Louisiana spirit" in the *Chronicle of Higher Education* "End Paper" excerpt from his and Philip Gould's collection of photographs (Gould and Berry 2000). Another source is Putumayo World Music's Cajun collection, which the producers tout as follows: "Like its cousin, zydeco, Cajun music's motto is 'laissez les bons temps roulez' [*sic*] or 'let the good times roll' " (2001, CD cover quote). And perhaps no clearer evidence can be found of the complete and unproblematic association of *laissez les bons temps rouler* with Louisiana than the expression's appearance in a clue on the quiz show *Jeopardy* (4 September 2000): "La Salle said 'laissez les bons temps rouler' as he claimed this territory for France."

3 Notably, "the disenchantment of the world" has an important function in the works of Max Weber. My thanks to Lawrence A. Scaff for guidance on this term's function in Weber.

4 A striking example of this juxtaposition of the promotion of tradition can be found in the column in the weekly *Times of Acadiana* by Kelly Strenge, in which she promotes the annual Festivals Acadiens as "more than a good time" under the heading "The Travel Biz—News from the Tourism Industry" (2000, 32–33). This intersection of industry and culture is highlighted at the end of the article with the description of the author's position as "public relations and special projects manager for the Lafayette Convention and Visitors Commission."

5 From the perspective of the diverse practices of local and global musics and subcul-

tures, I have been inspired, among other recent works, by the following studies: Aparicio 1998; Chow 1993; Dettmar and Richey 1999; Gilbert and Pearson 1999; Hazzard-Gordon 1990; Jensen 1998; Keil and Feld 1994; Keil, Keil, and Blau 1992; Kelly and McDonnell 1999; Lewis 1992; Lipsitz 1990 and 1994; Loza 1993; Romero 2001; Slobin 1993; J. Taylor 1998; T. Taylor 1997; Thornton 1996; Walser 1993; and Waterman 1990. Two recent works on French cultural studies have also been of great value: Rosello 1998 and the essays collected in Le Hir and Strand 2000.

6 The best-known sources on "minor literature" are Deleuze and Guattari, *Kafka: Toward a Minor Literature* (1986) and *A Thousand Plateaus* (1987), and also Deleuze's essays on literature in *Essays Critical and Clinical* (1997). See also the essays in JanMohammed and Lloyd 1990, as well as Bogue 1997.

7 No doubt it would have been important to examine the works and performances of many other contemporary groups and musicians in order to show the broad range of Cajun music. However, reasons of space, time, and access to materials have forced me to make strategic choices with which some readers and fans may rightly take issue. As a result of these choices, I regretfully acknowledge omitting or paying scant attention to many local Louisiana groups and musicians—some of which are my favorites, like Filé, Jambalaya, and D. L. Menard. For the same reasons, I have not addressed the phenomenon of the burgeoning number of Cajun groups outside Louisiana.

8 One consideration raised by an astute reader of this manuscript is the absence of an audio CD of Cajun music to accompany my study. Questions of cost and permissions preclude this undertaking, but fortunately an array of compilation CDs are readily available. Certainly, no compilation recording exactly reproduces the music to which I refer in this study, but for a sample of representative recordings I suggest *Cajun Spice: Dance Music from South Louisiana* (1989), *La Musique Chez Mulate's* (1986), *Putumayo Presents Cajun* (2001), *Allons en Louisiane* (1999), and *Cajun Music and Zydeco* (1992).

I should add that the selection of artists and lyrics in chapter 2 is but a slim glimpse of the field of Cajun musical expression, and to begin to represent this field fairly the chapter would need to be expanded considerably and many more excerpts would need to be added. Even then, I could not pretend that such an extended discussion does justice to this field. Hence, the analyses in this chapter should be taken as an invitation to readers to begin their own exploration and appreciation of the Cajun musical and thematic field.

9 In chapter 6 particularly, as well as the book in general, I try to maintain the currency of recordings and cultural initiatives. However, given the vitality of this cultural domain, there will inevitably be a gap between this currency and the book's date of publication.

10 A remarkable study by Mark Mattern (1998) explores the important links between cultural initiatives and local political alliances, with two chapters devoted to the Louisiana Cajun and African American communities.

11 Barry, of course, takes her title from the 1975 documentary and from the 1979 Nathan Abshire album and song of the same name, "The Good Times Are Killing Me."

1 Becoming-Cajun

1 A body of personal and critical essays and books, designated a bit glibly as "moi-critique" (Begley 1994), has invested the personal with new significance for academic life. Several writers working in this vein have had particular importance for my work, notably Alice Kaplan (1993), Nancy K. Miller (1991), Gerald MacLean (1989), and in different yet congruent ways, Jane Gallop (1995 and 1997).

2 See Veeser 1996 on personal criticism. On the term "strategic," Candace Lang cautions that "autobiographical writing is not and cannot be an innocent, naive form of expression: it is a strategic one that mobilizes particular 'experiences' and 'events' into narratives—or antinarratives—with a view to particular effects" (1996, 50).

3 Del Sesto makes a careful distinction between the *fais do-do*, which "is a relatively large, informal, public dance held once a week in a dancehall, a night club, a saloon, a barn, or in a large outdoor area such as a churchyard," and the *bal de maison*, which is "limited to family, neighbors, and close friends. It is held in the home and outsiders are usually restricted from attending" (1975, 127). Del Sesto comments that besides helping to "maintain close family ties and serve to distinguish various family identities," the *bal de maison* had another purpose: "Although there are no written records, the author has learned from local informants that the *bal de maison* was merely a way of excluding various groups within the community" (127). He also distinguishes these venues from the wedding dance (the *bal de noce*), the public dance, the *bal de band* (dating to the New Orleans Jazz Age) with its traditional Dixieland music "sung in the various French dialects used by Louisiana Blacks" (128), and the various festival events of southern Louisiana, of which the best known is Mardi Gras (128–33). On the different Cajun dance locales, see also Comeaux 2000.

4 See the documentary tribute to Balfa, *Dewey Balfa: The Tribute Concert* (1993). It should be noted that Balfa appeared at Newport "as a last minute replacement on guitar to accompany Gladius Thibodeaux on accordion and Louis 'Vinesse' Lejeune.... An editorial in the local [Louisiana] newspaper commented condescendingly about the notion of festival talent scouts finding talent among Cajun musicians, and predicted embarrassing consequences if indeed Louisiana was so represented in Newport" (Ancelet 1999, 121). Three years later, Balfa and his brothers Rodney and Will appeared at the Newport festival. The previous year, 1966, the Creole musicians Canray Fontenot and Bois Sec Ardoin appeared at the festival (Tisserand 1998, 71). See also documentaries by Les Blank (1971) and Yasha Aginsky (1983a and 1983b), which include the music of the Balfas.

5 This summary relies on Ancelet 1989a and 1992a; Ancelet, Edwards, and Pitre 1991; Pierre Daigle 1987; and A. Savoy 1984. Ancelet 1998 provides a brief overview of research on Louisiana French folklife. See also Conrad 1986 and 1983, and Binder 1998. One additional initiative that bears mention is Warren A. Perrin's efforts in the 1990s to lead a legal campaign to compel the queen of England to acknowledge and apologize for the Acadians' expulsion (see http://www.acadianmuseum.com/warren.html for extensive documentation of these efforts). I return in chapter 6 to consider the active engagement of other Cajuns in recent cultural initiatives.

6   I want to be careful here to distinguish North American French studies, to which I am referring, from French studies as practiced in France. I also have to distinguish the circumstances described in this analysis from Canadian French studies because many of the issues that I discuss are specific to the complex tensions between French and U.S. intelligentsias. Jean-Philippe Mathy has traced French accounts of American society and mutual intellectual differences throughout this century, noting that "the love-hate relationship between French and American cultures" is far from over, because "powerful forces on both sides of the Atlantic resist adoption of viewpoints foreign to their national traditions" (1993, 259). For further discussion of tensions between American and French perceptions of their cultures, especially French resistance to American popular culture, see Mathy 1997 and 2000; also Stivale 1997b.

7   The key texts in this debate are Apostolidès 1993; Compagnon 1991; Hullot-Kentor 1993; Pavel 1992, 1995, 1997; and Schor 1992, 1993, 1995a. One volume in particular, Hollier 1989, raised the ire of some commentators (most notably, Compagnon) for its culturally based approach to French literary history as an alternative to traditional French literary anthologies. Moreover, despite the waning of this debate, and indeed Pavel's apparent reconciliation (however partial) with cultural studies (1997), some scholars still seem determined to defend "the discipline of French . . . from the cultural studies onslaught" (Schwartz 2000, 130). Meanwhile, other scholars have moved forward with more productive initiatives. See, in particular, Le Hir 1995–96 and Stanton 1997 for reviews of French and American perspectives in French studies; Compagnon 1996 for a concise overview of French studies in the United States; the introduction by Fourny and Schehr (1997, 1–4) to a special issue of *Contemporary French Civilization* with essays that juxtapose "cultural studies" and "culture wars" in the American French Studies context; the introduction by Richard Klein (1998, 5–11) to the special issue of *Diacritics*, "Doing French Studies"; and the collection of essays on French cultural studies edited by Le Hir and Strand (2000). For a thorough retrospective view on the French-American culture wars, see Mathy 2000.

8   Stivale 2000 provides a detailed account of a number of these positions. See, in particular, Petrey 1995; Kritzman 1995; R. Chambers 1996; and Yaari 2000.

9   I should note that Le Hir's approach to French cultural studies relies, often too heavily in my view, on the arguable promotion of Pierre Bourdieu's work as a preeminently French form of cultural studies (see Le Hir 2000). On Bourdieu's relationship to cultural studies, see Shiach 1993 and Readings 1996 (105–11).

10   Note the contrast between Le Hir's affirmative position and Schwartz's defensive posture on behalf of "disciplines under attack from cultural studies" (2000, 130): "A genuinely forward-looking French cultural studies would then be both conceptually broader and historically deeper than what is currently put forward under this name, and would situate cultural studies in its American incarnation as a symptom of the very phenomena—the rise of individualism and the globalized marketplace and the accompanying collapse of local and collective norms—that now require study in French as elsewhere. In this form, French cultural studies will be able to claim legitimately to have comprehended the cultural phenomenon of cultural studies long after the latter has disappeared from the scene" (132).

11 On the purpose of the volume, Conley states that it is meant "to show how both French *and* culture studies can be meshed in such a way that the sharp focus of disciplinary inquiry in the former (literature, cinema, new historicism) will assure breadth and perspective by appeal to the latter (where many boundaries have yet to be redrawn)" (1996, 273). One should note that in employing the term "culture studies," Conley nuances his argument by distinguishing implicitly between this French subdisciplinary turn and the broader competitive domain of cultural studies—that is, between two complementary, yet particular, approaches.

12 Petrey here modifies considerably the position he outlined in his earlier *French Review* essay (1995). See Bell 1997; Furman 1998; and Yaari 1996 for alternate views.

13 Among other fields that have been influenced, not without controversy, by cultural studies are history (see "Hot Type" 1997; Ruark 1999), sociology (Shapiro 2000), black studies (Schneider 2000), women's studies (Heller 1990), and, of course, literary studies in English and American studies (Coughlin 1989; Cain 1996; Fleishman 1995; Berlant 1998; Heller 1998; Modleski 1998; Monaghan 1998; and Felski 1999). On cross-disciplinarity, see Wissoker 2000.

14 Although by citing other examples of such research projects that trace new parameters for research in French studies I run the risk of inevitable omissions, I wish to note Apter 1999; Bongie 1998; Kaplan and Roussin 1994; Lionnet 1989; Lionnet and Scharfman 1993; Christopher Miller 1998; Rosello 1998; Ross 1995; and the essays collected in Le Hir and Strand 2000 and in Marks and McCaffrey 2001.

15 Deleuze and Guattari designate this kind of event with the term "haecceity" (1987, 260–65); see also Stivale 1997a and chapter 4 of this volume.

16 Deleuze relates this expressive force of the "minor" to "the task of the fabulating function to invent a people," a struggle in which becoming-Cajun participates (Deleuze 1997, 4–5). See Bogue 1997 for a lucid development of "minor" writing, and Nealon 1998 on the relation of "becoming-black" to the refrain.

17 My reflections on methodology for dance study have been informed by studies in Buckland 1999; Fraleigh 1987; and Fraleigh and Hanstein 1999, among others.

18 Taylor clarifies this: "Construction of 'natives' by music fans at the metropoles constantly demands that these 'natives' be premodern, untainted, and thus musically the same as they ever were" (1997, 21). See Hamm 1995 for a different yet compatible analysis of modernist "narratives of authenticity" (11–17, 23–27); and see Romero 2001 for an ethnographic study of memory, identity, and authenticity in Andean music of the Mantaro Valley.

19 See, among others, Bendix 1989; Chi 1997; Golomb 1995; Hamm 1995; Jensen 1998; MacCannell 1999; T. Taylor 1997; and Thornton 1996. Bendix 1997 provides a detailed overview of the notion of authenticity in folklore studies; Filene 2000 examines the construction of the cult of authenticity during the twentieth century in the context of American "roots music"; and Graham 2001 considers the trope of authenticity in the Irish context.

20 On "charismatic closure," Grossberg calls this "another strategy that closes off the terrain of cultural studies by identifying it with a particular speaking position" (1997b, 345). Timothy Taylor identifies a third authenticity in world music, the "au-

thenticity of emotionality," a concept that "is often bound up with constructions of spirituality," and particularly with "listeners' demands for authentic spirituality [that] apply to Others, whose perceived enigmatic qualities are often interpreted as spiritual" (1997, 23–24).

21 MacCannell cites Goffman 1959 in distinguishing "front regions"—"the meeting place of hosts and guests or customers and service persons"—from "back regions," "the place where members of the home team retire between performances to relax and to prepare" (1999, 92). MacCannell maintains that in the tourist's desire for authentic experiences, "it is always possible that what is taken to be entry into a back region is really entry into a front region that has been totally set up in advance for touristic visitation" (1999, 101). Extrapolating from Goffman's front/back dichotomy, MacCannell develops a six-stage continuum, from Goffman's front region, through different stages of decorated back regions somehow "organized" for tourists, to Goffman's back region, "the kind of social space that motivates touristic consciousness" (101–2).

22 The issue of cultural assimilation has been raised in stark terms by the U.S. Census Bureau, which has claimed that new data reveals a population drop among Cajuns "to about 44,000 from more than 407,000 in just ten years" (Bragg 2001, A1), a claim rejected by Cajuns interviewed in the *New York Times* article. According to a census analyst, the discrepancy may lie in how the survey forms were worded and interpreted. In response, the executive director of CODOFIL (Council for the Development of French in Louisiana) replies, "I don't see 9 out of 10 people denying they are Cajun" at a time "when there are so many people working to preserve their history and way of life" (qtd. in Bragg 2001, A20).

23 As a term, *zydeco* is a regional pronunciation of "les haricots," derived from the Clifton Chenier title, "Les Haricots Est Pas Salés" (The snapbeans aren't salted). Ancelet notes: "The spelling of *zydeco* was coined in 1960 by Mack McCormick, an ethnomusicologist in Houston who was attempting to render phonetically the term that black Creole musicians were using to identify their music" (1989a, 1). An alternate spelling, *zarico*, is a French phonetic rendering proposed by French Canadian André Gladu (Ancelet 1989a, 1). As a musical form, zydeco is distinct from Cajun music in emphasizing a jazz, blues, and R&B mix usually with fundamental instrumentation of fiddle, piano or button accordion, rubboard, and guitar, frequently enhanced through amplification and added instruments. As a dance form, zydeco inspires a more syncopated eight-count step than either the Cajun two-step or jitterbug, and the many blues numbers inspire a close slow-dance shuffle not necessarily as stylized as the Cajun waltz. See the indispensable opening chapter, "What's In A Name," in Tisserand 1998, 9–21; and also Orteza 1999; Caffrey 2000d; and Blagg 2001 (on the Ardoin family legacy). On broader questions of *créolité* in Francophone music, see Grenier and Guilbault 1997; and Rosello 2000.

24 I should state that while I have a passion for all forms of zydeco music as well as dance, I have spent a considerably greater amount of time, energy, and sweat in Cajun dance and music venues. However, for anyone who may have read Ken Wells's *Wall Street Journal* profile of zydeco on the occasion of the 2001 Mardi Gras celebra-

tion, let me dispel the definition given there that zydeco is "essentially Cajun music done up with African-American funk, syncopation, and flair, with some blues thrown in" (2001, A1). Few statements could be more insulting than to render zydeco a derivative of Cajun music, and there are strong arguments to suggest that the relationship is quite the reverse. I can do no better than to refer to two recent sources, Olivier and Sandmel's *Zydeco!* (1999) and Tisserand's *The Kingdom of Zydeco* (1998) with the accompanying CD from Rounder, *The Music from the Zydeco Kingdom* (2000). For additional representative compilations, see *Putumayo Presents Zydeco* (2000), *Zydeco Festival* (1988), and *Zydeco Live* (1989, 2 vols.). See also Mattern (1998, 108–17), who addresses directly the controversial issue of the assimilation of black Creoles into Cajun identity.

25 Savoy (born in 1940) may also be distinguished from Richard and Doucet by their age differences (Richard was born in 1950, Doucet in 1951). All three hail from the rural area in and around Lafayette (Savoy from near Eunice, Richard and Doucet from Lafayette, with relatives in Scott), and all three have university degrees—Savoy with a B.S. in chemical engineering, Richard with a B.A. from Tulane University, and Doucet with a B.A. from Louisiana State University (Ancelet 1999, 93, 129–32, 141–42). In 1975, Doucet received an NEA Folk Arts Apprenticeship grant to study Cajun fiddle styles, and thus sought out and learned fiddle from all the living legends of Cajun fiddle, especially Dennis McGee: "Those experiences helped me musically, culturally, historically, linguistically (Dennis never speaks to me in English). I gave up graduate school in English to come and do my own version of graduate work in Cajun French language and music here. When I went to France [with Richard in 1974], I had plans to come back to go to graduate school in New Mexico to study the romantics. I traded Blake for Balfa and came home instead" (Ancelet 1999, 145; see also Mouton 1997). Although the first BeauSoleil album was released in 1976, the group members took ten years before deciding to work full time in the band. In spite of the gradual start, their successes include a Grammy (for *L'Amour ou la Folie* 1997), numerous Grammy nominations, and international exposure—for example, Garrison Keillor's *A Prairie Home Companion*; the 1997 Superbowl and other televised events backing Mary Chapin Carpenter on "Down at the Twist and Shout"; and the Grammy awards ceremony (Huggs 1992, 16). Doucet and the members of his band of the mid-1970s, Coteau, have also released a reunion album, *Highly Seasoned Cajun Music* (1997). See also Caffrey 2001f on the finale of BeauSoleil's twenty-fifth anniversary tour at the Heymann Performing Arts Center in Lafayette (15 November 2001).

26 For reviews of this documentary, see Carlson 1998 and Mouton 1999.

27 In chapter 2 I consider the important thematics of "home" as developed in Richard's poetry and its relation to *Cap Enragé*. Although completely unknown in the United States, *Cap Enragé* has had extraordinary success in the francophone world (particularly in Québec), going double platinum in 2000. Since *Cap Enragé*, Richard has released two compilation albums of music from his entire career, one for the American market on Rhino Records (Richard 2000a) and a double CD for the francophone market (2000b). For the former, Richard states that he tried "to include as much song writing material [as possible], . . . trying to tell people that, like, I can do the energetic

Cajun thing, but there's also a sensitive side to Zack" (qtd. in Mouton 1999, 38). For the latter, he wanted to illustrate "the evolution of myself as a songwriter and musician" (qtd. in Mouton 1999, 38). Richard has also released a recording of new compositions (Richard 2000c), as well as a set of early recordings dating to 1974 that were never released (Richard 2001b). See also http://www.zacharyrichard.com.

28 Doucet presents the introduction in the liner notes to another Savoy collaboration, with award-winning fiddler Ken Smith: "Performing and recording with the Savoys is a life endeavor, but with BeauSoleil's touring schedule, I sometimes find that I can't be in two places at once. So in my absence Marc and Ann hit the road with Ken Smith" (*Savoy-Smith* 1996).

2 (Geo)graphies of *(Dé)paysement*: Dislocation and Unsettling in the Cajun Music Repertoire

1 This renaissance itself was prepared by the revival of traditional Cajun music following World War II under the inspiration of the accordionist Iry LeJeune in the late 1940s as well as by efforts to develop the local recording industry. As a result, traditional dance bands became increasingly popular in the 1950s, and subsequent initiatives of the folk revival movement led to increased interest in Louisiana French music (Ancelet 1999, 27–29). See Rickels 1975 on Acadiana folklore; Whitfield 1969 and Fields 1986–87 for analyses of the Louisiana French folk song; and Hannusch 2002 for a portrait of Iry LeJeune.

2 On Dewey Balfa as "the inspirational force behind the Cajun music renaissance," see Aginsky 1983b. This first wave of the renaissance sparked a number of initiatives in the 1960s and 1970s, notably the creation of the Louisiana Folk Foundation, of CODOFIL (Council for the Development of French in Louisiana), the Center for Acadian and Creole Folklore (later the Folklore and Folklife Program) at the University of Southwestern Louisiana's Center for Louisiana Studies, and the festival Tribute to Cajun Music, which would become an annual event (Ancelet 1999, 31–33).

3 Ann Savoy's volume provides a detailed overview of Cajun, Creole, and zydeco forms of instrumentation, origins of the music repertoires, and profiles of artists accompanied by versions of the different songs, all interspersed with interviews. Similarly, Ancelet's book (originally published in 1984 and reissued and expanded in 1999) consists of interview profiles of approximately two dozen Cajun, Creole, and zydeco musicians, including Zachary Richard, Marc Savoy, and Michael Doucet. Along with the volumes by Savoy and Ancelet, I should mention additional works published in the mid-to-late 1970s and early 1980s: Reed 1976; Conrad 1986 and 1983; Rushton 1979; Gould 1980; Broven 1983; and Dormon 1983.

4 I should note that Andy Edmonds's volume of the same (main) title, *Let the Good Times Roll! The Complete Cajun Handbook*, was published in 1984, the same year as Ancelet's and Savoy's volumes. However, rather than focusing primarily on Cajun music, Edmonds attempts to provide an overview of Cajun culture under the main headings "Life-Style," "Folklore," and "Through the Back Door" (referring to the Cajun saying, "You can only be a Cajun in one of three ways—by birth, by the ring, or through the back door").

5 See Reed, Tate, and Bihm 1969 and Blanchet 1970 on the role of the singer's *cri* in relation to the instruments of Cajun music.

6 In her seminal study of Cajun folk songs from 1939, Whitfield 1969 provides a typology of the themes of these songs, which Fields summarizes as follows: "Many of these forty-eight songs are sad and tell of lost loved ones and hard times. Singing about their trials seemed to have helped relieve frustration. The themes in these songs may be grouped into those of (1) love and marriage, (2) the lover going to Texas, (3) carefree manner in okaying cards, drinking, and dancing, (4) animals that are often in foolish predicaments, (5) people or places, (6) the Civil War, and (7) miscellaneous subjects. Songs of religion, nationalism, or the type of hero worship found in broadside ballads are conspicuously absent" (1986–87, 16).

7 In the following song titles I indicate the toponyms with an asterisk:

Filé, *Cajun Dance Band* (1987). Side A: "Allons Rock 'n Roll," "*The Catawomp Stomp," "*Pont de Vue," "*Pine Grove Blues," "J'ai Fait Mon Idée," "T'en As Eu, T'en Auras Plus." Side B: "*Allons Aller Chez Fred," "Chanson de Mardi Gras," "*La Valse de Kaplan," "Z'Haricots Gris Gris," "Sugar Bee."

Bruce Daigrepont, *Stir Up the Roux* (1987). Side A: "Laissez Faire," "*La Valse de la Rivière Rouge," "Disco et Fais Do-Do," "Les Traces de Mon Bogué," "*Bayou Teche Two-Step." Side B: "*Marksville Two-Step," "Les Filles Cadjines," "Un Autre Soir Ennuyant," "*Frisco Zydeco," "Stir Up the Roux."

Steve Riley and the Mamou Playboys (1990). Side A: "*La Pointe aux Pins," "*Eunice Waltz," "Ton Papa et ta Maman m'Ont Jeté Dehors," "Chers Petits Yeux Bleus," "*Mamou Hot Step," "Indien sur le Chicot." Side B: "*Blues de Port Arthur," "Valse de la Belle," "*High Point Two-Step," "La Valse des Vachers," "*Grand Bois," "*Blues de Port Arthur (part 2)."

Savoy-Doucet Cajun Band, *Les Harias—Home Music* (1983). Side A: " 'Tits Yeux Noirs," "*Port Arthur Blues," "Depuis l'Age de 15 Ans," "*La Chère 'Tite Fille de la Campagne" (translated as "With the California Cajuns"), "La Grosse Erreur," "Jongle à Moi." Side B: "Quoi Faire?" "Une Vielle [*sic*] Valse," "Chère Bassette," "*Melville Two-Step," "Jolie Blonde," "*Eunice Two-Step," "Le Pauvre Hobo."

8 Recorded examples of the home tradition were made by John and Alan Lomax and recently released in a record produced by Doucet and Ancelet (1987). Morthland notes that the Lomax recordings "feature members of the Hoffpauir family of New Iberia, who sing tortured a cappella story-songs of exile and solitude," and that more recent performances of this home music by Lula Landry and Inez Catalon have taken place at the American Folklife Festival in Washington, D.C., and at the annual Lafayette Festivals Acadiens (1988, 19–20). See also Ancelet 1999 (43–49). Note also that the first album of the Savoy-Doucet Cajun Band (1983) evokes this home tradition, and it is revived in the more recent work of Marce Lacouture (2000).

Clearly, the home song tradition, understood as a distinct mode of women's musical practice, bears witness to the particular experience by Cajun women in rural Louisiana culture. As I will note in chapter 5 in summarizing Alan Lomax's film *Cajun Country: Don't Drop the Potato* (1990), the destiny of Cajun women as wives of settlers on the prairies, swamps, and bayous of southern Louisiana was (and, until relatively recently, has remained) extremely limited, usually impoverished, and often quite bleak. In this sense, then, the thematics of *(dé)paysement* addressed in this chapter constitute only a partial expression through music of the Cajun experience, especially as these musical compositions and themes encompass gender issues.

9   Unless otherwise noted, I faithfully follow the transcriptions and translations of all lyrics in Cajun French presented here as indicated on the album, tape, and CD notes, with apparent inconsistencies of spelling and grammar included. For a thorough examination of Cajun Mardi Gras, including the lyrics of "La Chanson de Mardi Gras," see Ancelet 1989b. Ancelet maintains that "in the early 1950s, a group of cultural activists in the Mamou area, under the leadership of Paul Tate and Revon Reed, undertook to revive the traditional Mardi Gras run. They sought guidance from older members of the community . . . who remembered running Mardi Gras and even remembered the words of that community's version of the traditional Mardi Gras song" (1989b, 5–6). See also Ancelet 1980a, Roshto 1992, and the special issue of the *Journal of American Folklore,* "Southwestern Louisiana Mardi Gras Traditions," edited by Carl Lindhal (2001). See especially the different versions of "La Chanson de Mardi Gras" explained by Sexton and Oster (2001).

10 Christopher Miller argues for a critical, indeed skeptical, view of the "nomad thought" developed by Deleuze and Guattari in *A Thousand Plateaus.* Calling their approach a "happy-talk revolution" ("the benefits are advertised in the text, while the bodies are hidden, not even in the footnotes, but in the original source material" [1998, 195]). Miller concludes that Deleuze and Guattari "want to have it both ways: to propose a 'pure idea' of nomads" (possible only if they eschew actuality) "mixed with 'actual' information" introduced by Deleuze and Guattari in their extensive footnote apparatus (198). Although I recognize the limitations of "nomadology" that Miller identifies in the referential context adopted by Deleuze and Guattari, my engagement with the Deleuze-Guattarian concept of the nomad serves to underscore the paradox inherent to the Cajun *(dé)paysement,* particularly as it relates to the thematics of Cajun music.

11 As Fields notes, summarizing Whitfield (1969), "the songs show the Cajun as frank and unafraid. He is romantic and adventurous; he makes love ardently, is intensely jealous, and if he does not win, he is willing to *aller au Texas* [go to Texas]—that far-distant country of the great unknown—there to drown his sorrows, to seek forgetfulness, and probably to love again" (1986–87, 16).

12 The Web page devoted to the Avoyelles French family name origins states: "Marksville's founder, Marc Éliché, was a native of Venice, Italy. He was a peddler, and legend states he was in the area of Marksville when his wagon wheel broke, so he just stayed and set up a store on what is today the northwest corner of Main and Ogden Streets in Marksville. Ironically, another Avoyelles area carries the name of yet another Italian immigrant of early Avoyelles. The area of Cocoville, south of Marksville, is named after the son of Dominique Coco who, like his comrade Marc Éliché, was an Italian peddler" (http:www.geocities.com/~avoyelles).

The lyrics to the songs on all Bruce Daigrepont albums are located at http://www.brucedaigrepont.com/lyrics.htm.

13 Steve Riley and the Mamou Playboys (1998) attribute "Voyage d'Amour" to Dewey

Balfa, whereas on the BeauSoleil album (1984) the attribution is "a traditional tune as learned from the late Rodney Balfa."

14 In the final stanza, the very words that the fiancée speaks include one lexical detail that may have struck alert readers as peculiar at the very least, the use of the potentially pejorative term *nègre* (black, nigger). We should note that this term, modified by *cher vieux* (dear old), constitutes a term of endearment, often without necessary racial distinction. It is interesting to note, though, that the term defies translation on the BeauSoleil album and is rendered simply as "my dear," which is a problem to which I return, along with other racial issues, in chapter 5.

15 Hunter Hayes's rendition of "Rockin' Flames" (2000) is a tribute to Toups's own version (1991), and the overall sound of Hayes's recording bears a striking resemblance to the early Toups and ZydeCajun albums. With a much more mature voice and accordion style, Damon Troy (2001) seems inspired by the later, more mature, and reflective Toups recordings (see Fuselier 2001). I return to Hunter Hayes in the context of the new generation of Cajun musicians in chapter 6.

16 Of the five CDs released since *Fish Out of Water* during the 1990s, only *Down Home Live!* (1992) is not listed in the discography on the Wayne Toups Web site (http://www.waynetoups.com), presumably because the live songs, recorded at the Crowley (Louisiana) Rice Festival (Toups's home town) in October, 1987, were released by Toups's original label which had the rights to the early recordings.

17 Although Peter Schwarz is no longer announced as a band member, Riley, Greely, and Kevin Dugas have added guitarists Roddie Romero and Kyle Hébert. Riley and Greely have also joined the revival of Louisiana swamp pop in the stellar L'il Band of Gold (2000).

18 A striking juxtaposition of photographs in Philip Gould's collection *Cajun Music and Zydeco* (1992) shows a young Steve Riley at the 1984 Festival de Musique Acadienne standing at the edge of the stage, gazing intently at the musicians; the following page shows a young boy standing equally at the edge of the stage, staring at Steve Riley. A photo of Riley in profile is on the following page (1992, 28–30). Both this and Gould's earlier collection (1980) contain a number of photographs of the makers of Cajun music.

19 Both "home" and "gone" are familiar terms in Cajun and Creole dialects, with the expression "je suis gone" being an idiomatic replacement for "je suis allé" (I went, as in "je suis gone au marché [to market]) and "je suis parti" (I left).

20 Perhaps one reason for the raised consciousness in Doucet's composition is its chronological coincidence with preparations for the yearlong 1999 Francofête and the World Acadian Congress (Congrès Mondial Acadien) that took place in August 1999. This congress continued the deliberate initiative begun in the 1994 congress in New Brunswick to unite the descendants of the Acadians worldwide. I should note, however, that another song on *Cajunization*, "Chanson pour Tommy" (Song for Tommy), is an extremely personal composition that the band dedicates to the former and founding member Tommy Comeaux, who passed away in 1997 at age forty-five.

21 My thanks to Sue Daigrepont for pointing out the importance of the song "Acadie à la Louisiane" in this context.

22 Heylen notes that *Mille misères*, originally published by Marcantel in 1979 under the pseudonym Marc Untel de Gravelles as a Louisiana Project at Laval University in Québec, was "the very play that defined the original company [preceding Le Théâtre 'Cadien, called], *Nous Autres*, as 'other.' . . . *Nous Autres* conceived of Cajun theatre as defined and constructed within its own ethnic boundary. *Le Théâtre 'Cadien*, on the contrary, now offers a theatre content to reconcile its constituency's difference with that of the surrounding communities of multi-ethnic America" (1994, 454, 463). See Allain 1998 on the importance of this theatrical engagement for the construction of the Cajun past.

23 For a thorough review of Richard's musical career, see Mouton 1999 and 2000, and the liner note text by Laurent Saulnier in Richard 2000b. Richard contributed to the poetry collection recognized as being responsible for the "birth of Cajun poetry," *Cris sur le bayou: Naissance d'une poésie acadienne en Louisiane*, edited by Barry Jean Ancelet (1980b) and inspired by a poetry reading organized in 1978 in Québec City during the Rencontre des Francophones de l'Amérique du Nord, published as *Acadie tropicale* (Ancelet 1983). Zachary Richard had a great influence on this volume: not only did he contribute the poem "La Ballade de Beausoleil" that he had presented at the 1978 Québec festival, he provided twenty-five other poems that he would in-clude subsequently in his own first volume of poetry, *Voyage de nuit: Cahiers de poésie, 1975–79* (2001c). However, the major omissions from his own collection are two poems with a militant edge, "La Ballade de Beausoleil" and "Réveille," which Janis Pallister describes as "a Cajun call to arms 'pour sauver l'héritage' [to save their heritage]" (1988, 20). Of the several accounts of *Cris sur le bayou*, two are by col-leagues of Ancelet at the (then) University of Southwestern Louisiana, Mathé Allain 1989 and D. Barry 1988 and 1998. The most recent and thorough study, by Dianne Guenin-Lelle (1997), situates these poems within the context of cultural assimilation in Acadiana. See also Allain (1998) for a study of literary efforts to construct the Cajun past.

24 From Richard's Acadian roots, the song "Cap Enragé" evokes a location in southern New Brunswick; "Dans le Nord Canadien" (In the great Canadian north) evokes a time before modern civilization destroyed the purity of the wilderness; and "Au Ranch à Willy" is a tribute to the French Canadian country and western singer Willy Lamothe, on whose television show, *Willy's Ranch*, Richard appeared in 1974. From his Louisiana roots, "Au Bord du Lac Bijou" is a beautiful love ballad evoking the mystery of the Atchafalaya Basin; "Aux Natchitoches," says Richard in the translation notes, "is my version of an old Ballade, perhaps the oldest song of the Louisiana Cadien repertoire not brought from Canada or France," about the trading post near the junction of the Red and Cane rivers.

25 In the translated lyrics, Richard states: "This song is the only one which I did not write or co-write. There can be no translation since the verses contain only place names, while the chorus is a list of resistance fighters dear to Native American and Acadian history. The Petit Codiac is the river which runs through New Brunswick. Kouchibouguac is now a Canadian national park in Northeastern New Brunswick. It was the scene of a controversial expropriation by the Canadian government of the

local Acadian population in 1976. The expropriation was contested by a group of residents led by Jackie Vautour. While he was away, the RCMP arrived at his home and arrested his wife and children and bulldozed his house. After over 10 years of resistance including time spent in prison, Jackie Vautour finally settled with the government of Canada. Crazy Horse was an Oglala Sioux leader bayoneted by an American soldier while attempting to evade capture in the late 19th century. Beausoleil Broussard was the leader of the only successful Acadian revolt during the deportation of 1755. Fleeing from British imprisonment he was able to lead his band of followers to Southwestern Louisiana. The town of Broussard was named in his honor. Louis Riel (misspelled in the French text) was the leader of the mixed-blood metis revolt of Manitoba of the late 19th century. He was tried and hanged for treason by the government of Canada. The last line of the chorus ["Asteur c'est mon tour"] means, 'Now it's my turn'" (1996). The author of "Petit Codiac," Yves Chiasson, is a member of the French Canadian group Zéro Degré Celsius, which first recorded this song.

26   Yet another material sign of Richard's growth is the inclusion in the volume of a CD on which the poet recites twenty-three of the poems, thus providing the oral complement of the written texts. As Orteza notes, besides taking a featured role in the French-Canadian French-language miniseries *Juliette Pomerlau* (as a middle-aged Czechoslovakian), Richard is in full bloom during this period because "insecure musicians don't pursue two recording careers . . . or publish books of poetry . . . or receive culturally prestigious decorations (the Ordre des Francophones d'Amérique for his contribution to the vitality of the French language in North America) while taking the time to found and/or champion cultural organizations (Action Cadienne, CODOFIL) and events (Congrès Mondial, FrancoFête)" (1998a, 21). See also Alciatore 1998 and Simoneaux 2000 on the diverse projects in Richard's career.

27   The manifesto for the Action Cadienne organization is located at http://www.action cadienne.org/manifesto.html. See also Caffery 2000. On different "pragmatic" forms of "acting in concert" among the Cajuns, see Mattern 1998 (79–100).

3   "J'ai Été au Bal":
Cajun Sights and Sounds

1   For information on the Cajun heritage villages, see the Web pages for Vermilionville (http://www.vermilionville.org/) and Acadian Village (http://www.coonass.com/ acadian.htm). On the Jean Lafitte National Park sites, which include the Liberty Theater, see Campbell 1999; and see also http://www.epinions.com/content_ 51310136964 for a review of the *Rendez-vous des Cajuns* radio show.

2   The phenomenon of the World Wide Web has produced a wide range of Web sites devoted solely to Cajun dance and music as well as zydeco, with links to events and bands located well beyond the United States. A sample of representative sites includes Jeremy Rice's Cajun/Zydeco page, http://www.bme.jhu.edu/~jrice/cz.html; Gary Hayman's Cajun/Zydeco Music and Dance site, http://users.erols.com/ghayman/; Crazygator's Zydeco and Cajun Hall of Fame, http://zydeco.crazygator.com/ roadhome.html; L'Espace Cajun/Acadien at Globegate (links to French- and English-

language resources), http://globegate.utm.edu/french/globegate_mirror/cajun.html; *Louisiana Music Online's* musicians and bands, http://www.louisianaradio.com/lmo/musicians/index.html; and LSU–Eunice's site for contemporary Louisiana Cajun, Creole, and zydeco musicians, http://www.lsue.edu/acadgate/music/musicmain.htm. See also Gilliam 1992 describing a Cajun dance and music event in the United Kingdom, and Caffery 2001b about Cajun music as a global phenomenon.

3 Deleuze and Guattari initially discuss the notion of the minor in their *Kafka: Towards a Minor Literature* (1986), then later in *A Thousand Plateaus* (1987). See also Deleuze's discussion of the minor in *Essays Critical and Clinical* (1997).

4 Two specific traits of this use of language (or representation), says Jameson, are the limits "designated by the excess of intensity" articulated through pitch and intonation, and the disappearance of the individual subject "behind the beleaguered collective which thus speaks all the more resonantly through it" (1992, 173).

5 I obtained my copy of *Southern Comfort* from the United Kingdom where the film is available both on VHS and DVD, as is now the case in North America. Oddly enough, on one Web site where movies are rated, IMDb (http://us.imdb.com), the less-available film has a slightly higher rating: 6.9 stars (out of 10) for *Southern Comfort* (381 votes cast) versus 6.6 stars for *The Big Easy* (1260 votes cast).

6 Vincent Canby's assessment is quite succinct: "Whoever 'fixed' 'The Big Easy' has fixed it by making essential story points fuzzy, and by pouring soundtrack music over it under the mistaken impression that it was a hot fudge sundae. . . . If one doesn't demand narrative coherence, it's possible to enjoy 'The Big Easy' for the performances of Quaid . . . and Barkin" (1987, C6). Pauline Kael is more severe; summing up McSwain and Osborne's efforts to bring the guilty to justice, Kael jibes, "That should have included the scriptwriters. . . . The picture has an amateurish, fifties-B-movie droopiness" (1987, 100). See also Ansen (1987) and Schickel (1987) for more positive, albeit brief, reviews.

7 Without questioning the sincerity of Doucet's assessment of *The Big Easy's* impact, I should note that he and his group BeauSoleil make a significant contribution to the film's soundtrack—the syrup on what Canby refers to as the film as "hot fudge sundae" (1987, C6). Thus, BeauSoleil holds the privileged place of providing the opening Cajun sound for the film—the driving two-step "Zydeco Gris Gris"—which accompanies the impressively beautiful aerial shots of Louisiana in the initial credit sequence.

8 Among his many credits dating back to the early 1970s, Walter Hill directed the cult favorite *The Warriors* (1979), *48 Hours* and *Another 48 Hours* (1982 and 1990, respectively) and *Last Man Standing* (1996). The case of *Southern Comfort* includes notable actors Keith Carradine, Powers Boothe, Fred Ward, and a brief appearance (as the first man killed) by Peter Coyote. Moreover, Ry Cooder, besides his renown as a guitarist, has an impressive career as a film soundtrack composer.

9 A brief synopsis of the film is in order here: on weekend maneuvers in the Louisiana swamps, a hapless group of National Guardsmen anger local Cajuns by stealing canoes to cross a stretch of water. When their commander is shot in retaliation for one of the men shooting blank rounds at an invisible Cajun, an escalation begins

with the unit members being killed off one by one. Even a lone Cajun trapper that they capture manages to escape, and the two surviving unit members (Carradine and Boothe) arrive at the encampment hoping to make contact with civilization. Instead, they barely escape from a final confrontation with the hunters who have been tracking them; this encounter coincides with a raucous *bal de maison* in a nearby cabin that masks the noise of gunshots.

10 One might also associate these scenes with John Boorman's film *Deliverance* (1972), in which the conflict between rural and urban cultures occurs against a backdrop of raw wilderness, ethnic music, local dialect, and defensive responses from the rural inhabitants. My thanks to Louise Speed for pointing out these parallels.

11 The music selections—performed by the quartet of Dewey Balfa, Marc Savoy, Frank Savoy, and John Stelly—are the two-step "Allons à Lafayette" (corresponding to the soldiers' arrival up to Spencer's line, "Relax, Hardin, these are the good Cajuns"), then the two-step "Parlez-Nous à Boire" (during the dance and stalking sequences, up to Hardin being shot in the left shoulder by the first hunter), and a waltz the title of which I could not identify (performed through the killing sequence to the soldiers' escape).

12 *The Big Easy* is the unlikely tale of a Cajun family related through service in the New Orleans Police Department at all ranks. Detective Remy McSwain seduces city district attorney Ann Osborne early on, but when McSwain is charged with taking a bribe (caught on film), Osborne—motivated also by a sense of having been betrayed—must prosecute him. The *bal de maison* sequence, immediately following his successful acquittal, prepares his turnabout toward following an honest path that will lead, with Osborne's help, to the exposure of corruption in the very heart of McSwain's unit.

13 One of the earliest examples of this research is Naomi Griffiths's study of Cajun origins (1973). The Center for Louisiana Studies (at the University of Louisiana at Lafayette) has provided continued support for study in this field, notably by James Dormon (1983), and for collections edited by the center's director, Glenn Conrad (1979 [1986]; 1983). More recently, the work of Conrad's colleague, Carl Brasseaux, systematically extends this work and provides further insight into the origins and development of Cajun society (1987, 1992). To these versions, one must add several studies of more specific scope: on the one hand, there are several studies that provide details of diverse folk practices (Post 1962; Ancelet, Edwards, and Pitre 1991), and on the other hand, several studies noted in chapter 2 examine the origins and artists of the music/dance culture (Ancelet 1999 and 1989a; A. Savoy 1984; Plater, Speyrer, and Speyrer 1993). The most recent contributions to this corpus offer guides to Cajun and zydeco cultures (Nyhan, Rollins, and Babb 1997; Olivier and Sandmel 1999; and Tisserand 1998). Finally, three other forms of documentation complement the aforementioned texts: one can gain immense understanding, not to mention pleasure, from the photographic studies of Cajun society by Philip Gould (1980, 1992; and Gould and Berry 2000). Moreover, Rhonda Case Severn (1991) has developed an abundant array of written materials on Cajun linguistics, history, music, and folklore for use in the French classroom, an audiocassette with selections from Cajun music (written lyrics also available), and two videocassettes that not only include oral history

but also video music and dance selections as well as local Cajun French television interviews. Severn's work with video relates to the third, perhaps most abundant, array of documents, the numerous audiovisual studies of Cajun culture now available on video: concert footage with interviews, including *Clifton Chenier and His Redhot Louisiana Band* (1987), *Dewey Balfa: The Tribute Concert* (1993), and *Hot Pepper: The Life and Music of Clifton Chenier* (1973); and studies of Louisiana (Cajun and Creole) cultural practices, including *Cajun Country: Don't Drop the Potato* (1990), *Dance for a Chicken: The Cajun Mardi Gras* (1993), *The Good Times Are Killing Me* (1976), *Louisiane Francophone: Lache Pas la Patate!* (n.d.), *Spend It All* (1971), *Zydeco* (1984), and *Zydeco Nite 'n' Day* (1991).

14 According to Barry Jean Ancelet, Les Blank's *Spend It All* (1971; Blank's first documentary devoted to Cajun culture), "portrayed the Cajuns as a hard-living, hard-playing people who enjoyed a wonderfully exotic cuisine and danced uninhibitedly to intense, soulful music sung in French" (1990, 12). While praising Blank's technique, Ancelet maintains that Blank "did not make a film about the Cajuns, he made a film about what he found unusual and exciting and different about the Cajuns" (12). In the same article, Ancelet describes the results of another documentary (not connected to Les Blank), *The Good Times Are Killing Me* (1976), that "portrayed the Cajuns as a strange tribe of vulgar, hard-partying drunks" and the renowned accordionist Nathan Abshire as "an impoverished, alcoholic musician, despondent over his son's recent arrest" (12). That community leaders assisted this production added insult to injury, and Ancelet notes that "local contact person Dewey Balfa wept when he saw the result of his collaboration" (13). Judging from the portrayal of Cajun musicians in *Southern Comfort*, the 1976 documentary would not be the last time that Balfa would be disappointed by his collaboration with filmmakers.

15 Pierre Daigle states that there are three camps: the "ultra-traditionalists," those who "want Cajun music played as it was in the 1920's and early 30's when it finally reached full bloom"; the "ultra-modernists," those who "want to take it closer to rock music, or country music, or whatever"; and "those who fall somewhere in between" (1987, 77–78). My fusion/traditionalist pairing presumes the overlapping, middle ground that Daigle suggests. However, these distinctions certainly do vary based on fans' tastes: in a letter to the *Times of Acadiana*, the Lafayette dance instructors Miriam Fontenot and Paula Lafleur defend Filé for their choice *not* to pursue a "progressive" or "zydeco" sound on their first album (1987), in order "to keep their traditional sound, . . . a 'must' for instructing Cajun dance classes, the [sound] that has lasted for generations" (1987, 3). What is unusual about this perspective is that the Filé album in question actually includes a number of zydeco-style and rock songs (e.g., "Allons Rock 'n Roll," "Sugar Bee," and "Z'Haricots Gris Gris") alongside interpretations of Cajun standards.

16 For examples of Toups's "new wave" Cajun music, see especially *Johnnie Can't Dance* (1988), *Blast from the Bayou* (1989), and *Fish Out of Water* (1991).

17 Whereas BeauSoleil has increasingly sought to expand its stylistic range beyond Cajun musical forms and instrumentation, Daigle and Cajun Gold situated themselves squarely within the Cajun music repertoire yet expanded it with compositions

by Paul Daigle's father, Pierre. See the profile on Cajun Gold in Nyhan, Rollins, and Babb (1997, 47).

18 I refer to "filmmaker" in the singular for *Marc and Ann* because Les Blank alone produced this documentary.

19 For examples of this style, see the Savoy-Doucet Cajun Band's *Les Harias—Home Music* (1983), *With Spirits* (1986), and *Two-Step d'Amédé* (1989).

20 For a biography and filmography of Les Blank, see the Flower Films site at http://www.lesblank.com/les_blank_bio.htm.

21 As for Marc Savoy's own evolution, a recent interview shows the extent to which he has become extremely reluctant to tour or to play in concert venues (Fuller 2001b).

22 See Marc Savoy (1988) in which he presents the personal and professional background that is the source of his conservative—that is, "preservative"—cultural stance.

23 Nuancing Nora's insights, Savage points out that "the modern need to objectify collective memory in tangible traces . . . [indicates] the presence of a certain hierarchy of memory activities, in which 'enduring' (and properly documented) testimonials take on the greatest value and cultural prestige," making real both "collective memory, physically rooted" and "the collective" itself (1994, 146).

24 Among BeauSoleil's recordings, see "BeauSoleil Boogie" on *Bayou Boogie* (1986b); "Hey Baby, Quoi Ca Dit?," "Bunk's Blues," and "Bayou Cadillac" on *Bayou Cadillac* (1989a); "Danse Caribe" on *L'Amour ou la Folie* (1997); and "Cubano Bayou" on *Cajunization* (1999). With a group called Cajun Brew, Doucet also recorded an album consisting mainly of Cajun cover versions of songs such as "Wooly Booly," "Louie Louie," and "Do You Want to Dance?" (1987). To Doucet is attributed responsibility with Floyd Soileau for the sound editing on *Louisiana Cajun and Creole Music, 1934: The Lomax Recordings* (1987), originally made by Alan Lomax and John Avery Lomax for the Library of Congress in 1934. On the pioneering work of Lomax father and son in the 1930s, see Filene 2000.

25 Ancelet also pointed to other indicators of this self-consciousness (which I will discuss in chapter 5): the failed attempt within the Cajun French Music Association to "regulate" the kind of dance step their members could practice to the two-step beat (the two-step rather than the jitterbug). He also emphasized the self-consciousness of local dancers in small, rural dance halls, aware and sometimes resentful of dance styles imported from nonlocals to the weekly events (Ancelet 1992b).

26 In presenting Speyrer's video, I should mention that I collaborated with him on a number of occasions between 1987 and 1990 in the dance instruction and performance setting. I must also acknowledge that while Speyrer was among the first entrepreneurs to introduce dance instruction to the New Orleans area, the Cajun dancer who initiated this instruction in the Lafayette area was Miriam Fontenot. My thanks also go to Barry Ancelet and Paula Lafleur for their help in discussing Cajun dance in southern Louisiana.

27 Ancelet (1992b) specifically named the development of the troika step (two women with one man) and the two-couple step as initiatives by dancers in the Cajun dance restaurants that indicated their deliberate creation of Cajun dance. The late Dennis McGee recalled, "[people] stopped dancing to reels when I was young [McGee was

born in 1893]. They continued to dance *contredanses* during my courting days" (Ancelet 1999, 35). See Plater, Speyrer, and Speyrer for troika and two-couple steps (1993, 139–62), as well as Speyrer 1993b. See also Brenda Daigle (1972) for details on dance practices at *fais do-dos* as recalled by Dennis McGee.

28 Mattern 1998 (92–100) locates the importance of the Lafayette Festivals Acadiens in its focal role as collaborative community building from its inception in 1974.

29 Three other instructional videos are available for zydeco steps. Two of these—*Learn to Zydeco Dance Tonight* (1995) and *Advanced Zydeco Dance* (2000)—focus almost solely on instructions for the dance steps while providing the minimum of cultural context. Also, while the music in each video consists of recordings by Louisiana Creole zydeco musicians, the dance instruction is provided by two Caucasian dancers, Ben Pagac and Debbie Shaw, who teach zydeco in the Washington, D.C., area. This racial idiosyncrasy actually reflects the emergence of zydeco in the 1990s as a hugely popular crossover dance form nationwide (see Wells 2001). The third video, by Mona "Zydeco Queen" Wilson, titled "*Zydeco*-robics *Mona*-robics Style," presents itself as "specializing in *truly authentic* and quality *creole* zydeco dance lessons," with zydeco instruction linked to aerobic exercise (Wilson 2001).

4   Feeling the Event: Spaces of Affects
and the Cajun Dance Arena

1 See Stivale 1995, 1997a, and 2000. Considerable work has been done, of course, on the terms space and affect. On space, see, among others, de Certeau 1984; Grossberg 1996b; Lefebvre 1991; Massey 1994; Soja 1989; and Wise 1997. On affect, see Grossberg 1992 (69–111) and Massumi 1995.

2 While the conceptual framework and terminology used here might seem to obscure rather than clarify consideration of something as apparently accessible as dance practices, the dearth of analysis in cultural studies precisely of these practices and their modes of representation suggests that such accessibility is indeed only apparent. I agree with Jane Desmond that we have only begun to assess dance practices, which need to be placed on the agenda of cultural studies (1997, 33). Desmond argues that the text- and object-based orientation of cultural studies as well as "the academy's aversion to the material body, and its fictive separation of mental and physical production," contribute to the marginalization of dance scholarship, although she cites as hopeful signs of change Foster 1986; Franko 1993; and the 1992 "Choreographing History" initiative collected in Foster 1996 as well as in Foster 1995. To these, we can add, among others, Aparicio 1998; Banes 1994; Desmond 1999; Foster 1992; Fraleigh 1987; Gilbert and Pearson 1999; Gotfrit 1991; Lopez 1997 (and other essays in Delgado and Muñoz 1997); J. Taylor 1998; and the links between music and dance established in Keil and Feld 1994 and in Keil, Keil, and Blau 1992.

3 The archetypal example of this type of space and audience response was in the PBS broadcast of *Austin City Limits* of a concert by BeauSoleil in 1990. In the BeauSoleil performance, the cameras focused either on the band members or on the seated audience members, never (or only incidentally) on the few participants who chose to dance, necessarily off-camera.

4   The Ark has long since responded to its customers' demands for dance space, particularly for Cajun music performances, but often with difficulty because open space for dancing means fewer seats available for paying customers (and hence possibly lower revenue). At one performance at The Ark where a dance space had been located stage right, Michael Doucet of BeauSoleil remarked on the inconvenient arrangement of dancers hidden off to the side. The Ark's management now has responded by providing more centrally located dance space.

5   These steps are quite distinct: the Cajun jitterbug resembles the swing in the upper body movements (twirls, turn-outs, side-by-side moves) but differs in its simpler footwork, without the rock step. The zydeco style, corresponding to the Louisiana African American music of the same name, resembles the swing in the couple's closer body contact but differs somewhat in the basic, eight-count foot step and almost completely with the near absence of upper body moves. To distinguish between the two styles, dancers sometimes describe the Cajun jitterbug as unfolding in the head (through intricate leads and upper-body movements) while the zydeco step(s) unfold through the body. See Plater, Speyrer, and Speyrer 1993 for descriptions of the jitterbug; Olivier and Sandmel 1999 for zydeco images and descriptions; and Tisserand 1998 for a history of zydeco. For broader histories of different traditions in social country dancing, see Shaw 1949 and 1950; and Nevell 1977.

6   I adapt and develop this example from Stivale 1998, 162–63.

7   Furthermore, it is not only in relation to the individuation of a life vis-à-vis individuation of a subject that the in-between admixture is operable, but in the thisness of haecceities themselves: "It should not be thought that a haecceity consists simply of a décor or backdrop that situates subjects, or of appendages that hold things and people to the ground. It is the entire assemblage in its individuated aggregate that is a haecceity; it is this assemblage that is defined by a longitude and a latitude, by speeds and affects, independently of forms and substances, which belong to another plane. It is the wolf itself, and the horse, and the child, that cease to be subjects to become events, in assemblages that are inseparable from an hour, a season, an atmosphere, a life" (Deleuze and Guattari 1987, 262).

8   Although quite a number of different line-dance (or freeze) steps exist, line-dance dancers agree on one uniform step in performance, often in response to particular musical compositions. On country line dancing (in the context of women's festivals), see Armstrong and Jewell 1992.

9   Michaul's moved from Algiers a few years later to an initial location in the New Orleans Central Business District (CBD), then to its current location nearby. It was in the first CBD location that the dance instructional tape examined in chapter 3 was filmed.

10   Deleuze and Guattari develop these traits with reference to mother-child relations, among other examples (1987, 169–70). See Patricia Sotirin forthcoming; my thanks to her for considerable assistance in understanding faciality. For another examination of faciality, see Welchman 1988.

11   On home and spatial politics, see Massey 1994; and on home and territory, see Wise 2000.

12   Although Deleuze speaks of the "haptic function" in painting, he tends to do so in terms of the modulation of colors in visual representation (Deleuze 1981, 79–86).

13 On "haptic visuality" and "haptic cinema," see Marks 2000 (62–193).

14 While the usual convention for dancing in Cajun dance and music venues is men leading and women following, I am using gender neutral language here, to the extent possible, to acknowledge that not all dance venues for this music limit partners to male-female couples.

15 Plater, Speyrer, and Speyrer 1993 designate as the "conversational step" the move that helps one pause to navigate in crowds: "The man goes forward L-2-3 and back R-2-3, while the woman mirrors his step (back R-2-3 and forward L-2-3). Eventually, they break out into the normal waltz pattern" (53). The same holds true with the two-step (57).

16 These difficulties frequently relate to issues of what are considered traditional dance steps in contrast to the creative variations that I have described, to which I return in this chapter's conclusion. One experience of such difficulty to which I contributed occurred in 1995 at the New Orleans branch of the Cajun dance and music restaurant, Mulate's. At one point during the evening, I approached a table of men and women who, I learned quickly, were visiting the city for an academic conference. I invited one woman to waltz, on a dance floor that included a number of couples waltzing with embellished waltz movements (some borrowed from jitterbug moves). After only a few steps on the floor, my partner told me in no uncertain terms, "I want fancy!" indicating some of the other "fancy" waltzers. Rather than follow my first impulse—to return her to her table and friends—I obliged her with "fancy" moves, after which I did accompany her back to her place. My resistance came as much from the breach of the implicit conventions between the lead and the follower (clearly, my own control issues) as from the assumption that "fancy" style is in some ways better than the simple, unadorned waltz style. Throughout the 1990s, the embellished waltz movements have become the norm on many dance floors, especially in New Orleans, but for newer dancers unfamiliar with the dynamics of flow and the cultural conventions on the Cajun dance floor, the embellished style may be mistaken for the sole mode of dancing movement to the waltz.

17 Given the context of this scene—the documentary on Cajun and zydeco and the rural dance and music venue—one should not necessarily construe two women dancing together as an overt disruption of social norms and sexual politics, as described by Gotfrit 1991. Rather, in many venues two women dancing the jitterbug (or the zydeco), the waltz, or the two-step is usually viewed as an acceptable alternative to women not being able to dance for lack of male partners.

18 Plater, Speyrer, and Speyrer 1993 present explanations of the full repertoire of these waltz, two-step, and jitterbug moves as well as the three-person (two women, one man) combination known as the troika and the two-couple routine. See also the two-cassette video that accompanies the book (Speyrer and Speyrer, 1993a and 1993b).

19 Deleuze (1990, 257) explores this question, which is raised by Spinoza in his *Ethics* (1992). See also Deleuze and Guattari 1987 (252–72).

20 It is tempting here to consider, with Grossberg (1997a, 245–52), distinctions between "fans, fanatics, and ideologues." A list of global Web sites for Cajun and zydeco bands is given in Caffery 2001b; see also the list I offer in chapter 3, note 2. See J. Taylor 1998 for a description of the ongoing tango arena.

21 I use the term "fold" in order to undermine the outside/inside binary on which Iain Chambers seems to insist (1986, 135).

5 Disenchanting *Les Bons Temps*

1 In fact, references to *les zaricos* (that is, to *les haricots*, or snap beans, pronounced with an emphatic *z* to connect the article to the substantive) are evident in the first two songs in the Creole section of *Louisiana Cajun and Creole Music, 1937: The Lomax Recordings* (Doucet and Ancelet 1987): "Dégo" is a shouted *juré* improvisation, its title referring to an Italian worker in the song, and "J'ai Fait Tout le Tour du Pays" combines a *juré* verse with a conversational bridge between the singer asking for "les haricots" from his mother who replies that "les haricots sont pas salés" ("the snap beans aren't salty"), meaning she is so poor that there is no salt pork or meat in the pot.

2 See Ancelet 1999, 100–5; and Nyhan, Rollins, and Babb 1997, 23–24, for more information on Nathan Abshire.

3 This version is from *A Cajun Legend: The Best of Nathan Abshire* (1986) recorded with the Balfa Brothers, the lyrics of which are included in the album. Other versions are noted by Nyhan, Rollins, and Babb 1997, 24.

4 For example, the final verse of "Madame Young, Donnez-Moi Votre Plus Jolie Blonde" ends with the singer referring to himself, "fais pas ça avec ton nèg', / Tu vas me faire, mais, mourir, / Toujours, toujours, malheureuse" (Don't do that with your man, / You're going to make me, but, die, / Always, always, [an] unhappy one). Similarly, in "Lafayette," the singer cries in the final verse, "Mais je mérite pas, / Tout ça mais t'après faire, / T'après quitter, ton nèg', / Mais pour, mais t'en aller" (I don't deserve / All you are doing to me, / You're leaving your friend, / To go away).

5 "Black Gal" has also been recorded by a number of other zydeco musicians; for example, by Boozoo Chavis on *Boozoo, That's Who!* (1993) and Nathan Williams and the Zydeco Cha-Chas on *Creole Crossroads* (1995). Moreover, the term *nèg'* appears in lyrics of various songs on different Cajun and zydeco albums (e.g., "Oh Bye, Mon Neg" on Boozoo Chavis's *Boozoo, That's Who!* and "Bye Bye, Mon Neg" on Geno Delafose's *That's What I'm Talking About!* [1996]). Also, on one of several Web sites devoted solely to the Cajun genre known as "Boudreaux jokes" (for example, http://home.att.net/~phantom-guy/ilo__boudreaux.htm), the term *nèg'* appears several times as the vernacular for "guy," "pal," or "dude." This is the sense of the opening words in *The Big Easy*, "Hey, 'tit nèg, where y'at?" spoken by Dennis Quaid as Remy McSwain to his sergeant, played by Ned Beatty.

6 These tensions are, of course, not limited to Cajun dance and music practices, as we shall see from sociocultural practices considered in the following sections. A specific nexus of tensions related to issues considered here has been examined closely in a special issue of the *Journal of American Folklore* on Louisiana Mardi Gras traditions (2001), notably about the practice of wearing blackface in the Cajun Mardi Gras rides (*courirs*). The traditional role played by the character in blackface is that of the *nègre*, a male who acts as disciplinarian to other revelers (known as *soldats*, or soldiers). As Carl Lindhal notes, in some Mardi Gras *courirs* the *nègre* is accompanied by a *négresse*,

a role also filled by a white male. Lindhal's commentary on these practices relates to matters of language as well: "Outsiders find it difficult to perceive in the nègre and négresse anything other than virulent racism; insiders often find nothing racist in these interpretations. For many members of Mardi Gras communities, the blackface figures are so familiar, their annual appearance so expected, that they do not possess the power of social provocation that incites such negative reactions in those who view them from a greater cultural distance" (2001, 250). This distinction between proximity and distance can help us understand the otherwise surprising comments by Catherine Blanchet on the Filé album (1987).

7   The first part of this segment starts with the scenes of Marc and Ann Savoy in performance that I examine closely in chapter 3, taken from Les Blank's documentary *Marc and Ann* (1991). Ann Savoy then discusses the role of Cleoma Falcon, with her husband Joe Falcon, as the first musicians to record a Cajun music record in 1928. This first section closes with the beautiful tune sung a cappella by one of the Falcon descendants, Odile Falcon, seated in her daughter's kitchen.

8   For example, Cajun fiddler Wade Frugé explains to Ann Savoy that "when we wanted to get Amédé [Ardoin] to play at a party with us, we'd get permission from the person giving the party to bring him," but this would not prevent what Frugé calls "them old Frenchmen" from drinking heavily and then "caus[ing] trouble for Amédé." Frugé says that Ardoin "liked to play with my uncle because nobody would mess around with him when he was with my uncle" (1984, 46). And Dennis McGee mentions that "there was a black man who played the fiddle and he wanted to play with Amédé. And Amédé told him, 'I'm not gonna' play with you. If you and I play together, two blacks, the whites are gonna' kill us. There would be nothing to save us. I like to have Mr. McGee with me because Mr. McGee's gonna' help me'" (1984, 52).

9   This celebratory practice derives from a tradition of misbehavior and revelry as the all-male riders travel from farm to farm on the eve of Lent to dance for payment from the farmer of a contribution (usually a chicken) to the gumbo to be prepared for that evening. See Ancelet 1980a, 1989b, and 2001 (as well as other essays in the *Journal of American Folklore* on Mardi Gras traditions [2001]).

10 This subject is emphasized in the film by Dennis McGee's wife (his third wife, whom he married when she was thirteen and he was thirty-two) who is clearly uninspired by the younger Dennis's girlfriends and appears resigned to having given birth to ten children, eight of whom survived. On this distinct role for Cajun women in the Mardi Gras celebrations, see Ware 2001. I return to the issue of Cajun women's place in Louisiana society in chapter 6.

11 Examples are the first book in Cajun French, Revon Reed's *Lâche pas la patate* (1976) (Don't drop the potato; i.e., don't give up); in the weekly radio broadcasts in Cajun French from Fred's Lounge in Mamou; and in the accolades following the performance of Dewey Balfa, Vinesse Lejeune, and Gladius Thibodeaux at the 1964 Newport Folk Festival.

12 The Cajun French Music Association's Web site logo reads: "Dedicated to Promote and Preserve Cajun Music and Culture." Founded in 1984, the CFMA organization admits Cajuns and non-Cajuns to promote all aspects of the Cajun cultural heritage

including "authentic Cajun language and the traditions of [Cajuns'] Acadian ancestry" (http://www.cajunfrenchmusic.org/cfma.htm).

13 On the different conceptions of community in Cajun and Creole groups in southern Louisiana, see Mattern (1998, 79–117).

14 This reference to the CFMA "colors" means the dress shirts (sometimes white, sometimes yellow) bearing the circular logo of the association, which are frequently worn both by men and women members. In a number of the video clips of different Cajun bands and dancers filmed at Randol's Restaurant and included in Rhonda Case Severn's documentary compilation (1991), one can see the valiant efforts of several CFMA members performing the two-step around the edge of the jitterbug dance floor. On these initiatives by the CFMA, see also Mattern 1998 (103–5).

15 Although the term "jig" is certainly a legitimate dance term, even if considerably inaccurate as a reference to the jitterbug, the term also possesses a distinctly pejorative racial connotation. Although not all who use the term jig in referring to the jitterbug mean it in the pejorative sense, the appellation nonetheless can serve as a signal to denigrate the dance practice as more than merely nontraditional—that is, as distinctly and racially "other."

6   *Laissez les Bons Temps Rouler*, or, Death and Life in the Cajun Dance Arena

1 See the Web site on contemporary Louisiana Cajun, Creole, and zydeco musicians at http://www.lsue.edu/acadgate/music/musicman.htm.

2 See http://www.lafolkroots.org.

3 Toups was scheduled to appear at the 2002 New Orleans Jazz and Heritage Festival performing with "the Zydecajuns" (http://www.nojazzfest.com/schedules/friday _5_03.html), and the current Toups Web site lists "Wayne Toups and Zydecajun" on the banner.

WORKS CITED

Abshire, Nathan. 1979. *Pine Grove Blues*. Swallow 6014.

—. 1986. *A Cajun Legend: The Best of Nathan Abshire*. Swallow 6061.

Abshire, Nathan, and the Balfa Brothers. 1979. *The Good Times Are Killing Me*. Swallow LP-6023-4.

"Action Cadienne." 1995. *Times of Acadiana*, 14 June, 3.

Advanced Zydeco Dance. 2000. Prod. Ben Pagac. Insectefex, Inc.

Against the Tide: The Story of the Cajun People of Louisiana. N.d. [1999]. Prod. Zachary Richard. Louisiana Public Broadcasting.

Aginsky, Yasha. 1983a. *Cajun Visits*. Flower Films 1123.

—. 1983b. *Les Blues de Balfa*. Flower Films 1124.

Alciatore, Angelie. 1998. "Back Talk with Zachary Richard." *OffBeat*, February, 92–94.

Alcoff, Linda. 1991–92. "The Problem of Speaking for Others." *Cultural Critique* 20: 5–32.

Allain, Mathé. 1989. "Littérature et mentalité populaire en Louisiane." *Vie française* 41.1: 29–38.

—. 1998. " 'Quatre hectares de passé': La Réinvention du passé dans la Louisiane contemporaine." *Francophonies d'Amérique* 4: 7.

Allons en Louisiane. 1999. Produced and written by Scott Billington. Rounder 11661-6093-2.

Ancelet, Barry Jean. 1980a. "Courir du Mardi Gras." *Attakapas Gazette* 15.4: 159–64.

—, ed. 1980b. *Cris sur le bayou: Naissance d'une poésie acadienne en Louisiane*. Montréal: Les Éditions Intermède.

—, ed. 1983. *Acadie tropicale*. Lafayette, La.: Éditions de la Nouvelle Acadie.

—. 1988. "A Perspective on Teaching the 'Problem Language' in Louisiana." *The French Review* 61.3: 345–56.

—. 1989a. *Cajun Music: Its Origins and Development*. Lafayette: Center for Louisiana Studies, University of Southwestern Louisiana.

—. 1989b. *"Capitaine, voyage ton flag": The Traditional Cajun Country Mardi Gras*. Lafayette: Center for Louisiana Studies, University of Southwestern Louisiana.

—. 1990. "Drinking, Dancing, Brawling Gamblers Who Spend Most of Their Time in the Swamp." *Times of Acadiana*, 20 June, 12–15.

—. 1992a. "Cultural Tourism in Cajun Country: Shotgun Wedding or Marriage Made in Heaven?" *Southern Folklore* 49: 256–66.

—. 1992b. Interview by author. 4 June.

—. 1996. "From Evangeline Hot Sauce to Cajun Ice: Signs of Ethnicity in South Louisiana." *Folklife in Louisiana: The Louisiana Folklife Program*. http://www.crt/state/la.us/folklife/main_misc_hot_sauce.html. Rpt. from *Louisiana Folklore Miscellany*.

—. 1998. "Research on Louisiana French Folklore and Folklife." In *Creoles and Cajuns: French Louisiana—La Louisiane Française*, ed. Wolfgang Binder. Frankfurt: Peter Lang. 83–90.

—. 1999. *Musiciens cadiens et créoles/The Makers of Cajun Music*. Austin: University of Texas Press. 1984. Rpt. and rev. as *Cajun and Creole Music Makers*. Jackson: University Press of Mississippi.

—. 2001. "Falling Apart to Stay Together: Deep Play in the Grand Marais Mardi Gras." *Journal of American Folklore* 114.452: 144–53.

Ancelet, Barry Jean, Jay Edwards, and Glen Pitre. 1991. *Cajun Country*. Jackson: University of Mississippi Press.

Angers, Trent. 1989. *The Truth about the Cajuns*. Lafayette, La.: Acadian House Publishing.

Ansen, David. 1987. "An August Heat Wave." *Newsweek*, 24 August, 60–61.

Aparicio, Frances R. 1998. *Listening to Salsa: Gender, Latin Popular Music, and Puerto Rican Cultures*. Hanover, N.H.: Wesleyan University Press/University Press of New England.

Apostolidès, Jean-Marie. 1993. "'This Group Is Both Male and Foreign.'" *Stanford French Review* 16.2: iii–vii.

Apter, Emily. 1999. *Continental Drift: From National Characters to Virtual Subjects*. Chicago: University of Chicago Press.

Ardoin, Bois Sec, with Balfa Toujours. 1998. *Allons Danser*. Rounder 6081.

Armstrong, Toni Jr., and Terri Lynn Jewell. 1992. "Country Line Dancing with Maile and Marina." *Hot Wire: The Journal of Women's Music and Culture* 8.1: 24–26.

Bakhtin, M. M. 1981. *The Dialogic Imagination*. Trans. Caryl Emerson and Michael Holquist. Austin: University of Texas Press.

Balfa Toujours. 1993. *Pop, Tu Me Parles Toujours*. Swallow 6110-4.

—. 1995. *A Vieille Terre Haute*. Swallow 3121.

—. 1996. *Deux Voyages*. Rounder 6071.

—. 1998. *La Pointe*. Rounder 6068.

—. 2000. *Live at Whiskey River Landing*. Rounder 6096.

La Bande Feufollet. 1999. *La Bande Feufollet*. Swallow 6154.

—. 2001. *Belle Louisiane*. Feufollet Records.

Banes, Sally. 1994. *Writing Dancing in the Age of Postmodernism*. Hanover, N.H.: Wesleyan University Press.

Barry, A. David. 1988. "La Renaissance poétique en Louisiane: Reflets culturels." *Vie française* 40.1: 31–44.

——. 1998. "De l'oral à l'écrit: La problématique louisianaise." In *Creoles and Cajuns: French Louisiana—La Louisiane Française*, ed. Wolfgang Binder. Frankfurt: Peter Lang. 287–300.

Barry, Lynda. [1988] 1998. *The Good Times Are Killing Me*. Seattle: Sasquatch Books.

BeauSoleil, with Michael Doucet. 1976. *The Spirit of Cajun Music*. Swallow 6031.

——. 1984. *Parlez-Nous à Boire*. Arhoolie 5034.

——. 1986a. *Allons à Lafayette*. Arhoolie 308.

——. 1986b. *Bayou Boogie*. Rounder 6015.

——. 1986c. *Christmas Boogie*. Swallow 6004.

——. 1986d. *Belizaire the Cajun*. Arhoolie 5038.

——. 1989a. *Bayou Cadillac*. Rounder 6025.

——. 1989b. *Allons à Lafayette and More, with Canray Fontenot*. Arhoolie 308.

——. 1991. *Live from the Left Coast*. Rounder C-6035.

——. 1997. *L'Amour ou la Folie*. Rhino R2-72622.

——. 1999. *Cajunization*. Rhino R2-75633.

——. 2001. *The Best of the Crawfish Years, 1985–1991*. Rounder 6099-2.

BeauSoleil, with Marcia Ball. 1990. *Austin City Limits*. PBS program 1502.

Begley, Adam. 1994. "The 'I's' Have It: Duke's Moi Critics Expose Themselves." *Lingua Franca* 4.3: 54–59.

Bell, David. 1997. "Disciplining the Disciplines Means Saying What One Means." *Contemporary French Civilization* 21.2: 113–30.

Bendix, Regina. 1989. "Tourism and Cultural Displays: Inventing Traditions for Whom?" *Journal of American Folklore* 102: 131–46.

——. 1997. *In Search of Authenticity: The Formation of Folklore Studies*. Madison: University of Wisconsin Press.

Benjamin, Walter. 1968. *Illuminations*. Trans. H. Zohn. New York: Schocken.

Bennett, Tony. 1993. "Being 'in the True' of Cultural Studies." *Southern Review* 26: 217–38.

——. 1998. "Cultural Studies: A Reluctant Discipline." *Cultural Studies* 12.4: 528–45.

Berlant, Lauren. 1998. "Collegiality, Crisis, and Cultural Studies." *Profession 1998*. New York: Modern Language Association. 105–16.

Berman, Russell. 1997. "Reform and Continuity: Graduate Education toward a Foreign Cultural Literacy." *Profession 1997*. New York: Modern Language Association. 61–74.

Berry, Jason. 2000. "Bayou Tapestry." *Chronicle of Higher Education*, 22 September, B19.

Bhabha, Homi. 1994. *The Location of Culture*. New York: Routledge.

Bier, Charlie. 1999. "Second That Emotion." *Times of Acadiana*, 15 September, 30–33.

The Big Easy. 1987. Dir. Jim McBride. Kings Road Entertainment.

Binder, Wolfgang, ed. 1998. *Creoles and Cajuns: French Louisiana—La Louisiane Française*. Frankfurt: Peter Lang.

Black, Baxter. 2000. "Cajun Dance." *On the Edge of Common Sense*, 17 July.

Blagg, Christopher. 2001. "Spilling the (Snap) Beans on Zydeco: An Ardoin Family Perspective." *OffBeat*, September, 60–63.

Blanchet, Catherine. 1970. "Acadian Instrumental Music." *Louisiana Folklore Miscellany* 3.1: 70–75.

Blank, Les, dir. 1971. *Spend It All*. Flower Films.

—, dir. 1973a. *Dry Wood*. Flower Films.

—, dir. 1973b. *Hot Pepper: The Life and Music of Clifton Chenier*. Flower Films.

—, dir. 1990. *Yum, Yum, Yum!* Flower Films.

—, dir. 1991. *Marc and Ann*. Flower Films.

Blank, Les, and Chris Strachwitz, dirs. 1989a. *French Dance Tonight*. Ed. Maureen Gosling. Brazos Films.

—, dirs. 1989b. *J'ai Été au Bal (I Went to the Dance): The Cajun and Zydeco Music of Louisiana*. Ed. Maureen Gosling, narr. Barry Jean Ancelet and Michael Doucet. Brazos Films.

Bogue, Ronald. 1997. "Minor Writing and Minor Literature." *Symploké* 5.1–2: 99–118.

Bongie, Chris. 1998. *Islands and Exiles: The Creole Identities of Post/Colonial Literature*. Stanford, Calif.: Stanford University Press.

Bragg, Rick. 2001. "Reported to Be Vanishing, Cajuns Give a Sharp 'Non.'" *New York Times*, 16 August, A1, A20.

Brasseaux, Carl A. 1987. *The Founding of New Acadia: The Beginning of Acadian Life in Louisiana, 1765–1803*. Baton Rouge: Louisiana State University Press.

—. 1991. "Oral History of Acadiana." In *Discovering Acadiana*, ed. and prod. Rhonda Case Severn, vol. 2, videocassette.

—. 1992. *Acadian to Cajun: Transformation of a People, 1803–1877*. Jackson: University Press of Mississippi.

Broven, John. 1983. *South to Louisiana: The Music of the Cajun Bayous*. Gretna, La.: Pelican Publishing.

Buckland, Theresa J., ed. 1999. *Dance in the Field: Theory, Methods, and Issues in Dance Ethnography*. New York: St. Martin's Press.

Buckwheat Zydeco. 1987. *On a Night Like This*. Island 90622-1.

—. 1999. *The Buckwheat Zydeco Story: A Twenty Year Party*. Tomorrow Recordings B00000JCBS.

Caffery, Josh. 2000. "Students 'Immersed' in French." *Advocate Online*, 24 July.

—. 2001a. "Dirk's Due." *Times of Acadiana*, 21 February, 49–52.

—. 2001b. "The Travels of Magellan Breaux." *Times of Acadiana*, 14 March, 14–18.

—. 2001c. "The Stomp in the Swamp." *Times of Acadiana*, 18 April, 55–56.

—. 2001d. "All Hail the King." *Times of Acadiana*, 25 April, 34–42.

—. 2001e. "Belle Louisiane: La Bande Feufollet Releases Its Second Album." *Times of Acadiana*, 30 May, 35–38.

—. 2001f. "Sit and Listen." *Times of Acadiana*, 7 November, 24–29.

—. 2001g. "You Could Win a Grammy." *Times of Acadiana*, 28 November, 43–44.

Cain, William E. 1996. "English Courses Should Focus on Reading, Not Cultural Studies." *Chronicle of Higher Education*, 13 December, B4.

Cajun Country: Don't Drop the Potato. 1990. Dir. Alan Lomax. Pacific Arts Video.

Cajun Dance Instruction. N.d. [1992]. Prod. Michaul's Restaurant.

Cajun Music and Zydeco. 1992. Rounder C-11572.

Cajun Spice: Dance Music from South Louisiana. 1989. Rounder C-11550.

Campbell, Cynthia V. 1999. "Jean Lafitte National Park." *Advocate Online,* 11 September.

Canby, Vincent. 1987. " 'The Big Easy,' Comedy about a Police Case." *New York Times,* 21 August, C6.

Carlson, Shala. 1998. "Cinema Vérité." *Times of Acadiana,* 28 January, 6–8.

Cecil, Betty. 1988. *I Love to Cajun Dance.* (No producer indicated).

Chambers, Iain. 1986. *Popular Culture: The Metropolitan Experience.* London: Methuen.

Chambers, Ross. 1996. "Cultural Studies as a Challenge to French Studies." *Australian Journal of French Studies* 33.2: 137–56.

Chavis, Boozoo. 1993. *Boozoo, That's Who!* Rounder 2126.

———. 2001. *Down Home on Dog Hill.* Rounder 2166-2.

Chenier, Clifton. 1990. *Bon Temps Roulet and More.* Arhoolie 345.

Chi, Robert. 1997. "Toward a New Tourism: Albert Wendt and Becoming Attractions." *Cultural Critique* 37: 61–105.

Chow, Rey. 1993. *Writing Diaspora: Tactics of Intervention in Contemporary Cultural Studies.* Bloomington: Indiana University Press.

Clifford, James. 1988. *The Predicament of Culture.* Cambridge: Harvard University Press.

Clifton Chenier and His Redhot Louisiana Band. 1987. Dir. Chris Strachwitz. Arhoolie Productions.

Comeaux, Malcolm L. 1978. "The Cajun Accordion." *Revue de Louisiane/Louisiana Review* 7.2: 117–28.

———. 2000. "The Cajun Dance Hall." *Material Culture* 32.1: 37–56.

Compagnon, Antoine. 1991. "The Diminishing Canon of French Literature in America." *Stanford French Review* 15.1–2: 103–15.

———. 1996. "A la recherche d'un nouveau statut." *France-Amérique,* 24 February: L–N.

Conley, Tom. 1996. "Afterword/Identity: Never More." In *Identity Papers: Contested Nationhood in Twentieth-Century France,* ed. Steven Ungar and Tom Conley. Minneapolis: University of Minnesota Press, 272–82.

———. 1998. "Putting French Studies on the Map." *Diacritics* 28.3: 23–39.

Conrad, Glenn R., ed. [1979] 1986. *New Iberia: Essays on the Town and Its People.* Lafayette: Center for Louisiana Studies, University of Southwestern Louisiana.

———, ed. 1983. *The Cajuns: Essays on Their History and Culture.* Lafayette: Center for Louisiana Studies, University of Southwestern Louisiana.

Cormier, Sheryl, and Cajun Sounds. 1992. *Queen of Cajun Music.* Swallow 6098-2.

Coteau. 1997. *Highly Seasoned Cajun Music.* Rounder 6078.

Coughlin, Ellen K. 1989. "In Face of Growing Success and Conservatives' Attacks, Cultural-Studies Scholars Ponder Future Directions." *Chronicle of Higher Education,* 18 January, A4–A5, A12.

Courville, Matthew. 1999. *Avec un Coeur Pour Mon Pa Pa.* Swallow 6158.

Daigle, Brenda. 1972. "Acadian Fiddler Dennis McGee and Acadian Dances." *Attakapas Gazette* 7.3:124–43.

Daigle, Pierre V. 1972. *Tears, Love, and Laughter: The Story of the Cajuns and Their Music.* Ville Platte, La.: Swallow Publishing.

Daigrepont, Bruce. 1987. *Stir Up the Roux.* Rounder 6016.

——. 1989. *Coeur des Cajuns*. Rounder 6026.

——. 1994. *Petit Cadeau*. Rounder 6060.

——. 1999. *Paradis*. Rounder 6090.

Dance for a Chicken: The Cajun Mardi Gras. 1993. Dir. Pat Mire. Attakapas Productions.

de Certeau, Michel. 1984. *The Practice of Everyday Life*. Trans. Steven F. Rendall. Berkeley: University of California Press.

Delafose, Geno, and French Rockin' Boogie. 1996. *That's What I'm Talking About*. Rounder 2141.

——. 1998. *La Chanson Perdue*. Rounder 2151.

Deleuze, Gilles. 1981. *Francis Bacon: Logique de la sensation*. Paris: Éditions de la Différence.

——. 1988. *Spinoza: Practical Philosophy*. Trans. Robert Hurley. San Francisco: City Lights Books.

——. 1990. *Expressionism in Philosophy: Spinoza*. Trans. Martin Joughin. New York: Zone.

——. 1995. *Negotiations*. Trans. Martin Joughin. New York: Columbia University Press.

——. 1997. *Essays Critical and Clinical*. Trans. Daniel W. Smith and Michael A. Greco. Minneapolis: University of Minnesota Press.

——. 2000. *Proust and Signs*. Trans. Richard Howard. Minneapolis: University of Minnesota Press.

Deleuze, Gilles, and Félix Guattari. 1986. *Kafka: Toward a Minor Literature*. Trans. Dana Polan. Minneapolis: University of Minnesota Press.

——. 1987. *A Thousand Plateaus*. Trans. Brian Massumi. Minneapolis: University of Minnesota Press.

Deleuze, Gilles, and Claire Parnet. 1996. *L'Abécédaire de Gilles Deleuze*. Dir. Pierre-André Boutang. Video Editions Montparnasse.

Delgado, Celeste Fraser, and José Estaban Muñoz, eds. 1997. *Everynight Life: Culture and Dance in Latin/o America*. Durham: Duke University Press.

Del Sesto, Steven L. 1975. "Cajun Social Institutions and Cultural Configurations." In *The Culture of Acadiana*, ed. Steven L. Del Sesto and Jon L. Gibson. Lafayette: University of Southwestern Louisiana. 121–42.

Desmond, Jane C. 1997. "Embodying Difference: Issues in Dance and Cultural Studies." In *Everynight Life: Culture and Dance in Latin/o America*, ed. Celeste Fraser Delgado and José Estaban Muñoz. Durham, N.C.: Duke University Press. 33–64.

——. 1999. "Engendering Dance: Feminist Inquiry and Dance Research." In *Researching Dance: Evolving Modes of Inquiry*, ed. Sondra Horton Fraleigh and Penelope Hanstein. Pittsburgh: University of Pittsburgh Press. 309–33.

Dettmar, Kevin J. H., and William Richey. 1999. *Reading Rock and Roll: Authenticity, Appropriation, Aesthetics*. New York: Columbia University Press.

Dewey Balfa: The Tribute Concert. 1993. (No director indicated). Motion, Inc.

Doane, Mary Ann. 1986. "The Voice in the Cinema: The Articulation of Body and Space." In *Narrative, Apparatus, Ideology*, ed. Philip Rosen. New York: Columbia University Press. 335–48.

Dormon, James H. 1983. *The People Called Cajuns*. Lafayette: Center for Louisiana Studies, University of Southwestern Louisiana.

Doucet, Michael. 1988. Reply to letter by Rudy Markl. *Times of Acadiana*, 3 August, 3–4.

Doucet, Michael, and Barry Jean Ancelet, prods. 1987. *Louisiana Cajun and Creole Music, 1934: The Lomax Recordings*. Swallow 8003-2.

Doucet, Michael, and Cajun Brew. 1987. *Michael Doucet and Cajun Brew*. Rounder 6017.

Druon, Michèle. 2000. "In Search of a Postmodern Ethics of Knowledge." In *French Cultural Studies: Criticism at the Crossroads*, ed. Marie-Pierre Le Hir and Dana Strand. Albany: State University of New York Press. 103–21.

Duke, Jerry. 1988. *Dances of the Cajuns (Louisiana and Texas)*. San Francisco: Duke Publishing Co.

Edmonds, Andy. 1984. *Let the Good Times Roll! The Complete Cajun Handbook*. New York: Avon Books.

Felski, Rita. 1999. "Those Who Disdain Cultural Studies Don't Know What They Are Talking About." *Chronicle of Higher Education*, 23 July, B6.

Fields, James C. 1986–87. "Analysis of Forty-Eight Cajun Folk Songs." *Louisiana Folklore Miscellany* 6.2: 15–24.

Filé. 1987. *Cajun Dance Band*. Flying Fish Records 418.

Filene, Benjamin. 2000. *Romancing the Folk: Public Memory and American Roots Music*. Chapel Hill: University of North Carolina Press.

Fisher, Jennifer. 1997. "Relational Sense: Towards a Haptic Aesthetics." *Parachute* 87: 4–11.

Fleishman, Avrom. 1995. "The Condition of English: Taking Stock in a Time of Culture Wars." *College English* 57.7: 807–21.

Fontenot, Miriam L., and Paula Lafleur. 1987. "Filé is Good for Cajun Music Gumbo." *Times of Acadiana*, 23 September, 3.

Foster, Susan Leigh. 1986. *Reading Dancing: Bodies and Subject in Contemporary American Dance*. Berkeley: University of California Press.

—. 1992. "Dancing Bodies." In *Incorporations 6*, ed. Jonathan Crary and Sanford Kwinter. New York: Zone. 480–95.

—, ed. 1995. *Choreographing History*. Bloomington: Indiana University Press.

—, ed. 1996. *Corporealities: Dancing Knowledge, Culture, and Power*. New York: Routledge.

Fourny, Jean-François, and Lawrence Schehr. 1997. "Introduction: Haven't We Been Through All This Before?" *Contemporary French Civilization* 21.2: 1–4.

Fraleigh, Sondra Horton. 1987. *Dance and the Lived Body: A Descriptive Aesthetics*. Pittsburgh: University of Pittsburgh Press.

Fraleigh, Sondra Horton, and Penelope Hanstein, eds. 1999. *Researching Dance: Evolving Modes of Inquiry*. Pittsburgh: University of Pittsburgh Press.

Franko, Mark. 1993. *Dance as Text: Ideologies of the Baroque Body*. Cambridge: Cambridge University Press.

French Dance Tonight. 1989. Dir. Les Blank and Chris Strachwitz. Ed. Maureen Gosling. Brazos Films.

Les Frères Michot. 1987. *Elevés à Pillette*. AR-ZED 1014.

Fuller, R. Reese. 2001a. "A Genuine Buzz." *Times of Acadiana*, 21 February, 11–13.

—. 2001b. "Marc of Distinction." *Times of Acadiana*, 4 April, 18–23.

—. 2001c. "A Cajun Twist." *Times of Acadiana*, 4 July, 9–10.

Furman, Nelly. 1998. "French Studies: Back to the Future." *Profession 1998*. New York: Modern Language Association. 68–80.

Fuselier, Herman. 2000. "Trahan's Music Is for Everybody." *OffBeat*, November, 51–52.

——. 2001. "The Cajun Elvis." *OffBeat*, August, 18–19.

Gallop, Jane. 1995. "The Teacher's Breasts." In *Pedagogy: The Question of Impersonation*, ed. Jane Gallop. Bloomington: Indiana University Press, 79–89.

——. 1997. *Feminist Accused of Sexual Harassment*. Durham, N.C.: Duke University Press.

Gaudet, Marcia. 2001. " 'Mardi Gras, Chic-a-la-Pie': Reasserting Creole Identity Through Festive Play." *Journal of American Folklore* 114.452: 154–74.

Gilbert, Jeremy, and Ewan Pearson. 1999. *Discographies: Dance Music, Culture, and the Politics of Sound*. New York: Routledge.

Gilliam, Clare. 1992. "The Good Times Roll." *English Dance and Song* 54.2: 5.

Gillis, John R. 1994a. "Memory and Identity: The History of a Relationship." In *Commemorations: The Politics of National Identity*, ed. John R. Gillis. Princeton: Princeton University Press. 3–24.

——, ed. 1994b. *Commemorations: The Politics of National Identity*. Princeton: Princeton University Press.

Glissant, Edouard. 1997. *Poetics of Relation*. Trans. Betsy Wing. Ann Arbor: University of Michigan Press.

Goffman, Erving. 1959. *The Presentation of Self in Everyday Life*. Garden City, N.Y.: Doubleday.

Golomb, Jacob. 1995. *In Search of Authenticity: From Kierkegaard to Camus*. New York: Routledge.

The Good Times Are Killing Me. 1976. (No director indicated). TVTV New York.

Gotfrit, L. 1991. "Women Dancing Back: Disruption and the Politics of Pleasure." In *Postmodernism, Feminism, and Cultural Politics: Redrawing Educational Boundaries*, ed. Henry Giroux. Albany: State University of New York Press. 174–95.

Gould, Philip. 1980. *Les Acadiens d'asteur/Today's Cajuns*. Baton Rouge: Louisiana State University Press.

——. 1992. *Cajun Music and Zydeco*. Baton Rouge: Louisiana State University Press.

Gould, Philip, and Jason Berry. 2000. *Louisiana Faces: Images from a Renaissance*. Baton Rouge: Louisiana State University Press.

Graham, Colin. 2001. " 'Blame It on Maureen O'Hara': Ireland and the Trope of Authenticity." *Cultural Studies* 15.1: 58–75.

Granger, Courtney. 1999. *Un Bal Chez Balfa*. Rounder 6089.

Greenblatt, Stephen. 1995. "Culture." In *Critical Terms for Literary Study*, 2d ed., ed. Frank Lentricchia and Thomas McLaughlin. Chicago: University of Chicago Press. 225–32.

Grenier, Line, and Jocelyne Guilbault. 1997. "Créolité and Francophonie in Music: Socio-Musical Repositioning Where It Matters." *Cultural Studies* 11.2: 207–34.

Griffiths, Naomi E. 1973. *The Acadians: Creation of a People*. Toronto: McGraw-Hill Ryerson.

Grossberg, Lawrence. 1986. "Teaching the Popular." In *Theory in the Classroom*, ed. Cary Nelson. Urbana: University of Illinois Press. 177–200.

——. 1988. "Putting the Pop Back into Postmodernism." In *Universal Abandon: The Politics of Postmodernism*, ed. Andrew Ross. Minneapolis: University of Minnesota Press. 167–90.

——. 1992. *We Gotta Get Out of This Place*. New York: Routledge.

—. 1996a. "Toward a Genealogy of the State of Cultural Studies." In *Disciplinarity and Dissent in Cultural Studies*, ed. Cary Nelson and Dilip Parameshwar Gaonkar. New York: Routledge. 131–47.

—. 1996b. "The Space of Culture, The Power of Space." In *The Post-Colonial Question: Common Skies, Divided Horizons*, ed. Iain Chambers and Lydia Curti. New York: Routledge. 169–88.

—. 1997a. *Dancing in Spite of Myself.* Durham, N.C.: Duke University Press.

—. 1997b. *Bringing It All Back Home.* Durham, N.C.: Duke University Press.

—. 1998. " 'The Cultural Studies' Crossroads Blues." *European Journal of Cultural Studies* 1.1: 65–82.

Grossberg, Lawrence, Cary Nelson, and Paula Treichler, eds. 1992. *Cultural Studies.* New York: Routledge.

Guenin-Lelle, Dianne. 1997. "The Birth of Cajun Poetry: An Analysis of *Cris sur le bayou: Naissance d'une poésie acadienne en Louisiane*." *French Review* 70.3: 439–51.

Guillory, Kristi, and Bill Grass. 1995. *Réveille.* Swallow 6119.

Guillory, Kristi, and Réveille. 1996. *La Dance des Ancêtres.* Swallow 6136.

Hamm, Charles. 1995. *Putting Popular Music in Its Place.* Cambridge: Cambridge University Press.

Hannusch, Jeff. 1985. *I Hear You Knockin': The Sound of New Orleans Rhythm and Blues.* Ville Platte, La.: Swallow Publications.

—. 2002. "Masters of Louisiana Folk Music: Iry LeJeune." *OffBeat*, January, 20–22.

Hayes, Hunter. 2000. *De Mes Yeux/Through My Eyes.* Sugartown LRHR IIII.

Hazzard-Gordon, Katrina. 1990. *Jookin': The Rise of Social Dance Formations in African-American Culture.* Philadelphia, Pa.: Temple University Press.

Heller, Scott. 1990. "Cultural Studies: Eclectic and Controversial Mix of Research Sparks a Growing Movement." *Chronicle of Higher Education*, 31 January, A4–A5, A9.

—. 1998. "Weary of Cultural Studies, Some Scholars Rediscover Beauty." *Chronicle of Higher Education*, 4 December, A15.

Heylen, Romy. 1994. "Kill the Devil or Marry an American: Descent and Consent among the Cajuns." *French Review* 67.3: 453–65.

Hollier, Denis, ed. 1989. *A New History of French Literature.* Cambridge: Harvard University Press.

Hot Pepper: The Life and Music of Clifton Chenier. 1973. Dir. Les Blank. Flower Films.

"Hot Type: Intellectual Historians Debate Direction of the Field." 1997. *Chronicle of Higher Education*, 14 February, A16.

Huggs, Katrinna. 1992. "Surprising Success." *Times of Acadiana*, 20 May, 16–18.

Hullot-Kentor, Odile. 1993. "Profession Forum: Breaking Ranks." *Profession 93*. New York: Modern Language Association. 68–71.

Jackson, Jean E. 1995. "Culture, Genuine and Spurious: The Politics of Indianness in the Vaupés, Colombia." *American Ethnologist* 22.1: 3–27.

Jacquot, Martine. 1988. "De l'acadianité à l'américanité: Une poésie de l'errance." *Dalhousie French Studies* 15: 134–42.

J'ai Été au Bal (I Went to the Dance): The Cajun and Zydeco Music of Louisiana. 1989. Dir. Les

Blank and Chris Strachwitz. Ed. Maureen Gosling. Narr. Barry Jean Ancelet and Michael Doucet. Brazos Films.

J'ai Été au Bal (I Went to the Dance). 1990. 2 vols. Arhoolie C331–332.

Jameson, Fredric. 1992. *Signatures of the Visible*. New York: Routledge.

———. 1993. "On 'Cultural Studies.'" *Social Text* 34: 17–52.

JanMohammed, Abdul R., and David Lloyd, eds. 1990. *The Nature and Context of Minority Discourse*. Oxford: Oxford University Press.

Jensen, Joli. 1998. *Nashville Sound: Authenticity, Commercialization, and Country Music*. Nashville, Tenn.: Vanderbilt University Press.

Les Jeunes Cajun. 2000. *Notre Manière*. Acadiana Records 0131.

Kael, Pauline. 1987. "The Big Easy." *New Yorker*, 7 September, 100.

Kaplan, Alice. 1993. *French Lessons*. Chicago: University of Chicago Press.

Kaplan, Alice, and Philippe Roussin, eds. 1994. "Céline, USA." *South Atlantic Quarterly* 93.2.

Keil, Charles, and Steven Feld. 1994. *Music Grooves*. Chicago: University of Chicago Press.

Keil, Charles, Angeliki V. Keil, and Dick Blau. 1992. *Polka Happiness*. Philadelphia: Temple University Press.

Kelly, Karen, and Evelyn McDonnell, eds. 1999. *Stars Don't Stand Still in the Sky: Music and Myth*. New York: New York University Press.

Klein, Richard. 1998. "The Object of French Studies—*Gebrauchkunst*." *Diacritics* 28.3: 5–11.

Kritzman, Lawrence D. 1995. "Identity Crises: France, Culture, and the Idea of Nation." *SubStance* 76–77: 5–20.

Lacouture, Marce. 2000. *La Joie Cadienne*. Cut-Up Records.

Lang, Candace. 1996. "Autocritique." In *Confessions of the Critics*, ed. H. Aram Veeser. New York: Routledge. 40–54.

Learn to Zydeco Dance Tonight. 1995. Prod. Ben Pagac. Insectefex, Inc.

Lefebvre, Henri. 1991. *The Production of Space*. Trans. Donald Nicholson-Smith. Oxford: Blackwell.

Le Hir, Marie-Pierre. 1995–96. "Bridging National Fields: Nineteenth-Century Scholarship in French and American Perspectives." *Nineteenth-Century French Studies* 24.1–2: 13–33.

———. 1997. "French Cultural Studies in the United States: A Case Study." *Sites* 1.1: 171–90.

Le Hir, Marie-Pierre. "The 'Popular' in Cultural Studies." In *French Cultural Studies: Criticism at the Crossroads*, ed. Marie-Pierre Le Hir and Dana Strand. Albany: State University of New York Press. 123–42.

Le Hir, Marie-Pierre, and Dana Strand, eds. 2000. *French Cultural Studies: Criticism at the Crossroads*. Albany: State University of New York Press.

Lentricchia, Frank, and Thomas McLaughlin, eds. 1995. *Critical Terms for Literary Study*. 2nd ed. Chicago: University of Chicago Press.

Lewis, J. Lowell. 1992. *Ring of Liberation: Deceptive Discourse in Brazilian Capoeira*. Chicago: University of Chicago Press.

L'il Band of Gold. 2000. *L'il Band of Gold*. Shanachie 6047.

Lindhal, Carl. 2001. "A Note on Blackface." *Journal of American Folklore* 114.452: 248–54.

Lionnet, Françoise. 1989. *Autobiographical Voices: Race, Gender, Self-Portraiture.* Ithaca, N.Y.: Cornell University Press.

Lionnet, Françoise, and Ronnie Scharfman, eds. 1993. "Post/Colonial Conditions: Exiles, Migrations, and Nomadisms." *Yale French Studies* 82/83.

Lipsitz, George. 1990. *Time Passages: Collective Memory and American Popular Culture.* Minneapolis: University of Minnesota Press.

——. 1994. *Dangerous Crossroads: Popular Music, Postmodernism, and the Poetics of Place.* New York: Verso.

Lomax, Alan, dir. 1990. *Cajun Country: Don't Drop the Potato.* Pacific Arts Video.

Lopez, Ana M. 1997. "Of Rhythms and Borders." In *Everynight Life: Culture and Dance in Latin/o America,* ed. Celeste Fraser Delgado and José Estaban Muñoz. Durham: Duke University Press. 310–44.

Louisiane francophone: Lache pas la patate! n.d. pics/University of Iowa.

Lowenthal, David. 1994. "Identity, Heritage, and History." In *Commemorations: The Politics of National Identity,* ed. John R. Gillis. Princeton: Princeton University Press. 41–57.

Loza, Steven. 1993. *Barrio Rhythm: Mexican American Music in Los Angeles.* Urbana: University of Illinois Press.

"LPB Shows Gain Two nete Honors." 2001. *Advocate Online,* 21 January.

MacCannell, Dean. 1999. *The Tourist: A New Theory of the Leisure Class.* New York: Schocken. 1976. Rpt. Berkeley: University of California Press.

MacLean, Gerald. 1989. "Citing the Subject." In *Gender and Theory: Dialogues on Feminist Criticism,* ed. Linda Kaufmann. New York: Blackwell. 140–57.

Magnolia Sisters. 1995. *Prends Courage.* Arhoolie 439.

——. 2000. *Chers Amis.* Rounder 6070.

Marc and Ann. 1991. Dir. Les Blank. Flower Films.

Marks, John, and Enda McCaffrey, eds. 2001. *French Cultural Debates.* Melbourne: Monash University; Newark: University of Delaware Press.

Marks, Laura U. 2000. *The Skin of the Film: Intercultural Cinema, Embodiment, and the Senses.* Durham, N.C.: Duke University Press.

Massey, Doreen. 1994. *Space, Place, and Gender.* Minneapolis: University of Minnesota Press.

Massumi, B. 1995. "The Autonomy of Affect." *Cultural Critique* 31: 83–109.

Mathy, Jean-Philippe. 1993. *Extrême-Occident: French Intellectuals and America.* Chicago: University of Chicago Press.

——. 1997. "The Popularity of American Culture." *Sites* 1.1: 141–55.

——. 2000. *French Resistance: The French-American Culture Wars.* Minneapolis: University of Minnesota Press.

Mattern, Mark. 1998. *Acting in Concert: Music, Community, and Political Action.* New Brunswick, N.J.: Rutgers University Press.

McKeon, Ed, dir. 1997. *The Savoy-Doucet Band: Pour on the Pepper.* Motion Inc.

Miller, Christopher. 1998. *Nationalists and Nomads: Essays on Francophone African Literature and Culture.* Chicago: University of Chicago Press.

Miller, Nancy K. 1991. *Getting Personal.* New York: Routledge.

Modleski, Tania. 1998. "Questioning Scholars' Torrid Romance with Popular Culture." *Chronicle of Higher Education*, 13 November, B8.

Monaghan, Peter. 1998. "American-Studies Scholars Plumb 'Tensions of Empire' in Asia-Pacific Region." *Chronicle of Higher Education*, 11 December, A22.

Morthland, John. 1985. "The 'Toot-Toot' Wars." *Village Voice*, 6 August, 39–41.

——. 1988. "Preserving the Cajun 'Home' Tradition." *Louisiana Life* 8.3: 19–20.

Mouton, Todd. 1994a. "The Creole Mardi Gras." *Times of Acadiana*, 9 February, 19–20.

——. 1994b. "Talkin' 'Bout an Evolution." *Times of Acadiana*, 7 September, 36–37.

——. 1997. "Love or Folly? Cajun Trailblazers BeauSoleil Celebrate Twenty Years." *OffBeat*, February, 44–47.

——. 1999. "Checking the Rear View." *OffBeat*, July, 37–41.

Music from the Zydeco Kingdom. 2000. Comp. Michael Tisserand. Rounder 11579.

La Musique Chez Mulate's. 1986. With Dewey Balfa, BeauSoleil, Hector Duhon and Octa Clark, Filé, and D. L. Menard. Flat Town Music Co., MLP-8601.

Nealon, Jeffrey T. 1998. "Refraining, Becoming-Black: Repetition and Difference in Amiri Baraka's *Blues People*." *Symploké* 6.1–2: 83–95.

Nelson, Cary. 1997. *Manifesto of a Tenured Radical*. New York: New York University Press.

Nevell, Richard. 1977. *A Time to Dance: American Country Dancing from Hornpipes to Hot Hash*. New York: St. Martin's Press.

Nora, Pierre. 1996. "General Introduction: Between Memory and History." In *Realms of Memory: Rethinking the French Past. Vol. 1: Conflicts and Divisions*, ed. Pierre Nora, English-language ed. Lawrence D. Kritzman, trans. Arthur Goldhammer. New York: Columbia University Press.

Nyhan, Pat, Brian Rollins, and David Babb. 1997. *Let the Good Times Roll! A Guide to Cajun and Zydeco Music*. Portland, Maine: Upbeat Books.

Olivier, Rick, and Ben Sandmel. 1999. *Zydeco!* Jackson: University of Mississippi Press.

Orteza, Arsenio. 1997. "Soul Man." *Times of Acadiana*, 26 November, 56–57.

——. 1998a. "A Little Bit of Zack's World." *Times of Acadiana*, 24 June, 18–24.

——. 1998b. "Taking on the Big Boys." *Times of Acadiana*, 22 April, 29–31.

——. 1999. "Eat Their Poussière: Zydeco's Louisiana Purchase Inch toward Raunch." *Village Voice*, 11 May, 119–20.

——. 2001. "Good Sons of the Swamp." *Times of Acadiana*, 31 October, 60.

Pallister, Janis L. 1988. "New Departures in Cajun Poetry: Zachary Richard's *Voyage de nuit*." *Revue francophone de Louisiane* 3.1: 19–23.

Patton, Paul, ed. 1996. *Deleuze: A Critical Reader*. Cambridge: Blackwell.

Pavel, Thomas. 1992. "Les études culturelles: Une nouvelle discipline?" *Critique* 545: 731–42.

——. 1995. "Profession Forum: The Righting of French Studies." *Profession 1995*. New York: Modern Language Association. 110–11.

——. 1997. "Forum." *PMLA* 112.2: 267–68.

Petrey, Sandy. 1995. "French Studies/Cultural Studies: Reciprocal Invigoration or Mutual Destruction?" *The French Review* 68.3: 381–92.

——. 1998. "When Did Literature Stop Being Cultural?" *Diacritics* 28.3: 12–22.

Phillips, Hosea. 1983. "The Spoken French of Louisiana." In *The Cajuns: Essays on their*

History and Culture, ed. Glenn R. Conrad. Lafayette: Center for Louisiana Studies, University of Southwestern Louisiana. 145–55.

Plater, Ormonde, Rand Speyrer, and Cynthia Speyrer. 1993. *Cajun Dancing*. Gretna, La.: Pelican.

Post, Lauren C. 1962. *Cajun Sketches: From the Prairies of Southwest Louisiana*. Baton Rouge: Louisiana State University Press.

Putumayo Presents Cajun. 2001. Putumayo World Music PUT 184-2.

Putumayo Presents Zydeco. 2000. Putumayo World Music PUT 160-2.

Readings, Bill. 1996. *The University in Ruins*. Cambridge: Harvard University Press.

Reed, Revon. 1976. *Lâche pas la patate: Portrait des Acadiens de la Louisiane*. Ottawa: Editions Parti Pris.

Reed, Revon, Paul Tate, and Kathy Bihm. 1969. "The Voice in the Soul of Cajun Music." *Louisiana Heritage* 1.4: 14–15.

Richard, Zachary. 1977. *Mardi Gras*. RZ Records 1005.

—. 1980. *Live in Montreal*. Polydor GFS 90623.

—. 1988. *Zack's Bon Ton*. Rounder 6027.

—. 1989. *Mardi Gras Mambo*. Rounder 6037.

—. 1990. *Women in the Room*. A&M 75021-5302-2.

—. 1992. *Snake Bite Love*. A&M 70521-5387-2.

—. 1996. *Cap Enragé*. ADCD 10093.

—. 1997. *Faire récolte*. Moncton, Can.: Éditions Perce-Neige.

—. 2000a. *Silver Jubliee: The Best of Zachary Richard*. Rhino R2-75836.

—. 2000b. *Zachary Richard, Travailler C'est Trop Dur—Anthologie 1976–1999*. ADCD 10116.

—. 2000c. *Coeur Fidèle*. ADCD 10135.

—. 2001a. *Feu*. Montréal: Les Éditions des Intouchables.

—. 2001b. *High Time: The Elektra Recordings*. Rhino RHM2-7727.

—. 2001c. *Voyage de nuit: Cahier de poésie, 1975–79*. Lafayette: Center for Louisiana Studies, University of Southwestern Louisiana. 1987. Rpt. and rev. ed., Montréal: Les Éditions des Intouchables.

Rickels, Patricia. 1975. "The Folklore of Acadiana." In *The Culture of Acadiana*, ed. Steven L. Del Sesto and Jon L. Gibson. Lafayette: University of Southwestern Louisiana. 144–74.

Riley, Steve, and the Mamou Playboys. 1990. *Steve Riley and the Mamou Playboys*. Rounder C-6038.

—. 1992. *'Tit Galop pour Mamou*. Rounder 6048.

—. 1993. *Trace of Time*. Rounder 6053.

—. 1994. *Live!* Rounder 6058.

—. 1995. *La Toussaint*. Rounder 6068.

—. 1997. *Friday at Last*. Swallow 6139.

—. 1998. *Bayou Ruler*. Rounder 6083.

—. 2001. *Happytown*. Rounder 6098.

Rodman, Gilbert B. 1996. *Elvis after Elvis: The Posthumous Career of a Living Legend*. New York: Routledge.

Romero, Raúl R. 2001. *Debating the Past: Music, Memory, and Identity in the Andes*. New York: Oxford University Press.

Rosello, Mireille. 1998. *Declining the Stereotype: Ethnicity and Representation in French Cultures*. Hanover, N.H.: University Press of New England.

—. 2000. "Rap Music and French Cultural Studies: For an Ethics of the Ephemeral." In *French Cultural Studies: Criticism at the Crossroads*, ed. Marie-Pierre Le Hir and Dana Strand. Albany: State University of New York Press. 81–102.

Roshto, Ronnie E. 1992. "Georgie and Allen Manuel and Cajun Wire Screen Masks." *Louisiana Folklore Miscellany* 7: 33–49.

Ross, Kristin. 1995. *Fast Cars, Clean Bodies: Decolonization and the Reordering of French Culture*. Cambridge: MIT Press.

Ruark, Jennifer K. 1999. "A Place at the Table." *Chronicle of Higher Education*, 9 July, A17.

Rushton, William F. 1979. *The Cajuns: From Acadia to Louisiana*. New York: Farrar, Straus and Giroux.

Sacaulait. 2001. *Sac-à-Lait Jig*. Swallow 6165.

Samluk, Melissa. 2001. Masters Degree Examination. Dept. of Romance Languages and Literatures, Wayne State University.

Savage, Kirk. 1994. "The Politics of Memory: Black Emancipation and the Civil War Monument." In *Commemorations: The Politics of National Identity*, ed. John R. Gillis. Princeton: Princeton University Press. 127–49.

Savoy, Ann Allen. 1984. *Cajun Music: A Reflection of a People*, vol. 1. Eunice, La.: Bluebird Press.

—. 2002. *Evangeline Made: A Tribute to Cajun Music*. Vanguard Records 79585–2.

Savoy, Marc. 1988. "Maintaining Traditions." *Louisiana Folk Life* 12: 9–12.

Savoy-Doucet Cajun Band. 1983. *Les Harias—Home Music*. Arhoolie C-5029.

—. 1986. *With Spirits*. Arhoolie 5037.

—. 1989. *Two-Step d'Amédé*. Arhoolie C-316.

—. 1994. *Live! At the Dance*. Arhoolie 418.

—. 2000. *Sam's Big Rooster*. Arhoolie 481.

Savoy-Smith Cajun Band. 1996. *Now and Then*. Arhoolie 457.

Schickel, Richard. 1987. "Deep City Blues in New Orleans." *Time*, 24 August, 65.

Schneider, Alison. 2000. "Black Studies 101: Introductory Courses Reflect a Field Defining Itself." *Chronicle of Higher Education*, 19 May, A20.

Schor, Naomi. 1992. "The Righting of French Studies: Homosociality and the Killing of 'La pensée 68.'" *Profession 1992*. New York: Modern Language Association. 28–34.

—. 1993. "Response." *Profession 1993*. New York: Modern Language Association. 71.

—. 1995a. "Reply: The Righting of French Studies." *Profession 1995*. New York: Modern Language Association. 111–13.

—. 1995b. *Bad Objects: Essays Popular and Unpopular*. Durham, N.C.: Duke University Press.

Schwartz, Stephen Adam. 2000. "Everyman an Übermensch: The Culture of Cultural Studies." *SubStance* 29.1: 104–38.

Segura, Pearl Mary. 1983. "Amand Broussard *dit* Beausoleil." *Attakapas Gazette* 18.4: 146–53.

Severn, Rhonda Case. 1991. *Discovering Acadiana*. 2 vols., videocassette.

Sexton, Rocky L., and Harry Oster. 2001. "Une 'Tite Poule Grasse ou la Fille Aînée [A Little

Fat Chicken or the Eldest Daughter]: A Comparative Analysis of Cajun and Creole Mardi Gras Songs." *Journal of American Folklore* 114.452: 204–24.

Shapiro, Judith. 2000. "From Sociological Literacy to Sociological Imagination." *Chronicle of Higher Education*, 31 March, A68.

Shaw, Lloyd. 1949. *Cowboy Dances: A Collection of Western Square Dances.* Caldwell, Idaho: Caxton Printers.

——. 1950. *The Round Dance Book: A Century of Waltzing.* Caldwell, Idaho: Caxton Printers.

Sherman, Sharon R. 1998. *Documenting Ourselves: Film, Video, and Culture.* Lexington: University Press of Kentucky.

Shiach, Morag. 1993. " 'Cultural Studies' and the Work of Pierre Bourdieu." *French Cultural Studies* 4.3: 213–24.

Silverman, Kaja. 1983. *The Subject of Semiotics.* New York: Oxford University Press.

Simon, Paul. 1986. *Graceland.* Warner Brothers 25447–1.

Simoneaux, Angela. 2000. " 'Cajun Aristotle' Believes French Culture Must Be Saved." *Advocate Online*, 2 April.

Slobin, Mark. 1993. *Subcultural Sounds: Micromusics of the West.* Hanover, N.H.: Wesleyan University Press / University Press of New England.

Soja, Edward W. 1989. *Postmodern Geographies: The Reassertion of Space in Critical Theory.* London: Verso.

Sotirin, Patricia J. Forthcoming. "Representations of Breast Feeding Suckling Up to the Body without Organs." In *Animations (of Deleuze and Guattari)*, ed. Jennifer Daryl Slack. New York: Peter Lang.

Southern Comfort. 1981. Dir. Walter Hill. Cinema Group Venture.

"Southwestern Louisiana Mardi Gras Traditions." 2001. *Journal of American Folklore* 114.452.

Spell-Johnson, Sarah. 1997. "Les jeunes musiciens de la renaissance acadienne." *LA Life Magazine* 17.1: 30.

Spend It All. 1971. Dir. Les Blank. Flower Films.

Speyrer, J. Randolph. 1987. *Allons Danser.* (No producer indicated).

Speyrer, Rand, and Cynthia Speyrer. 1993a. *Introduction to Cajun Dancing.* Gretna, La.: Pelican.

——. 1993b. *Advanced Cajun Dancing.* Gretna, La.: Pelican.

Spinoza, Baruch. 1992. *The Ethics: Treatise on the Emendation of the Intellect; and Selected Letters.* Trans. Samuel Shirley. Indianapolis: Hackett Publishing.

Stanton, Domna. 1997. "Toward a Contextual Literary History: French Studies in the U.S." *Contemporary French Civilization* 21.2: 5–17.

Stivale, Charles J. 1994. " 'Spaces of Affect': Versions and Visions of Cajun Cultural History." *South Central Review* 11.4: 15–25.

——. 1997a. "Of *Heccéités* and *Ritournelles*: Movement and Affect in the Cajun Dance Arena." In *Articulating the Global and the Local*, ed. Ann Cvetkovich and Douglas Kellner. Boulder, Colo.: Westview. 129–48.

——. 1997b. "Of Cultural Lessons, French and Other." *Contemporary French Civilization* 21.2: 65–86.

—. 1998. *The Two-Fold Thought of Gilles Deleuze and Félix Guattari: Intersections and Animations*. New York: Guilford Publications.

—. 2000. "Becoming-Cajun." *Cultural Studies* 14.2: 147–76.

Stoekl, Allan. 1998. "Lanzmann and Deleuze: On the Question of Memory." *Symploké 6.1–2:* 72–82.

Strenge, Kelly. 2000. "Festivals Acadiens—More than a Good Time." *Times of Acadiana*, 13 September, 32–33.

Taylor, Julie. 1998. *Paper Tangos*. Durham, N.C.: Duke University Press.

Taylor, Timothy D. 1997. *Global Pop: World Music, World Markets*. New York: Routledge.

Terdiman, Richard. 1985. "Deconstructing Memory: On Representing the Past and Theorizing Culture in France since the Revolution." *Diacritics* 15.4: 13–36.

—. 1993. *Present Past: Modernity and the Memory Crisis*. Ithaca, N.Y.: Cornell University Press.

Thornton, Sarah. 1996. *Club Cultures: Music, Media, and Subcultural Capital*. Hanover, N.H.: Wesleyan University Press.

Tisserand, Michael. 1996. "Generation Z." *Times of Acadiana*, 25 September, 17–25.

—. 1998. *The Kingdom of Zydeco*. New York: Arcade Publishing.

Toups, Wayne. 1988. *Johnnie Can't Dance*. MTE 5035.

—. 1989. *Blast from the Bayou*. PolyGram/Mercury 236518-1.

—. 1990. "Interview." *Caliban* 9: 160–77.

—. 1991. *Fish Out of Water*. PolyGram/Mercury 848289-4.

—. 1992. *Down Home Live!* MTE 5043-2.

—. 1995. *Back to the Bayou*. Swallow SW 6124-2.

—. 1997. *Toups*. New Blues 77772.

—. 1998. *More than Just a Little*. BTM 0002.

—. 2000. *Little Wooden Box*. Shanachie SH 9024.

Toups, Wayne, and ZydeCajun. 1986. *ZydeCajun*. Kajun 5032.

Trahan, Horace. 1996. *Ossun Blues*. Swallow 6134.

—. 2001. *Reach Out and Touch a Hand*. Zydeco Hound 1010-2.

Trahan, Horace, and New Ossun Express. 2000. *Get On Board*. Zydeco Hound 1008-2.

Trahan, Kaleb. 1999. *La Prochaine Génération . . . C'est Dans Mon Sang (The Next Generation . . . It's in My Blood)*. Swallow 6161.

Troy, Damon, and Louisiana Beat. 2001. *Blowin' Like a Hurricane*. MTE 5071.

Turk, Leslie. 1995. "Eunice's Mardi Gras Shame." *Times of Acadiana*, 15 March, 16–17.

Ungar, Steven, and Tom Conley, eds. 1996. *Identity Papers: Contested Nationhood in Twentieth-Century France*. Minneapolis: University of Minnesota Press.

Van den Abbeele, George. 1980. "Sightseers: The Tourist as Theorist." *Diacritics* 10.4: 3–14.

Veeser, H. Aram, ed. 1996. *Confessions of the Critics*. New York: Routledge.

Viator, Moïse, and Alida Viator. 1999. *Mo Belle Créole*. Acadiana ACD-0120.

Walser, Robert. 1993. *Running with the Devil: Power, Gender, and Madness in Heavy Metal Music*. Hanover, N.H.: Wesleyan University Press/University Press of New England.

Ware, Carolyn E. 2001. "Anything to Act Crazy: Cajun Women and Mardi Gras Disguise." *Journal of American Folklore* 114.452: 225–47.

Waterman, Christopher Alan. 1990. *Jùjú: A Social History and Ethnography of an African Popular Music*. Chicago: University of Chicago Press.

Welchman, John. 1988. "Face(t): Notes on Faciality." *Artforum*, November, 130–38.

Wells, Ken. 2001. "Would that Kangaroo Be Hopping, or Is It Bopping to Zydeco?" *Wall Street Journal*, 6 February, A1, A10.

Westbrook, Laura. 1996. "Pretty, Little, and Fickle: Images of Women in Cajun Music." *Louisiana Folklore Miscellany* (online).

Whitfield, Irene Thérèse. 1969. *Louisiana French Folk Songs*. New York: Dover.

Willging, Dan. 2002. "Ann Savoy: Cajun Music's Cultural Ambassador." *OffBeat*, April, 56–67.

Williams, Nathan, and the Zydeco Cha Chas. 1995. *Creole Crossroads*. Rounder 2137.

Wilson, Mona. 2001. *Zydeco-robics Mona-robics Style*. Zydeco Dancing, Etc.!

Wise, J. MacGregor. 1997. *Exploring Technology and Social Space*. Thousand Oaks, Calif.: Sage.

——. 2000. "Home: Territory and Identity." *Cultural Studies* 14.2: 295–310.

Wissoker, Ken. 2000. "Negotiating a Passage between Disciplinary Borders." *Chronicle of Higher Education*, 14 April, B4.

Wynter, Sylvia. 1987. "On Disenchanting Discourse: 'Minority' Literary Criticism and Beyond." *Cultural Critique* 7: 207–44.

Yaari, Monique. 1996. "Culture Studies: A French Perspective." *Transculture* 1.1: 21–60.

——. 2002. "Toward a Cultural Curriculum for Graduate Studies: The Case of French." *ADFL Bulletin* 33.2: 33–49.

Zydeco. 1984. Dir. Nicholas R. Spitzer. Flower Films.

Zydeco Festival. 1988. Maison de Soul MdS-1024.

Zydeco Live! 1989a. Vol. 1., with Boozoo Chavis and the Magic Sounds and Nathan and the Zydeco Cha-Chas. Rounder 2069.

Zydeco Live! 1989b. Vol. 2., with John Delafose and the Eunice Playboys and Willis Prudhomme and the Zydeco Express. Rounder 2070.

Zydeco Nite 'n' Day. 1991. Dir. Robert Dowling. Island Visual Arts.

INDEX

Abshire, Nathan, 134, 136–39, 158; in *J'ai Été au Bal*, 143
Acadians: and exile, 10–11, 14, 25, 42, 69–70
Acadian Village, 74, 106, 108, 181 n.1
Action Cadienne. *See* Richard, Zachary
Against the Wind. See Richard, Zachary
Alcoff, Linda, 26, 35
Allain, Mathé, 180 nn.22, 23
"Allons à Lafayette," 91
Americanization of Cajuns, 11, 15
Ancelet, Barry Jean, 22, 25–26, 35, 40–41, 51–52, 57, 64–65, 101, 106, 135, 138, 140, 159, 176 n.3, 178 n.9, 184 n.14, 185 nn.25, 27; and authenticity, 149; in *J'ai Été au Bal*, 89, 142; and stereotypes of Cajuns, 82
Angers, Trent, 88
Ardoin, Amédé, 134, 136, 190 n.8; in *Cajun Country*, 146; in *J'ai Été au Bal*, 142; influence on Cajun music, 146
Ardoin, Bois Sec, 165, 171 n.4; in *J'ai Été au Bal*, 142
Arena: defined, 169 n.1
The Ark, 115, 187 n.4
Assimilation: cultural, 174 n.22
Austin City Limits, 30, 186 n.3
Authenticity, 173 nn.18–20; and Cajun

dance arena, 2–3; and Cajun music origins, 135–36; and Cajun music repertoire, 140–41; and constructing identity, 26–27; construction of, 153–57; defined, 24; Michael Doucet on, 99; and (geo)graphies, 48, 51; and globality and locality, 87; in documentaries, 147; in *Southern Comfort*, 80–81; linguistic, 85; as order words, 166–67; and performance, 32–33; and purity, 27, 33–34; and research, 23–24; role of dance in *The Big Easy*, 84–87; search for, 21; and social practices, 133; as strategy, 29–30; and toponyms, 44; and tourism, 24–25; and tradition, 76–77; and Horace Trahan, 149
Avoyelles parish, 178 n.12

Babb, David, 41
Bakhtin, M. M., 98
Bal de maison, 15; defined, 171 n.3; in *The Big Easy*, 81–88; in *Southern Comfort*, 80–81
Balfa, Christine, 7, 112, 149, 161–65
Balfa, Dewey, 16, 40, 52, 59, 89, 150, 171 n.4, 176 n.2; in *The Big Easy*, 81–85; in *J'ai Été au Bal*, 143; in *Southern Comfort*, 80; and tradition, 148

Falcon, Cleoma, 159, 161
Falcon, Odile, 190 n.7
Falcon, Solange Marie, 129, 159
Festivals Acadiens, 13, 101, 108, 186 n.28
Fields, James C., 177 n.6, 178 n.11
Filé, 90, 119, 139–40, 144; *Cajun Dance Band*, 177 n.7, 184 n.15
Filene, Ben, 133, 185 n.24
Fisher, Jennifer, 123
Fitzgeralds', 116–17
"Les Flammes d'Enfer," 31–32, 54–55, 57
Flower Films: Web site, 185 n.20
Fold: and inside/outside, 129
Folk music: and purity, 34
Fontenot, Canray, 165, 171 n.4; in *Cajun Country*, 146; in *J'ai Été au Bal*, 142
Fontenot, James, 64
Fontenot, Miriam, 184 n.15, 185 n.26
Franco-American relations, 172 n.6
Fred's Lounge, 190 n.11
Freeze, Cajun, 105, 118, 187 n.8
French Dance Tonight, 88–95
French studies, 2, 4, 17–20; distinctions in, 172 n.6
Frugé, Wade, 190 n.8; in *Cajun Country*, 146
Fuselier, Herman, 149–50

(Geo)graphies, 42–72; affective, 66–67; and authenticity, 48, 51; defined, 42
Glissant, Edouard, 65; and poetics of the Relation, 43–44, 48
Gillis, John, 97, 156
Globality, 5; and authenticity, 27
Goodman, John, 82
Gould, Philip, 179 n.18, 183 n.13
Le grand dérangement, 14, 42; and Beau-Soleil, 63
"Grand Texas," 51–52
Granger, Courtney, 112, 161–65
Greely, David, 59–60, 165
Greenblatt, Stephen, 36
Griffiths, Naomi, 183 n.13
Grossberg, Lawrence, 20, 38, 96, 173 n.20, 188 n.20
Guattari, Félix, 20–21, 48, 77, 111, 117–18, 121–22, 126–27, 166, 173 n.15; and faciality, 187 n.10; and nomadism, 178 n.10; and thisness, 187 n.7

Guenin-Lelle, Dianne, 180 n.23
Guillory, Chuck, 51
Guillory, Kristi, 160
Guillory, Queen Ida, 160

Haecceity. *See* Thisness
Hapticity: and dance performance, 123–26; and polylogue, 131; and thisness, 125–26
Hayes, Hunter, 57, 162–64, 179 n.15
Hayman, Gary: Cajun/zydeco Web page, 181 n.2
Heylen, Romy, 35, 180 n.22
Hill, Walter, 79, 182 n.8
History: and Cajun identity, 28
Home: and *(dé)paysement*, 58–62, 65; and family, 50–51; and identity, 46, 48; and toponyms, 45
Home song tradition, 159, 177 n.8
Houma Indians: in *Cajun Country*, 147
Hybridity, 31; cultural, 30; and identity, 25; and thisness, 33. *See also* In-between

Identity: and Cajun cultural practices, 108–9; and Cajun dance, 100–101; and Cajun history, 88; and Cajun social practices, 133; and community, 108; construction of, 5, 156; and cultural exploitation, 75; and family, 50–51; and home, 46, 48; and hybridity, 25; in *The Big Easy*, 87; in *Southern Comfort*, 87; and the minor, 82; and music and dance arena, 2–3, 87–88; and the outside, 34; and research, 23–24; and self-representation, 22; Wayne Toups on, 57
In-between, 30–31, 76–77, 96, 100; and commercialization, 106; and cultural heritage, 108; and dance instruction, 102; and dance performance, 128–31; and dance videos, 100; in *The Big Easy*, 87; in *Southern Comfort*, 87; and polylogue, 123; and style, 109
Innovation: in Cajun music, 89–90; and the in-between, 109

Jackson, Jean E., 26
Jacquot, Martine, 43
"J'ai été au Bal," 76
J'ai Été au Bal, 88–95, 129, 141–44, 190

Plater, Ormonde, 103, 188 n. 18
Polylogue: and dance performance, 131; and the in-between, 123; and music and dance, 116; and spectators, 128; and this-ness, 120–21
La Poussière Club, 152–53
Powell, Dirk, 40, 59, 112, 149, 161, 165–66
Purity: and authenticity, 27, 33–34; and tradition, 76

Quaid, Dennis, 81

Race: and cultural practices, 145
Racism: and folk music, 133
Randol's Restaurant, 13, 101
Reed, Lisa Trahan, 161
Reed, Revon, 88, 190 n.11
Refrain: and Cajun music, 119; and dance performance, 119; and territory, 49
Renaissance, Cajun cultural, 12, 16, 25, 40–41, 44, 74, 83, 113, 158, 176 nn.1, 2; and exclusion, 147; and zydeco, 41
Le Rendez-Vous des Cajuns, 25, 79
Restaurants, Cajun music, 101, 106
Rice, Jeremy: Cajun/zydeco Web page, 181 n.2
Richard, Belton, 160; in J'ai Été au Bal, 143
Richard, Wade, 58
Richard, Zachary, 1, 27–29, 40, 62, 164, 175 n.25, 175–76, n.27; and Action Cadienne, 7, 29, 76, 164, 181 n.27; Against the Tide, 28, 64, 70–71, 164; "La Ballade de Jean Batailleur," 74; Cap Enragé, 4, 29, 65–67, 175–76 n.27, 188 n.24; Coeur Fidèle, 29, 69, 71, 159; and commercialization, 73; and (dé)payse-ment, 67–69; and disenchantment, 70–71; and the earth, 68–69; Faire récolte, 67; Feu, 69–70; and home, 65; and innovation, 90, 96; and linguistic iden-tity, 71; and militancy, 28–29, 64–65; "Petit Codiac," 66–67, 188–89 n.25; poetry of, 188 n.23; and politics, 67, 70–71; "Réveille," 63–64, 70–71, 159; and rooted errantry, 68–69; and tactics, 28; and tradition, 130; Voyage de nuit, 64–65
Richardson, Dirk, 33
Riley, Steve, 162–63, 165, 179 n. 18
Riley Steve, and the Mamou Playboys: "Chez Personne," 60–61; and musical

thematics, 51; "Old Home Waltz," 59–60; and search for origins, 58–61; Steve Riley and the Mamou Playboys, topo-nyms, 177 n.7; Trace of Time, 59–60
Rockin' Dopsie, 41
Rockin' Sidney, 91; in J'ai Été au Bal, 143
Rodman, Gil, 37
Rollins, Brian, 41
Romero, Roddie, 162–63, 179 n.17
Rosello, Mireille, 3, 36
Rounder Records, 165–66

Samluk, Melissa, 36
Savage, Kirk, 185 n.23
Savoy, Ann, 31–32, 41, 44, 75, 92–94, 134–35, 139–40, 159–61, 176 n.3, 190 n.7
Savoy, Marc, 25, 27, 31–33, 45, 75, 92–95, 175 n.25, 185 nn.21, 22; and cultural integrity, 29–30, 95–96; in J'ai Été au Bal, 142; in Southern Comfort, 80; and strategy, 29; and tradition, 73–74, 95–96
Savoy-Doucet Cajun Band, 31–33, 185 n.19; Les Harias–Home Music, toponyms, 177 n.7, n.8; recordings, 185 n.19
The Savoy-Doucet Band: Pour on the Pepper, 31–33
Schwartz, Stephen Adam, 172 n.10
Schwarz, Peter, 59–60, 161, 179 n.17
Severn, Rhonda Case, 22, 183–84 n.13, 191 n.14
Shaw, Debbie, 186 n.29
Silverman, Kaja, 95
Simien, Terrance, 165
Simon, Paul, 41
Smith, Ken, 176 n.28
Soileau, Floyd, 91, 166
Southern Comfort, 6, 78–81; allegory in, 79–80; availability of, 78–79, 182 n.5; music in, 183 n. 11; popularity of, 182 n.5; synopsis of, 182–83 n.9
Spaces: and dance, 16; smooth, 114–16; striated, 118–19
Spaces of affects, 6, 17, 110; and dance style, 129–30; and the event, 114–15; in The Big Easy, 85 and music and dance arena, 20–21; and performance, 131; and polylogue, 122; and research, 22–23
Spectators: and polylogue, 128; and this-ness, 127–28

Charles J. Stivale is Professor of French at Wayne State University.

Library of Congress Cataloging-in-Publication Data
Stivale, Charles J.
Disenchanting les bons temps : identity and authenticity
in Cajun music and dance / Charles J. Stivale.
p. cm. — (Post-contemporary interventions)
Includes bibliographical references and index.
ISBN 0-8223-3033-4 (alk. paper)
ISBN 0-8223-3020-2 (pbk. : alk. paper)
1. Cajun music—Louisiana—History and criticism.
2. Folk dancing, Cajun—Louisiana.
3. Cajuns—Louisiana—Social life and customs.
I. Title. II. Series.
ML3560.C25 S75 2002   781.62′410763—dc21   2002006463